THOMAS AQUINAS ON VIRTUE

Thomas Aquinas produced a voluminous body of work on moral theory, and much of that work is on virtue, particularly the status and value of the virtues as principles of virtuous acts, and the way in which a moral life can be organized around them schematically. Thomas Osborne presents Aquinas's account of virtue in its historical, philosophical, and theological contexts, to show the reader what Aquinas himself wished to teach about virtue. His discussion makes the complexities of Aquinas's moral thought accessible to readers despite the differences between Thomas's texts themselves, and the distance between our background assumptions and his. The book will be valuable for scholars and students in ethics, medieval philosophy, and theology.

THOMAS M. OSBORNE, JR., is Professor in the Center for Thomistic Studies and the Department of Philosophy at the University of St. Thomas in Houston, Texas. His publications include several books on medieval ethics and moral psychology, and many articles in medieval, scholastic, and contemporary philosophy.

T0370731

THOMAS AQUINAS
ON VIRTUE

THOMAS M. OSBORNE, JR.
University of St. Thomas, Houston

CAMBRIDGE
UNIVERSITY PRESS

Shaftesbury Road, Cambridge CB2 8EA, United Kingdom

One Liberty Plaza, 20th Floor, New York, NY 10006, USA

477 Williamstown Road, Port Melbourne, VIC 3207, Australia

314–321, 3rd Floor, Plot 3, Splendor Forum, Jasola District Centre, New Delhi – 110025, India

103 Penang Road, #05–06/07, Visioncrest Commercial, Singapore 238467

Cambridge University Press is part of Cambridge University Press & Assessment, a department of the University of Cambridge.

We share the University's mission to contribute to society through the pursuit of education, learning and research at the highest international levels of excellence.

www.cambridge.org
Information on this title: www.cambridge.org/9781009054560

DOI: 10.1017/9781009053754

First published 2022
First paperback edition 2024

A catalogue record for this publication is available from the British Library

Library of Congress Cataloging-in-Publication data
NAMES: Osborne, Thomas M. (Thomas Michael), 1972– author.
TITLE: Thomas Aquinas on virtue / Thomas M. Osborne, Jr.
DESCRIPTION: Cambridge, United Kingdom : Cambridge University Press, 2022.
| Includes bibliographical references and index.
IDENTIFIERS: LCCN 2021970069 | ISBN 9781316511749 (hardback)
| ISBN 9781009053754 (ebook)
SUBJECTS: LCSH: Thomas, Aquinas, Saint, 1225?–1274. | Virtue.
| Ethics, Medieval. | Christian ethics – History – Middle Ages, 600–1500.
CLASSIFICATION: LCC B765.T54 O83 2022 | DDC 189/.4–dc23/eng/20220124
LC record available at https://lccn.loc.gov/2021970069

ISBN   978-1-316-51174-9   Hardback
ISBN   978-1-009-05456-0   Paperback

Contents

Acknowledgments

I would like to thank the anonymous readers and others who commented on parts of this book, in particular Maureen Bielinski, Carlos Casanova, Timothy Jacobs, and Steven Jensen.

Note on the Texts

In references to medieval works that are written in the "disputed question" style, "prol." stands for a prologue, "resp." or "sol." refers to the body or main response of an article, "s.c." to the *sed contra* or considerations "on the other hand," while "ad" designates responses to initial objections. References to other texts can include "Ord.," which refers to an "Ordinatio," "lib.," which indicates a book, "lect.," which signifies Thomas's lecture on that book, "cap.," which is for "chapter," and "dist.," which signifies a distinction number. Unless otherwise listed in the bibliography, all references to Thomas's works are from the critical Leonine edition. All references to the Marietti edition of Thomas's *Quaestiones Disputatae* are to vol. 2. Albert the Great is cited either in accordance with the edition published by Vivès in Paris (Paris) or the current critical edition that is being published in Cologne (Col.). Bonaventure is cited according to the Quaracchi edition (1882–1902), John Capreolus according to the Tours edition (1900–1907), John Duns Scotus according to the Vatican Edition (1950–), Peter Lombard according to the Rome edition (1971, 1981), Philip the Chancellor according to Nicolaus Wicki's edition (1985), and William of Auxerre according to the Paris/Rome edition (1980–87). Full bibliographical references can be found in the bibliography. Thomas de Vio Cajetan's commentary on the *Summa Theologiae* is cited according to its printing alongside the *Summa Theologiae* in the Leonine edition. John of St. Thomas is cited according to the Québec edition. Odon Lottin's *Psychologie et Morale aux XIIe et XIIIe Siècles* is cited according to the latest edition.

Abbreviations

Book Series and Editions

CCSL	Corpus Christianorum Series Latina
CSEL	Corpus Scriptorum Ecclesiasticorum Latinorum
PL	Patrologia Latina
PM	*Psychologie et Morale aux XIIe et XIII ^e Siècles*

Thomas Aquinas

DM	*Quaestiones Disputatae de Malo*
DSC	*Quaestio Disputata de Spiritualibus Creaturis*
DV	*Quaestiones Disputatae de Veritate*
DVC	*Quaestio Disputata de Virtutibus in Communi*
DVCard.	*Quaestio Disputata de Virtutibus Cardinalibus*
DVCarit.	*Quaestio Disputata de Caritate*
DVSpe	*Quaestio Disputata de Spe*
In Div. Nom.	*In Librum Beati Dionysii de Divinis Nominibus Expositio*
In Met.	*Sententia super Metaphysicam*
In Phys.	*In Libros Physicorum*
In Post. An.	*In Posteriorum Analyticorum*
In Sent.	*Scriptum super Libros Sententiarum*
QDA	*Quaestiones Disputatae de Anima*
Quod.	*Quodlibeta*
SBT	*Super Boetium de Trinitate*
SCG	*Summa Contra Gentiles*
SLDA	*Sentencia Libri de anima*
SLE	*Sententia Libri Ethicorum*
SLP	*Sententia Libri Politicorum*
S.T.	*Summa Theologiae*
I	First Part of the *Summa Theologiae*

I-II	First Part of the Second Part of the *Summa Theologiae*
II-II	Second Part of the Second Part of the *Summa Theologiae*
III	Third Part of the *Summa Theologiae*
Sup. I Cor.	*Super I Epistolam ad Corinthos*
Sup. Mat.	*Lectura Super Matthaeum*
Sup. Rom.	*Super Epistolam ad Romanos*
Sup. Tit.	*Super Epistolam ad Titum*

Aristotle

Categ.	*Categories*
De An.	*De Anima*
EN	*Ethica Nicomachea*
Met.	*Metaphysica*
Phys.	*Physica*
Pol.	*Politica*

Augustine

Confess.	*Confessionum Libri XIII*
De Civ. Dei	*De Ciuitate Dei*
De Div. Quaest. 83	*De Diuersis Quaestionibus Octoginta Tribus*
De Lib. Arbit.	*De Libero Arbitrio*
De Mor.	*De Moribus Ecclesiae Catholicae et de Moribus Manichaeorum*
De Serm. in Monte	*De Sermone Domini in Monte Libros Duos*
De Trin.	*De Trinitate*
Retr.	*Retractationum Libri Duo*

Introduction

Virtue plays a central role in Thomas Aquinas's moral theory. Agents are good because their acts are good. Virtues are capacities by which agents are able to produce these good acts consistently, pleasurably, and for their own sake. This book presents Thomas's more general account of virtue in its historical, chronological, philosophical, and theological contexts. It attempts to help the reader to understand what Thomas himself wished to teach about virtue, even if the material might seem at times distant from contemporary ethical discussions.

Many of Thomas's writings are on moral theory, and a large part of them is on the virtues. This importance of the virtues can be seen in Thomas's most significant work, the *Summa Theologiae*.[1] The Second Part of its three parts (hereafter *Secunda Pars*) is about moral matters, and it is much larger than the other parts. This *Secunda Pars* itself includes a First Part (hereafter *Prima Secundae*), which is on more speculative general topics, and a Second Part (hereafter *Secunda Secundae*), which covers moral matters that are relevant to every moral agent as well as to those that belong to particular kinds of life. Thomas himself describes the *Prima Secundae* as "a common consideration of virtues and vices and other things pertaining to moral matter."[2] It includes what the moral theorist must know before considering particular cases. The *Secunda Secundae* organizes the moral particulars that concern all moral agents around the four cardinal virtues, namely prudence, justice, courage or fortitude (*fortitudo*), and temperance, and the three theological virtues, namely faith, hope, and charity. The other virtues are all reduced to these virtues, and the various vices are considered in opposition to the virtues. Thomas states that by organizing particular moral theory in this way, "nothing of morals will be

---

[1] Leonard Boyle, "The Setting of the *Summa Theologiae* of St. Thomas – Revisited," in *The Ethics of Aquinas*, ed. Stephen J. Pope (Washington, DC: Georgetown University Press, 2002), 1–16.
[2] "communem considerationem de virtutibus et vitiis et aliis ad materialem moralem pertinentibus ..." Thomas, *S.T.*, II-II, prol.

passed over."[3] Thomas's Dominican predecessor William Peraldus (d. 1271) had written a *Summa de vitiis et virtutibus* that followed a similar plan; it covered the moral life according to the virtues, the beatitudes that Jesus Christ enunciated in the Sermon on the Mount, and the seven gifts of the Holy Ghost.[4] But it was not nearly as systematic and lacked the complete theological overview of Thomas's work.[5] Nevertheless, the *Summa Theologiae* largely is about what later theologians would describe as moral theology, and its moral teaching is mostly organized around the virtues.

In order to understand Thomas's account of virtue, we must first look at the relationship between theology and philosophy. Thomas's theology presupposes a developed moral philosophy.[6] He does not set out to develop his own new moral theory in these writings. He accepts as true much of what was written by established authorities, including not only previous Christian writers but also philosophers such as Aristotle, whose entire *Nicomachean Ethics* was recently translated into Latin. When Thomas was a student in Cologne (1248–1252), his teacher Albert the Great (c. 1200–1280) was among the first to comment on this new complete version, and Thomas seems to have assisted in compiling Albert's notes. Aristotle influences not only Thomas's understanding of particular moral topics but also his account of moral philosophy as a practical science.

An Aristotelian science can be described as knowledge of or a habit of knowing conclusions by demonstration from evident principles that are prior, universal, and necessary.[7] The conclusions are known to be true by means of other known truths. Such science is acquired by human effort and differs from the ordinary knowledge that comes from nature or experience. A practical science is widely speaking about what is subject to human action. The *Nicomachean Ethics* is a work on the practical science of ethics, which is that part of moral philosophy which is concerned with an individual's action.[8] The other two parts of moral philosophy are about human action in the context of the other two natural human unities.

---

[3] "nihil moralium erit praetermissum." Thomas, *S.T.*, II-II, prol.
[4] William Peraldus, *Summa aurea de virtutibus et vitiis* (Venice, 1497). John Inglis, "Aquinas's Replication of the Acquired Moral Virtues," *Journal of Religious Ethics* 27 (1999): 6–13.
[5] Boyle, "Setting of the *Summa Theologiae*," 9–10.
[6] For Aquinas's understanding of the relationship between faith, theology, and philosophy, see Thomas M. Osborne Jr., "Natural Reason and Supernatural Faith," in *Aquinas's Summa Theologiae: A Critical Guide*, ed. Jeffrey Hause (Cambridge: Cambridge University Press, 2018), 188–203; John Jenkins, *Knowledge and Faith in Thomas Aquinas* (Cambridge: Cambridge University Press), 1997.
[7] For the relationship between such science and theology, see Jenkins, *Knowledge and Faith*, 78–98.
[8] Thomas, *SLE*, lib. 1, lect. 1 (Leonine, 47.1, 4). For the subject of moral philosophy and moral theology, see William Wallace, *The Role of Demonstration in St. Thomas Aquinas: A Study of Methodology in St. Thomas Aquinas* (River Forest, IL: The Thomist Press, 1962), 143–162.

Household economics is about the family, and political science is about the political community. The individual's virtue, which is studied in ethics, is also considered in these other moral sciences.

Moral philosophy needs to be distinguished both from productive sciences or skills and from speculative sciences. Skills, such as boatbuilding or carpentry, are also practical, but they are more about making products than about human action as such. In contrast to the practical sciences, speculative sciences are about objects that are not subject to human action, such as movable being and mathematical being. Metaphysics is a speculative science whose subject is being as such. God, even if he is not part of the subject of metaphysics, is at the very least a principle of the subject of metaphysics. Consequently, metaphysics is a kind of philosophical theology.

Thomas's theological account of ethics draws greatly on Aristotle's *Nicomachean Ethics*. During his lifetime, Aristotle's works became foundational for philosophical education. Nevertheless, Aristotle is not his only philosophical authority, and he does not think that the development of philosophical knowledge ended with Aristotle's death. Thomas, along with his contemporaries and immediate predecessors, had great respect for Marcus Tullius Cicero (106–43 BC), who was the first to make Greek philosophy generally available to Latin readers. Although Cicero generally was a kind of Academic Skeptic, his moral philosophy largely reworked older Stoic notions.[9] His main targets seem to have been proponents of Epicureanism, who founded morality on pleasure. The Stoic Macrobius (c. 400) wrote a commentary on Cicero that contained an influential summary of the various virtues and their relation to each other. Thomas's taxonomy of virtue also relies heavily on the *De Virtutibus et Vitiis*, which was a somewhat Aristotelian part of the mostly Stoic *Peri Patheon*, which in his time was falsely attributed to the Aristotelian Andronicus of Rhodes.[10]

For Thomas and his contemporaries, theology is a science distinct from all of these philosophical sciences, including even that part of metaphysics that is concerned with God. The philosophical sciences can be acquired through human effort. In contrast, sacred science is a theology that requires the revelation of truth through Sacred Scripture. Thomas's understanding of Scripture was shaped by the authority of the Catholic Church as well as

[9] Raphael Wolf, *Cicero: The Philosophy of a Roman Skeptic* (London and New York: Routledge, 2015), 125–200.
[10] Michel Cacouros, "Le traité pseudo-Aristotélicien *De virtutibus et vitiis*," in *Dictionnaire des philosophes antiques, Supplément*, ed. Richard Goulet et al. (Paris: CNRS, 2003). 506–546.

by Church writers and earlier medieval theologians. Augustine of Hippo (d. 430) was the most important of the Latin Fathers, but Thomas was also influenced by Ambrose of Milan (d. 397) and Gregory the Great (d. 604). Through the writings he not only learned a kind of theology, but he also came into contact with their appropriation of Stoic and Neoplatonic philosophy. This Neoplatonism in particular shaped his reading of Stoic and Aristotelian philosophy.

Thomas was primarily a theologian who relied on the truths of Sacred Scripture. Philosophical writers were not his only authorities. However, in doing theology he practiced and developed a philosophy that has its roots in the traditions of ancient Rome and Greece. Like his contemporaries, he adopts the notion of theology as a science comparable to the philosophical sciences. In his period, theological studies were preceded by years of study in the philosophical sciences, perhaps in a university or in the religious houses of orders such as the Dominicans and the Franciscans. Not everyone who studied the philosophical sciences in a university went on to theology, but theologians were all proficient in philosophy. Theology, unlike metaphysics, considers not only God in himself but also all of creation in reference to God, including human actions. Consequently, theology includes theological ethics, which depends both on philosophical ethics and on Sacred Scripture.

It is difficult or even impossible to separate Thomas's theology from his philosophy if we think of philosophy as some sort of personal world-view. But if we think of theology and philosophy as distinct sciences, we can see how Thomas practices and develops both. Philosophical ethics studies human acts with the aid of human reason alone. Theology is concerned with such acts insofar as they are understood additionally through revelation. It is not clear that we should call Thomas's philosophy "Christian philosophy" just because he was a Christian or a theologian. Nevertheless, Thomas is primarily a theologian, who develops and uses moral philosophy in the context of his theological work.

Thomas's broader dialectical approach relies on earlier theologians and on Aristotle.[11] Previous scholastic theologians, such as Peter Abelard (d. 1142) and Peter Lombard (d. 1160), had developed a method of theology according to which the author must develop his own view in response to competing common opinions. In such cases, the authority of Augustine might be pitted against that of Gregory the Great or a quotation from one

---

[11] John Jenkins, "Expositions of the Text: Aquinas's Aristotelian Commentaries," *Medieval Philosophy and Theology* 5 (1996): 49–54.

of Augustine's works might be contrasted with a quotation from a different work. This use of conflicting authorities became the foundation of the disputed question format in which many scholastic works were written. Furthermore, Thomas's careful reading of Aristotle exposes him to the method whereby an enquiry begins with common opinions, and most especially the common opinions of the wise. From the perspective of a thirteenth-century reader, Aristotle's evaluation and use of such opinions fitted nicely with the use of authorities in the scholastic tradition. Thomas, like his contemporaries, would think it ridiculous to attempt to build one's own personal philosophy and theology apart from building on previous traditions of enquiry.

This book does not attempt to give a full account of Thomas's moral theology.[12] It does not fully address Thomas's position that the virtues are insufficient for the full Christian life. A complete picture of the moral life would explain how we need not only virtues but gifts of the Holy Ghost by which God moves us. Moreover, it does not discuss the central importance of the beatitudes, which are Jesus Christ's statements about happiness in his central discourse on morality, the Sermon on the Mount. Thomas's account of the virtues is to some extent separable from his account of the gifts and of the beatitudes, even though every acting Christian needs the gifts and should practice the acts described by the beatitudes.

It is important to keep in mind not only the theological context of Thomas's work but even his immediate historical context. Thomas, like any philosopher or theologian, often wrote in response to questions that were pressing at his time, and he addressed these questions by drawing on the conceptual resources that were available to him. For instance, we will see that Thomas does not attempt to pull a definition of virtue out of thin air but that he considers and adapts several traditional definitions that were used by his contemporaries. Were we to ignore the historical context, the variety of definitions and some of his remarks on them would be unintelligible. Similarly, we will later look at how Thomas distinguishes between acquired and infused moral virtue. If Thomas were faced with a variety of theories about how they interacted, we could expect a developed account. But since we know historically that he was among the first to distinguish clearly between them, it is unsurprising that his treatment of their cooperation is scanty. It was not well-travelled ground during his lifetime.

---

[12] For the importance of the gifts and beatitudes, see Servais Pinckaers, *The Sources of Christian Ethics*, 3rd ed., trans. Mary Thomas Noble (Washington, DC: The Catholic University of America Press, 1995), 134–164.

Similar insight can at times be gained from special attention to Thomas's own development. His writings on ethics cover nearly the whole of his roughly twenty-year working life.[13] We will see several instances of how in different works he can give different accounts of apparently the same topics. Sometimes these different accounts might be compatible with each other, but they might also indicate a change in his understanding or even a fuller development of his thought. In general, I attempt to use Thomas's different writings to shed light on each other. But at times we need to see how he changes in light of the various options that were available to him.

Thomas's earliest text on the ethics is his *Commentary on the Sentences*, which is a revised record of his teaching of Peter Lombard's *Sentences*, which was the standard textbook on theology. Thomas lectured on this work in the early 1250s, as part of his progress toward becoming a master in theology. This text is obviously less mature than his later writings, and it follows more or less the conventional order of theological studies. Thomas addressed several ethical issues in his disputed questions *De Veritate*, which he gave in the late 1250s, and the *Summa Contra Gentiles*, which was finished around 1265. In the late 1260s, when Thomas was teaching in Rome, he began his *Summa Theologiae*, which was meant to provide an alternative to Lombard's *Sentences* and perhaps to provide an alternative way of teaching moral theology. But most of his work on ethics was written after he returned to Paris in 1268. This Second Regency (1268–1272) in Paris was his most prolific period, and much of his work was on ethics.

During this Second Regency, Thomas seems to have composed several works that were complementary to the material that he was developing for the *Secunda Pars* of the *Summa Theologiae*. He compiled an outline on and then wrote a full commentary on the *Nicomachean Ethics*. This commentary contains no Christian theology, and it remains an important source not only for Thomas's thought but also for the study of Aristotle. There has been much disagreement over whether Thomas's philosophical commentaries should be seen as a guide to his own thought.[14] In this book I rely on this commentary in particular to show how Thomas understood Aristotle

[13] For Thomas's historical context and dates, I follow Jean-Pierre Torrell, *St. Thomas Aquinas*, vol. 1: *The Person and His Work*, rev. ed., trans. Robert Royal (Washington, DC: The Catholic University of America Press, 2005). A helpful chronology can be found in Porro Pasquale, *Thomas Aquinas: A Historical and Philosophical Profile*, trans. Joseph G. Trabbic and Roger W. Nutt (Washington, DC: The Catholic University of America Press, 2016), 439–443.
[14] For a history of disagreements concerning the nature of this commentary, see Tobias Hoffmann, Jörn Müller, and Mattias Perkams (eds), introduction to *Aquinas and the Nicomachean Ethics* (Cambridge: Cambridge University Press, 2013), 1–12.

during the Second Regency, and we will see that in his other works he uses Aristotle's work as a guide to philosophical moral science. In this book we will see how Thomas thinks that Aristotle gave a preliminary account of the moral and other sciences, at least insofar as they are attainable by human reason. However, he also uses the insights of later writers who add material to Aristotle's account and also give it greater accuracy and precision. Moreover, Aristotle did not have access to divine revelation. Thomas's primary concern is with theology, which is based on divine revelation.

During this same Second Regency, Thomas also gave disputed questions on the virtues, including a general treatment of virtue, the *De Virtutibus in Communi*, and a discussion of the cardinal virtues, the *De Virtutibus Cardinalibus*. Perhaps also in this period he put the final touches on his related disputed questions of sin and vice, the *De Malo*.

Often there is a stark contrast between what he wrote in his early *Commentary on the Sentences* and those texts on ethics that he wrote nearly twenty years later. We will see that at times themes from the *Sentences* commentary appear in some of his later works but not in others. We should keep in mind that opinions about whether and how Thomas develops his view or changes his mind are often conjectural. But the same caution should apply to descriptions of how earlier and later passages might be reconciled.

Although this book addresses all of the most significant texts in which Thomas writes on virtue, its structure follows the section on the virtues in general that we find in the *Prima Secundae*, qq. 56–67. The order of the discussion moves from the more general to the more specific and finishes with an account of the properties of virtue. Chapter 1 considers Thomas's definition of virtue as a good operative habit. To understand this definition, we must first consider how "habit" is a philosophical term that has no counterpart in ordinary English. Moreover, Thomas explains and defends this definition in light of the various authoritative definitions that are available to him, including especially definitions from Aristotle and Peter Lombard.

Chapter 2 is on the distinction between intellectual and moral virtue, which was first clearly delineated by Aristotle. The moral virtues correspond to what are most commonly recognized to be virtues, such as justice and courage. Intellectual virtues are habits of knowing that do not on their own make the agent good. Prudence, however, is significant as an intellectual virtue precisely because of its connection with the moral virtues. Prudence depends on moral virtue, and each moral virtue depends on prudence. Thomas emphasizes that the one virtue of prudence covers the material that belongs to all of the distinct moral virtues.

Chapter 3 considers the various divisions of moral virtue. This chapter describes Thomas's response to the Stoic thesis that the virtuous person lacks passions. Aristotle himself states that some moral virtues are about the passions. Thomas addresses this dispute in light of Augustine's account of the disagreement between the Stoics and the Peripatetics, who were Aristotle's later followers. He shows that he is willing to find some truth in different traditions, even though he primarily follows Aristotle. Moreover, he accepts from earlier Christian sources the originally Stoic and Neoplatonic doctrine that there are four cardinal virtues, namely prudence, justice, courage or fortitude, and temperance.

The topic of the cardinal virtues brings up a difficulty in translation that is best addressed in the beginning of this work. I will use both "courage" and "fortitude" to translate Thomas's use of the Latin word "*fortitudo*" to indicate this cardinal virtue. It seems to me that the word "*fortitudo*" has a wider use in Thomas's work than might be inferred from the sole use of the English word "courage." Although Aristotle uses courage to indicate a mean with respect to daring and the fear of death in battle, Thomas thinks that this habit is about difficult objects more generally.[15] Thomas often follows Aristotle's presentation of courage, but in the *Summa Theologiae* he explains that the principal act of courage or fortitude is endurance, which can also be a distinct virtue, and the primary exemplar of such courage is martyrdom.[16] For merely stylistic reasons, I will generally use "courage" to indicate the virtue insofar as it involves death in battle, and is a cardinal virtue, and I will use "fortitude" when a broader usage is needed. But for our purposes the terms are more or less interchangeable.

Chapter 3 ends with a discussion of the Neoplatonic thesis that there are different kinds or stages of virtue that lead to contemplation. The lowest level, the political, is merely about human affairs. But in the purgative stage, the subject is prepared for contemplation, and the highest human stage is a freedom from passion that is available only to those in heaven and the most perfect saints.

The focus on virtue as a preparation for contemplation prepares for Chapter 4's description of the distinction between natural and supernatural virtues. Natural virtues are acquired through human effort and are

---

[15] Aristotle, *EN* 3.6–7; Thomas, *S.T.*, II-II, q. 123. See Jennifer Herdt, "Aquinas's Aristotelian Defense of Martyr Courage," in *Aquinas and the Nicomachean Ethics*, 110–128.
[16] Thomas, *S.T.*, II-II, q. 124, art. 2.

studied by philosophical ethics. Supernatural virtues must directly come from God. Their existence is known only through revelation. Thomas's predecessors and most subsequent theologians typically identified these infused or supernatural virtues with the three theological virtues of faith, hope, and charity. The theological virtues are directly about God. But Thomas thinks that there must also be distinct infused moral virtues that exist alongside the acquired moral virtues. These infused virtues are specifically distinct from the acquired moral virtues that share the same matter and from the theological virtues that are about God. We will see that to understand much of what Thomas says about the virtues, we must delineate clearly between how such different virtues can be discussed in different contexts. Unfortunately, in some texts it is not clear whether Thomas is considering acquired or infused moral virtue, or even both together indistinctly.

Chapter 5 is about the properties of virtue. These properties follow upon a virtue by the simple fact that it is a virtue. There are four such properties that seem rather loosely connected: the mean of virtue, the connection between the virtues, the order of the virtues, and the duration of virtue after this life. Despite this somewhat loose ordering, each of these properties must be studied if we are to understand Thomas's account of virtue as a whole.

Chapter 6, which is the last chapter, considers the importance and contemporary relevance of Thomas's understanding of the virtues in light of what has been established in the previous chapters. The virtues are not basic to Thomas's understanding of moral goodness in the way that they are in some contemporary versions of virtue ethics. Nevertheless, they are needed to organize and account for the various ways of living a full life. Contemporary sciences might add precision or material to Thomas's account, but it is not clear that they require radical changes to it.

The goal of this book is to help the reader to learn from Thomas despite the differences between his texts themselves and the contemporary reader's tendency to hold background assumptions that make it difficult to assimilate what the various texts contain. I attempt to guide the reader through the various perils resulting from unfamiliarity with the relevant texts, as well as with the philosophical and historical contexts.

CHAPTER I

The Definition of Virtue

Thomas begins his discussion of virtue in the *Prima Secundae* by devoting q. 55 to its definition.[1] Peter Lombard had drawn from Augustine of Hippo's works the definition of virtue as a "good quality of the mind, by which we live rightly, which no one uses badly, which God alone works in a human."[2] In the first three articles of q. 55, Thomas argues that virtue is a good operative habit. In the fourth article he argues that Lombard's Augustinian definition of virtue is the most complete definition. This definition became widespread because the work in which it appeared, Lombard's *Sentences*, was the standard textbook for theology for many centuries. Thomas provides an account and defense of this standard definition not only in the *Summa Theologiae* but also in his early *Commentary on the Sentences* as well as in the roughly contemporaneous *De Virtutibus in Communi*, art. 1–2. However, in the *Summa Theologiae* Thomas more clearly connects this traditional definition with the more precise account of virtue as a good operative habit. His understanding of how the different definitions are related seems to be influenced by earlier writers such as Philip the Chancellor (d. 1236) and Albert the Great, who themselves inherited several definitions of virtue.[3] Thomas adds to this tradition in part by developing a lengthy and more sophisticated account of habits in general. Although his

---

[1] An earlier version of some of the material in Chapter 1 was published as "Operative Habits and Rational Nature," in *El Obrar Sigue Al Ser: Metafísica de la persona, la naturaleza y la acción,* ed. Carlos A. Casanova and Ignacio Serrano del Pozo (Santiago de Chile and Valparaíso: RIL, 2020), 189–208.

[2] "bona qualitas mentis qua recte vivitur et qua nullus male utitur, quam Deus solus in homine operatur": Lombard, *Sent.* lib. 2, d. 27, cap. 1 (1.2, 480). See Philip, *Summa de Bono,* 525; Albert, *De Bono,* tract. 13, q. 5, art. 1, n. 101 (Col., 28, 67). This is largely a compressed form of the description of virtue in Augustine, *De Libero Arbitrio,* 2.19 (CCSL 29, 271). See Lottin, *PM,* 3.1, 101.

[3] Philip, *Summa de Bono,* 525–542; Albert, *De Bono,* tract. 13, q. 5, art. 1, nn. 101–115 (Col., 28, 67–76). For Albert's discussion and dependence on Philip, see Stanley Cunningham, *Reclaiming Moral Agency: The Moral Philosophy of Albert the Great* (Washington, DC: The Catholic University of America Press, 2008), 159–161. For the influence of Philip on Albert and Thomas, see Rollen Edward Houser, introduction to *The Cardinal Virtues: Aquinas, Albert, and Philip the Chancellor* (Toronto: Pontifical Institute for Mediaeval Studies, 2004), 3–4, 42–56.

approach is heavily influenced by Aristotle's *Nicomachean Ethics*, the order of the discussion and the details seem to be Thomas's own.

Thomas's argument for his definition of virtue makes assumptions that might be unfamiliar to some contemporary readers. Some definitions include the causes of what is defined or even different nonessential properties. Among the various types of definition recognized by Thomas and his contemporaries, the most important kind places the species that is to be defined in its most proximate genus. Each intermediate genus itself is a species of another genus, until we ultimately arrive at one of the ten categories, which is composed of substance and nine accidents. For instance, a human being would be defined as a "rational animal." "Human being" is a species that can be defined by placing it in a genus and then indicating the difference that distinguishes it from other members of the genus. The species "human" itself has no species under it. It belongs to the genus "animal," which is a genus that includes every living thing that has sensation. The difference "rational" distinguishes humans from other animals. The genus "animal" includes various species of animals and itself is a species of the genus of living things. Just as there is a lowest species that includes no other species below it, so there are highest genera, which are members of no other genera. Ultimately the highest genus of human beings is a substance, which is something that is a being on its own. The nine accidents, such as quantity and quality, have their being in a substance immediately or through other accidents that have their being in a substance.

We will see that virtues are habits, which are accidents that come under the genus of quality. Powers are accidents that are often jointed to organs that are substantial parts of the substances. For instance, the power of sight is joined to the eye and parts of the brain. Individual humans are complete substances. A virtue is distinguished from many other habits by being an operative habit. It inheres in powers that are rational or in some way subject to reason, such as the intellect, the will, and the sense appetites, which are powers whose acts are passions, or what we might describe as emotions. An operative habit in some way causes operations, which generally speaking are actions and more narrowly speaking are living activities that somehow remain in the agents, such as seeing, hearing, and the peculiarly human activities of thinking and willing. Operative habits are needed because of the indeterminacy of human reason, and they cannot be present in nonrational animals. Typical human operations are proving a mathematical theorem, returning a borrowed item, and stealing. A virtue is distinguished from a vice by being a good operative habit, because it is a source of good operations, which make the agent good.

A virtue perfects a human power in its production of a good operation. We will see that Thomas draws on many different traditional definitions in order to argue for and explain what virtue is. But the overall trajectory of this chapter is to show why Thomas thinks that virtue is a good operative habit and what it means to define virtue in this way.

Habits

Thomas's understanding of habits is often neglected in accounts of his theory of virtues. Servais Pinckaers has argued that contemporary usage might mislead readers to think of habit as a kind of animal reflex or conditioning.[4] But according to Thomas, a habit is a particular kind of quality that other animals cannot possess, since habits inhere only in those powers that are either themselves rational or that participate in reason. Some habits inhere directly in the intellect and will, whereas others inhere in the sensitive appetites insofar as they are subject to reason. Habits are not what might now be described as a kind of physical habituation and conditioning, or "muscle memory." Such conditioning resembles a habit but falls short of it insofar as it does not involve the will in any way.[5] Thomas calls such conditioning a "custom" (*consuetudo*).

Thomas and his predecessors were familiar with many definitions of virtue, which were taken both from Catholic writers and from ancient philosophers.[6] According to Albert and Philip, Lombard's formulation is central even though it might seem to be incompatible with that of the philosophers. In particular, Philip and Albert state that the last part of this definition, which mentions God's agency, does not apply to those virtues that are described by the philosopher but instead to those that are given by God.[7] Nevertheless, they both think that the preceding parts of the definition apply to all virtue, and they argue for the definition's compatibility with Aristotelian definitions. Albert in particular connects the Augustinian definition to an Aristotelian moral and metaphysical understanding of virtue as a habit that inheres in the soul's powers. For example,

---

[4] Servais Pinckaers, "Le vertu est tout autre chose q'une habitude," *Nouvelle Revue Théologique* 82 (1960): 387–403. See also Nicholas Austin, *Aquinas on Virtue: A Causal Reading* (Washington, DC: Georgetown University Press, 2017), 23–36; Jean Porter, *The Perfection of Desire: Habit, Reason, and Virtue in Aquinas's Summa Theologiae* (Milwaukee, WI: Marquette University Press, 2018), 15–54.

[5] Thomas, *S.T.*, I-II, q. 50, art. 3, ad 2. Robert Miner, "Aquinas on Habitus," in *A History of Habit: From Aristotle to Bourdieu*, ed. Tom Sparrow and Adam Hutchinson (Lanham, MD: Lexington Books, 2013), 72–73.

[6] Lottin, *PM*, 3.1, 100–115.

[7] Philip, *Summa de Bono*, 530; Albert, *De Bono*, tract. 13, q. 5, art. 1, n. 110 (Col., 28, 73).

the definition describes virtue as a "good quality of the mind." According to Albert, this definition rightly indicates that virtue belongs to the genus "quality," since virtue is a habit.[8] Aristotelian habits are qualities. This quality belongs to the "mind" because it resides in either the rational part or those parts that obey reason.[9] Thomas seems to be influenced by Albert in his identification of the Aristotelian habit, which is a species of the category quality, with Lombard's quality.

In the *De Bono*, Albert gives two definitions of virtue from the philosophers. First, he mentions Cicero's definition of virtue as "a habit of the soul in the manner of a nature, in accordance with reason."[10] Although Cicero was not an Aristotelian, this definition brings out the Aristotelian theme that virtue resembles another nature. Second, Albert mentions Aristotle's definition of moral virtue in the *Nicomachean Ethics*, Book II, chapter 5, as "a voluntary habit consisting in a mean relative to us, determined by reason, and as the wise human will determine it."[11] Although Philip and Albert in their earlier years did not have access to the whole of the *Nicomachean Ethics*, they did have Latin translations of the first three books, which include Aristotle's definition of virtue. Both Philip and Albert adopt this definition of moral virtue and attempt to show how it is compatible with Lombard's definition and various texts from Augustine and other Catholic authorities.

The identification of the scholastic and Augustinian "quality" with Aristotle's "voluntary habit" might seem forced. For instance, Aristotle did not have the same explicit and well-developed notion of the will that was possessed by medieval philosophers.[12] Consequently, the notion of

---

[8] Albert, *De Bono*, tract. 13, q. 5, art. 1, n. 109 (Col., 28, 72). Philip considers this interpretation in *Summa de Bono*, 540.

[9] Albert, *De Bono*, tract. 13, q. 5, art. 1, n. 109 (Col., 28, 72). Philip seems to place them in the intellect and will in *Summa de Bono*, 529, 540.

[10] "animi habitus naturae modo rationi consentaneus": Cicero, *De Inventione*, lib. 2, c. 53, in Albert, *De Bono*, tr. 1, q. 5, art. 1, n. 101 (Col., 28, 66). For the exact quotation in Augustine, see *De Div. Quaest. 83*, q. 31 (CCSL 44A, 41).

[11] "habitus voluntarius in medietate consistens quoad nos, determinata ratione, et ut sapiens determinabit": Aristotle, *EN* 2.6.1106b36–1107a2, in Albert, *De Bono*, tr. 1, q. 5, art. 1, n. 101 (Col., 28, 66). For Philip's version, see *Summa de Bono*, 526, 537. The Greek would be better rendered as "of choice" or "elective" than "voluntary." Thomas had access to the more accurate translation of virtue as a "*habitus electivus*." See, among many passages, Thomas, *S. T.*, I, I-II, q. 50, art. 1, resp.

[12] For the role of this terminology in Thomas's account, see Bonnie Kent, "Losable Virtue: Aquinas on Character and Will," in *Aquinas and the Nicomachean Ethics*, ed. Tobias Hoffmann, Jörn Müller, and Matthias Perkams (Cambridge: Cambridge University Press, 2013), 99–102; Bonnie Kent, "Transitory Vice: Thomas Aquinas on Incontinence," *Journal of the History of Philosophy* 27 (1989): 218–219. For an argument that Aristotle was at least implicitly committed to the existence of the will as a faculty or power, see Terence Irwin, "Who Discovered the Will?" *Philosophical Perspectives* 6 (1992): 453–473; Terence Irwin, *The Development of Ethics*, vol. 1: *From Socrates to the Reformation* (Oxford: Oxford University Press, 2011), 173–175, 441–442.

voluntariness for Christians was at least verbally connected with a power of the soul that Aristotle did not mention. This verbal connection does not exist in Greek. For instance, medieval translations use the word "*voluntas*" to translate Aristotle's "simple wish" (*boulesis*), but Thomas and others recognized that this meaning of "*voluntas*" was distinct from its use as signifying the will.[13] Moreover, the related Latin term that can be translated as "voluntarily" or "willingly" (*voluntarie*) was used for action that has its source in the agent, and more narrowly an action that comes from the agent's intellect and will. Consequently, it was natural, if perhaps anachronistic, to identify Aristotle's notion of a voluntary action in its fullest sense with their own understanding of an action that has its source in the intellect and the will.

According to Aristotle, nonrational animals and children are capable of action that is voluntary in a wide sense even if it is not rational.[14] He contrasts voluntary action in a wide sense with that voluntary action which is the proper act of virtue, namely choice (*prohairesis/electio*). Aristotle mentions the act of choice but not the will as a faculty. In contrast, Philip's understanding of the importance of the will as a faculty can be seen in his defense of the Aristotle's statement that "Virtue is a habit by which someone is good and renders a work well."[15] Philip mentions as an objection that Aristotle's statement is too broad because it applies to both nonrational animals and children, who themselves are not able to use reason. Philip states that the last part of the definition, "[which] renders the work well," applies only to action that involves the will and intellect and not to the actions of those who lack reason.

In the *Summa Theologiae*, I-II, q. 55, art. 4, Thomas follows Albert and Philip on many of these points, especially in their way of reconciling Aristotle's account of virtue with Lombard's Augustinian definition. Nevertheless, before he discusses the Augustinian definition he devotes several questions to habits in general and several articles to the definition of virtue. In q. 55, art. 1–3, Thomas describes virtue as a good operative habit. This definition seems to be essential in that it gives the genus (operative habit) and a specific difference (good). However, we will see in Chapters 2 to 4 that not all virtues are good in the same way. For Thomas, as for his predecessors, the word "habit" is a technical term that subsumes

---

[13] Thomas, *S.T.*, I-II, q. 8, art. 2, ad 2. Cf. Thomas, *S.T.*, I, q. 83, art. 4.

[14] Aristotle, *EN* 3.2.1111b6-9. See Thomas, *SLE*, lib. 3, lect. 5 (Leonine, 47.1, 132).

[15] "Virtus est habitus a quo quis bonus est et bene reddit opus": Philip, *Summa de Bono*, 337–339. See Aristotle, *EN* 2.5.1102a22-23. Albert discusses the definition only briefly in his *De Bono*, tract. 13, q. 5, art. 1, ad 30, n. 114 (Col., 28, 75).

virtue under the Aristotelians quality of "habit," which helps the agent to act freely and with knowledge. In the immediately preceding qq. 49–54, Thomas discusses the nature of habits, the human powers in which they reside, how they are caused, and the way in which they are distinguished from each other. Thomas's lengthy discussion of habits surpasses previous accounts and illustrates his use of not only the *Nicomachean Ethics* but the Aristotelian corpus as a whole. He uses Aristotle's definition of a habit to explain why habits can be present only in rational powers and those powers that are subject to the rational ones.

Thomas uses different arguments to support the thesis that virtue is a habit. Sometimes he more or less follows Aristotle's arguments that virtue cannot be a passion. In other texts he develops further arguments, according to which virtue cannot be an act. For the most part, these arguments show not so much that virtue can be a habit but that it cannot be something other than a habit.

In the *Commentary on the Sentences*, Thomas states that virtue allows an act to be proportionate to its rational power not only according to its substance but also according to its mode.[16] Rational powers can without habits produce the kinds of acts that can be virtuous, but they will be done without pleasure and with difficulty, since such acts will not be connatural to the agent. A natural power does not need a habit, since a complete nature on its own is directed to a perfect act. God's power is capable of different acts and yet it is proportionate to any perfect act. Consequently, neither natural powers nor God needs habits to act well. In contrast, human powers on their own are not adapted and assimilated to virtuous acts. Habits are necessary because human powers are both undetermined and imperfect. Only a person who has the virtue of chastity chooses chaste acts in a way similar to that in which a heavy object falls downward.

In the *Summa Theologiae*, Thomas begins his argument for the conclusion that virtue is a habit by stating the premise that a virtue is a perfection of a power.[17] Since acts are perfections of powers, it follows that a perfection of a power is that which makes powers act. Habits are such a perfection. As in the *Commentary on the Sentences*, Thomas notes that powers need habits only if they lack determination on their own. In the *Summa Theologiae* he remarks that these undetermined powers are the rational powers that are proper to humans and not to animals or other intellectual creatures. Having argued in the previous questions that human powers

[16] Thomas, *In Sent.*, lib. 2, d. 27, q. 1, art. 1, sol. (Mandonnet-Moos, 2, 695–696).
[17] Thomas, *S.T.*, I-II, q. 55, art. 1, resp.

are perfected and determined by habits, he easily concludes that human virtues must be habits.

Thomas brings together a variety of Aristotelian texts in the *De Virtutibus in Communi*, art. 1. In the body of this question he cites three statements from Aristotle, namely the statement in the Latin of the *De Caelo* that virtue is "the peak of a power" (*ultimum potentiae*), Aristotle's remark in the *Nicomachean Ethics* that virtue renders well the agent and the work, and his statement in the *Physics* that it is a disposition of the perfect for the best.[18] Thomas connects these statements with each other by noting that a perfection of the power makes not only the act good but also the end, which is the agent's perfection. These three statements apply both to all human virtues and to virtue more broadly considered, such as the virtue of a horse or of a stone. In this text he considers human virtue as a kind of virtue taken in a wider sense. We can clearly see here the connection between the notion of virtue itself and that of an excellence or perfection.

Thomas's argument that human virtue is a habit is based on a description of the various kinds of powers. According to Thomas, powers can be divided into those that are only acting, those that are acted upon and acting, and those that are merely acting upon.[19] Instances of the first kind of power include God's power, the agent intellect, and merely natural powers. These powers do not need virtues because they are themselves complete. The virtues are the powers themselves. The third kind of powers, namely those that are merely acted upon, do not need habits either in order to act. The exterior senses belong to this group. For example, the eye perceives color when the eyes when it is opened and functioning properly. The power simply needs its object and the medium by which it sees. Powers that belong to this third group can themselves be called "virtues," in a different but related meaning of the term. The eye sees by the power of sight, which is its "virtue."

Virtuous habits are needed only for those powers of the second kind, that both act and are acted upon.[20] Insofar as they need habits, these powers lack determination to act. Thomas defends the same thesis that Aristotle argues for in the *Nicomachean Ethics*, Book II, chapter 5, in which Aristotle distinguishes virtues from passions and powers. But Thomas gives another

---

[18] Thomas, *DVC*, q. un, art. 1, resp. (Marietti, 708). See also Thomas, *In Sent.*, lib. 2, d. 23, q. 1, art. 3, sol. 1 (Mandonnet-Moos, 2, 706–707). See Aristotle, *De Caelo* 1.13.281a14-18; *Phys.* 7.3.246a13. The Marietti text states erroneously that the latter reference is from the *Met.*

[19] Thomas, *DVC*, q. un, art. 1, resp. (Marietti, 708–709).

[20] Thomas, *DVC*, q. un, art. 1, resp. (Marietti, 709).

argument for the distinction. He remarks that, since virtues are needed by the powers, they cannot be the powers themselves. Virtues are not passions because passions are acted upon, whereas virtues are a form that inheres in a power and helps it to act. Since they inhere in the power and do not belong to the other species of quality, they must be habits. Thomas states that virtue is needed in such powers in order for the operations to be uniform, prompt, and pleasurable. Since the powers are undetermined, they need habits in order to be inclined to one act rather than another. Since the agents are not inclined to the acts by the powers themselves, the agents will take longer to act, since they need to think more explicitly and at greater length about what they are going to do. Furthermore, habit makes a kind of act almost natural. Since an object is pleasurable because it is somehow suitable or fitting to a power, habits make their acts pleasurable for the agents. Thomas quotes Aristotle's *Nicomachean Ethics* in support of the position that virtue makes acts prompt and pleasurable.[21]

In all three texts, namely the *Commentary on the Sentences*, the *Summa Theologiae*, and the *De Virtutibus in Communi*, Thomas is primarily, if not only, concerned in his choice of objections with arguing that virtue is a habit and not an act or a power. He does not use the Aristotelian arguments for the position that it is a habit rather than a power or a passion. One reason might be that the argument in these texts is meant to establish that every virtue is a habit. Aristotle gives the argument in the part of his work that concerns moral virtue. Thomas gives the argument in contexts that include discussions of other kinds of virtue.

Whereas Aristotle argues in the *Nicomachean Ethics* that virtue is a habit by showing that it cannot be a passion or a power, Thomas also argues that it is not an act. This aspect of his discussion might reflect a Christian cultural context according to which virtue is identified with love and regarded as meritorious. Love is an act that can inform many acts, and merit accrues to acts rather than habits. Consequently, a person might be inclined to conclude that virtue is an act and not a habit. However, Thomas incorporates Augustine's description of virtue as love into his Aristotelian account of how virtues are habits. For instance, in *Prima Secundae*, q. 55, art. 1, the second and fourth objections appeal to definitions from Augustine in order to argue that virtue is an act or perhaps a relation. The second objection cites Augustine's claim that "virtue

---

[21] For promptness, see Aristotle, *EN* 3.7.1115a33-35; Thomas, *SLE*, lib. 3, lect. 14 (Leonine, 47.1, 162). For pleasure as a sign of virtue, see Aristotle, *EN* 2.3.1104b3; Thomas, *SLE*, lib. 2, lect. 3 (Leonine, 47.1, 83).

is the good use of free choice (*liberum arbitrium*)."[22] If virtue is a use, then it is an act and not a habit. Thomas replies by stating that this use is only the act of virtue. Augustine's statement is not about virtue itself but about its proper act. The fourth objection recalls Augustine's statements that "virtue is the order of love" and that "the ordering which is called virtue is to enjoy that which should be enjoyed, and to use that which should be used."[23] According to Augustine, use (*uti*) and enjoyment (*frui*) are kinds of love. We love a good through use when we love it for something else. We enjoy something when we love it for its own sake. Use is ultimately for the sake of enjoyment. In these passages Augustine seems to be saying that virtue is an act or relation of love and not a habit. Thomas replies to this interpretation by stating that virtue is the habit that orders this love. In objection three, it is argued that virtue is an act because it is meritorious. Thomas replies that virtue is meritorious insofar as it is a principle of acts and not an act itself.[24] He responds to each of these three objections not by rejecting the contents of Augustine's texts but by showing that when understood correctly they do not conflict with the Aristotelian account.

Subjects of Habits

Thomas holds the view that habits inhere in a power or a nature. Thomas's discussion of habits therefore presupposes the account of the human soul and its powers that he presents in the *Prima Pars* of the *Summa Theologiae*.[25] His whole ethical theory and his moral psychology in the *Secunda Pars* to some extent depend on this earlier discussion. Thomas's description of powers can be confusing, since there is a verbal connection in Latin between powers and potencies.[26] In Thomas's Latin, the word "*potentia*"

---

[22] "Virtus est bonus usus liberi arbitrii." For the probable source, see Augustine, *De Lib. Arbit.* 2.19 (CCSL 29, 271); *Retr.* 1. 9 (CCSL 57, 26–27). See the slightly different response in Thomas, *DVC*, q. un., art. 1, ad 1 (Marietti, 709).

[23] "virtus est ordo amoris." This quote seems to be loosely based on Augustine, *De Mor.*, 1.15 (CSEL 90, 29–30), and is also given by Albert, *De Bono*, tr. 1, q. 5, art. 1, n. 101 (Col. ed., vol. 28, 66). For a different use see Thomas, *DVC*, q. un., art. 1, ad 9 (Marietti, 710). "ordinatio quae virtus vocatur, est fruendis frui, et utendis uti": Augustine, *De Div. Quaest. 83*, q. 30 (CCSL 44A, 38).

[24] See also Thomas, *DVC*, q. un., art. 1, ad 2 (Marietti, 709).

[25] A good general introduction is Stephen L. Brock, *The Philosophy of Saint Thomas Aquinas: A Sketch* (Eugene, OR: Cascade Books, 2015), 51–82. For a more detailed discussion of the soul's powers, see Robert Pasnau, *Thomas Aquinas on Human Nature: A Philosophical Study of Summa Theologiae 1a 75–89* (Cambridge: Cambridge University Press, 2002), 143–170. A contemporary explanation and defense can be found in William Wallace, *The Modeling of Nature: Philosophy of Science and Philosophy of Nature in Synthesis* (Washington, DC: The Catholic University of America Press, 1996), 157–194.

[26] For different uses of "*potentia*," see Thomas, *In Met.*, lib. 5, lect. 14 (Marietti, 256–259).

can be translated in a general way as "potency" and more particularly as "power." Consequently, in order to understand how habits are related to powers, it is helpful in English to distinguish between a "power," which narrowly refers to the soul's capacities to act, and a "potency," which can be contrasted with act in a variety of ways. The wider act/potency distinction is fundamental to the physics and metaphysics of both Thomas and Aristotle, and as such is incapable of definition.[27]

The different kinds of change involve different kinds of potency. We can describe prime matter as in potency to first act, which is the act by which a substantial form determines it to a particular kind. Similarly, the substance itself, although already in first act, can be in potency to further act, as when we say that a substance such as a boy is potentially tall. The substantial form of living beings is the soul. It makes a particular body and its matter exist as a kind of thing that lives and, perhaps, senses and understands. It actualizes the matter so that the composite is a member of a living species. Only certain kinds of things can be changed substantially into a human being, such as eggs, water, and even bacon. Similarly, different substances are often in potency to different accidents. Only humans are in potency to becoming musical or mathematical. Gerbils lack such potencies.

More narrowly, potency covers not only a potency to being actualized by a form but it can also apply to a kind of ability, namely one whose actualization is an act or operation.[28] Such a potency or power of the soul is a principle that is capable of a certain kind of act. For instance, dolphins and gerbils can digest and reproduce, but they do not always do so. The substantial form cannot by itself be the immediate principle of digestion or reproduction, since it is always present and accounts for why the dolphin is a dolphin and a gerbil is a gerbil. Since the soul is a principle of first actuality, such acts require a potency that is intermediate between the soul and the act or operation. It is in this way that the Latin word (*potentia*) that is translated as "potency" is often also translated as "power" or "capacity." A power or capacity is the kind of potency that is a principle of operations. The soul makes the animal a kind of living substance, and a power makes it possible for an animal to perform a particular kind of act. Gerbils and dolphins are able to reproduce and eat because both gerbils and dolphins have the vital powers of nutrition and reproduction.

---

[27] My discussion of change follows in large part Thomas, *De principiis naturae*, ca 1–2 (Leonine, 43, 39–41). For an introductory overview and other texts, see Brock, *Philosophy of Saint Thomas Aquinas*, 25–50. For an explanation in a contemporary context, see Wallace, *Modeling of Nature*, 3–34.

[28] Thomas, *S.T.*, I, q. 54, art. 3; q. 77, art. 1; *DSC*, art. 11 (Marietti, 411–415); *Quod.* 10, q. 3, art. 1 (Leonine, 25. 1, 130–131).

In the *De Virtutibus in Communi* and to some extent the *Commentary on the Sentences*, Thomas clarifies the way in which habits such as virtues belong to powers.[29] He notes that accidents do not subsist and consequently their existence must be supported by a subject. Consequently, in a sense the soul or the soul-body composite is ultimately the subject of all accidents, including habits. Nevertheless, some accidents can belong to others insofar as they are related to them as potency to act and as effect to cause. These accidents belong to the substance by means of other accidents. For example, a color belongs to a substance by virtue of another accident, namely the color's surface, which belongs to the genus of quantity. The color actualizes the surface, even though ultimately both the color and the surface are supported by the substance composed of form and matter. Similarly, a habit is ultimately supported by the soul or soul-body composite by means of the power that it actualizes.

Habits do not belong immediately to the soul or the composite but rather to an accident that inheres in the soul. Whereas the soul belongs to the genus "substance" insofar as it is the formal principle of the substance, power belongs to the genus "quality," which is the genus of accidents that modifies substance in itself.[30] This genus "quality" has four species directly under it, namely power, habit or disposition, sensible quality, and figure or shape. For Thomas, an agent acts by means of her powers. The agent might be most properly the whole organism or less properly an organ or other subject.[31] For instance, we might say that a human sees with her eye but also that her eye sees. We might only very loosely say that her power of sight sees. Powers are principles that are intermediate between a living substance's essence and its operation. Properly speaking, operations and powers other than intellectual ones belong to the conjunct and not to the soul, and the subject of the powers is also in a way the subject of the operations. The conjunct, such as the human, has parts that can be subjects of operations and powers, such as the hand, the foot, and the eye. The non-intellectual powers inhere in the conjunct. The intellectual powers inhere directly in the soul. In this way we can say that a human understands with her soul in the way that she sees with her eye. Strictly speaking, a power that is in a bodily organ cannot be a subject because it is the wrong kind of part.

---

[29] Thomas, *DVC*, q. un. (Marietti, 715–716); *In Sent.*, lib. 3, d. 33, q. 2, art. 4, sol. 1 (Mandonnet-Moos, 3, 1062).
[30] Thomas, *S.T.*, I-II, q. 49, art. 2, resp.; q. 50, art. 2, ad 3.
[31] Thomas, *S.T.*, I, q. 75, art. 2, ad 2; q. 77, art. 5; *DSC*, art. 2, ad 2 (Leonine, 24.2, 30).

Powers are distinguished from each other by formal objects, or what they are about.[32] For instance, sight has color as its formal object, whereas hearing's formal object is sound. We might hear and see the same object, such as a rubber ball or an automobile, but the formal object is specific to a sense. For instance, I can see a yellow car and a blue automobile because redness and blueness are both species of color. Passive powers, such as seeing and hearing, have formal objects that are principles of their activity. Active powers, such as reproduction and moving in place, have formal objects that are goals to which they are directed. According to Thomas, there are five genera of vital powers: vegetative, sensitive, intellective, appetitive, and locomotive.[33] The vegetative powers are common to plants, nonrational animals, and human beings. These powers have as their subject the body to which the soul is united. For instance, nutrition and growth conserve and extend the living body, and reproduction produces another living body of the same kind and even with some of the same matter.[34] Such vegetative powers are not perfected by habits.

Some powers are common to both nonrational animals and humans, whereas others are present in humans alone.[35] It is worth considering the different species of human powers in order to understand why some can receive habits and others cannot. Some powers receive similitudes of external objects, whereas other powers incline the animal towards other objects. Cognitive powers, including the senses and the intellect, receive similitudes of external objects. The outer senses directly receive the sensible species, and the inner senses coordinate, store, and add aspects of suitability and time to them. Sensation is concerned with the accidental qualities of the material individual. There are about five external sense powers and four internal sense powers.[36] In contrast to sensation, which is about singulars, the human intellect is most apt to know adequately the natures of material substances.[37]

The intellect consists of two distinct powers, namely the agent intellect, which makes the individual material objects actually intelligible, and the possible intellect, which apprehends, judges, and reasons.[38] The possible

---

[32] *S.T.*, I, q. 77, art. 3; *SLDA*, lib. 2, ca 6 (Leonine, 45.1, 93–94); *QDA*, q. 13 (Leonine, 24.1, 113–122).

[33] Thomas, *S.T.*, I, q. 78, art. 1.

[34] Thomas, *S.T.*, I, q. 78, art. 2.

[35] For Thomas's account of sensation, see especially Anthony Kenny, *Aquinas on Mind* (New York and London: Routledge, 1993), 31–40; Pasnau, *Aquinas on Human Nature*, 171–199.

[36] *S.T.*, I, q. 78, art. 3–4; *QDA*, q. 13, resp. (Leonine, 24.1, 117–119). Touch in a way is a genus to which different sense powers belong.

[37] Thomas, *S.T.*, I, q. 84, art. 7; q. 87, art. 3; *SLDA*, lib. 3, ca 2 (Leonine, 45.1, 212–213).

[38] Thomas, *S.T.*, I, q. 79, art. 1–3. For Thomas's account of the intellect, see especially Kenny, *Aquinas on Mind*, 41–58, 89–128; Pasnau, *Aquinas on Human Nature*, 267–360.

intellect changes the functioning of two interior senses.[39] In animals the estimative sense judges by instinct the suitability or dangerousness of perceived objects, and the memory allows some sense of the past. For example, a sheep judges by instinct that wolves are dangerous and retains some notion of past experience with a wolf. In humans, two of the four internal senses are specifically distinct because of the way in which they depend on the intellect. The estimative sense is instead the cogitative sense, or particular reason, and the memory is reminiscence, which involves an intellectual grasp of time. The cogitative power is particularly important in human action and emotion, since it judges concerning particular actions and experiences.[40]

Two powers incline the living substance towards something else, namely the power of appetite and movement in place.[41] The appetitive powers are particularly important for Thomas's moral psychology. There are three appetitive powers. Two appetitive powers belong to the sense appetite, namely the concupiscible appetite and the irascible appetite.[42] As sense appetites, these powers are common to other animals, and they incline their possessors towards a sensibly perceived good or away from a sensibly perceived danger. The acts of the sense appetites can be described as "passions" or "emotions." The concupiscible appetite involves the sensible good in itself, whereas the irascible appetite involves this good under the aspect of difficulty. For instance, a dog through her concupiscible appetite might desire to eat a steak because she loves it. She is sad when the human eats the steak. Through the irascible appetite she might hope that she can have leftovers even while she is afraid that the steak might be completely eaten. The concupiscible appetite is capable of such passions as love, hate, desire, aversion, hope and sorrow. The irascible appetite is capable of passions

---

[39] Thomas, S.T., I, q. 78, art. 4, resp. and ad 4; SLDA, lib. 2, ca 13 (Leonine, 45.1, 121–122). Anthony Lisska, Aquinas's Theory of Perception: An Analytic Reconstruction (Oxford: Oxford University Press, 2016), 237–272.

[40] Rudolf Allers, "The Vis Cogitativa and Evaluation," New Scholasticism 15 (1941): 195–221; Daniel De Haan, "Moral Perception and the Function of the Vis Cogitativa in Thomas Aquinas's Doctrine of Antecedent and Consequent Passions," Documenti e studi sulla traditione filosofica medievale 25 (2014): 289–330.

[41] For the motive power, see Thomas, SLDA, lib. 3, ca 8-10 (Leonine, 45.1, 238–251).

[42] Thomas, S.T., I, q. 81, art. 2.; I-II, q. 22, art. 2; q. 24, art. 4. For Thomas's account of the appetitive powers, see especially Kenny, Aquinas on Mind, 59–88; Pasnau, Aquinas on Human Nature, 200–233. For an overview of the passions, see Kevin White, "The Passions of the Soul," in The Ethics of Aquinas, ed. Stephen J. Pope (Washington, DC: Georgetown University Press, 2002), 103–115. For monographs, see especially Nicholas Lombardo, The Logic of Desire: Aquinas on Emotion (Washington, DC: The Catholic University of America Press, 2010); Robert Miner, Thomas Aquinas on the Passions: A Study of Summa Theologiae 1a2ae 22–48 (Cambridge: Cambridge University Press, 2009).

such as hope, despair, daring, fear, and anger. In animals these appetites are directed by the estimative power, whereas in humans they are directed by the cogitative.

The rational appetite or will is capable of such passions but only in an extended way.[43] The will follows the good that is apprehended by the intellect.[44] Consequently, its object is the good in general rather than any one particular good, and it can freely choose between some particular goods. Unlike some of his predecessors and contemporaries, Thomas denies that there is a distinction of powers in the will between the concupiscible and the irascible.[45] His reasoning is that since the will, unlike the sense appetites, is concerned with the good that is generally perceived, its object cannot be divided in such a way that would entail a division of powers. Since humans are the only animals that have reason, they are the only animals that have a rational appetite or will. We will see that only some of these human powers are capable of being subjects of habits, namely those that are rational or those that participate in reason. The intellect and the will are essentially rational.

When Thomas describes virtue as a perfection of a power, he interprets "power" in this context as referring to powers for acting and to a potentiality for being. In this way "power" includes both matter and the powers of the soul.[46] Consequently, "virtue" includes both the form that actualizes matter and the habits that inhere in powers. An important premise of Thomas's argument is that human virtue is concerned with that which is proper to humans and not to other animals or bodies. Reason is the property that sets humans apart. Consequently, Aristotle and Thomas argue that human perfection involves rational activity. Although virtue in its wide sense might describe any sort of actualization of a potential, the human virtue under discussion is concerned with rational activity. Consequently, human virtue is neither a disposition of the body nor of some power that is common to the body and the soul but a habit that inheres either in rational powers or other powers insofar as they are

---

[43] Thomas, *S.T.*, I-II, q. 22, art. 3. For discussions, see Lombardo, *Logic of Desire*, 82–87; Miner, *Thomas Aquinas on the Passions*, 35–38; Peter King, "Aquinas on the Passions," in *Thomas Aquinas: Contemporary Philosophical Perspectives*, ed. Brian Davies (Oxford: Oxford University Press, 2002), 353–384, at 354–359. King's essay was originally published in *Aquinas's Moral Theory: Essays in Honor of Norman Kretzmann*, ed. Scott MacDonald and Eleonore Stump (Ithaca, NY: Cornell University Press, 1999), 101–132.

[44] Thomas, *S.T.*, I, q. 82, art. 1–2. Among many other texts, see especially Thomas, *DM*, q. 6 (Leonine, 23, 145–153). For an overview, see David Gallagher, "The Will and Its Acts," in *The Ethics of Aquinas*, 69–89.

[45] Thomas, *S.T.*, I, q. 82, art. 5; *In Sent.*, lib. 3, d. 17, art. 1, sol. 3, ad 4 (Mandonnet-Moos, 3, 533); *DV*, q. 25, art. 3 (Leonine, 22.3, 734–736); *SLDA*, lib. 3, ca 8 (Leonine, 45.1, 240–242).

[46] Thomas, *S.T.*, q. 55, art. 2, resp.

rational by participation. It is a power for acting. Since this habit is concerned with the activity of these powers, it follows that human virtue must be an operative habit. It is directly concerned with human operations.

Not all powers can be subjects of habits. According to Aristotle and Thomas, operative habits allow us to think, act, and feel better or worse than we would otherwise be able to. The habits that produce operations belong to those powers that are rational or in some way obedient to reason.[47] They are not unthinking bodily reflexes. Nonrational animals lack such habits because their powers function according to instinct. They might develop something like operative habits insofar as they have been trained to act in a particular way by human reason. But true habitual action is not instinctive but rather a result of a power that has been perfected by a habit. The sense powers and appetites are capable of being perfected by habits only to the extent that they are obedient to reason, as when someone habitually feels a passion such as anger or the desire for food.

Some habits can inhere in the possible intellect and in the will even if in some way they require bodily dispositions. Thomas states that the interior senses can be subject to habits only to the extent that they dispose the possible intellect to act. Such habits are principally in the intellect and only secondarily in the inner senses, such as the memory.[48] In another context, Thomas writes, "just as the act of the intellect is indeed principally and formally in the intellect itself, but materially and dispositively in the inferior powers, the same should be said of a habit."[49] In this life our intellectual activity uses sense information. Since this sense information is in the inner senses, the inner senses and most properly their organs are in a way subjects of intellectual habits.

Thomas's understanding of the virtues depends on his interpretation of the Aristotelian thesis that the sense appetites can have habits because they are in a wide sense obedient to reason.[50] Using Aristotelian terminology, he

---

[47] Thomas, *S.T.*, I-II, q. 50, art. 3–5; *In Sent.*, lib. 2, d. 23, a. 1, art. 1, sol. (Mandonnet-Moos, 2, 698–699); *DV*, q. 20, art. 2; q. 24, art. 4, ad 9 (Leonine, 22.2, 572–5765; 22.3, 691–692); *DVC*, art. 1, resp. (Marietti, 708–709).

[48] Thomas, *S.T.*, I-II, q. 50, art. 4, ad 3.

[49] "sicut actus intellectus principaliter quidem et formaliter est in ipso intellectu, materialiter autem et dispositive in inferioribus viribus, idem etiam dicendum est de habitu": Thomas, *S.T.*, I, q. 89, art. 5, resp.

[50] Thomas, *S.T.*, I, q. 81, art. 3; *DV*, q. 25, art. 4 (Leonine, 22.3, 736–737); *SLE*, lib. 1, lect. 20 (vol. 47.1, 72–73). This view can also be found in some way in Augustine, *De Sermone Domini in Monte*, 12.34 (CCSL 35, 36–38); *Confess.*, 8.5.11 (CCSL 27, 120). See Simo Knuuttila, *Emotions in Ancient and Medieval Philosophy* (Oxford: Clarendon, 2004), 169. For debates on whether the sense appetite is the subject of virtue, see Bonnie Kent, *Virtues of the Will: The Transformation of Ethics in the Late Thirteenth Century* (Washington, DC: The Catholic University of America Press, 1995).

describes this obedience as political and royal, as opposed to despotic.[51] The reason why this obedience is political and royal, is that the sensitive appetites are directed by the cogitative power, which itself participates in reason and obeys reasoning concerning universals. We can, for instance, influence our fear of flying by considering its relative safety in comparison with automobile travel. These passions do not obey reason in the way that our bodily members do. I can lift up my hand whenever I want, but I can quell fear or cause sensitive love at will sometimes only indirectly. Thomas thinks that many of these powers can be subjects of habits. Nevertheless, he thinks that only subjects with intellects and wills can have such habits, even though such sensitive powers are also possessed by nonrational animals. Moreover, he thinks that even some of these shared powers sometimes possess habits in a secondary way.

Some powers are capable of being modified by habits or dispositions, which are another species of quality.[52] According to Thomas, "A habit means a certain disposition with respect to the order to the nature of the thing, and to its own operation or its end, according to which the things is well or badly disposed to this."[53] Why do the powers need to be modified in some way in order to operate well or poorly? We can see and digest with the powers that we have at birth. Only some powers need to be disposed by habits. The reason is that many powers can be determined in different ways. For instance, we might develop the ability to do geometry or arithmetic, or we might consistently make certain mistakes. Similarly, we can learn how to paint or make music well or poorly. There can be a bodily component to these skills, but the bodily component itself results from the original decisions made by

---

[51] Aristotle, *Pol.* 1.5.1254b2-6; Lombardo, *Logic of Desire*, 99–101; Steven Jensen, "Virtuous Deliberation and the Passions," *The Thomist* 77 (2013): 203–208; Nicholas Kahm, *Aquinas on Emotion's Participation in Reason* (Washington, DC: The Catholic University of America Press, 2019); Pasnau, *Aquinas on Human Nature*, 257–264; Santiago Ramirez, *De Actibus Humanis: In I-II Summa Theologiae Expositio (QQ. VI-XXI)* (Madrid: Instituto de Filosofia "Luis Vives," 1972), 135–160. For general discussions of the regulation of passions by reason, see also Claudia Eisen Murphy, "Aquinas on Our Responsibility for Our Emotions," *Medieval Philosophy and Theology* 8 (1999): 163–205; Elisabeth Uffenheimer-Lippens, "Rationalized Passion and Passionate Rationality: Thomas Aquinas on the Relation between Reason and the Passions," *The Review of Metaphysics* 56 (2003): 525–558; Guiseppe Butera, "On Reason's Control of the Passions in Aquinas's Theory of Temperance," *Medieval Studies* 68 (2006): 133–160; Leonard Ferry, "Sorting Out Reason's Relation to the Passions in the Moral Theory of Aquinas," *Proceedings of the American Catholic Philosophical Association* 88 (2015): 227–244.

[52] *S.T.*, I-II, q. 49, art. 1–2; *DVC*, art. 1 (Marietti, 707–710). For a general discussion, see Bernard Inagki, "Habitus and Natura in Aquinas," in *Studies in Medieval Philosophy*, ed. John F. Wippel (Washington, DC: The Catholic University of America Press, 1987), 166–172.

[53] "habitus importat dispositionem quandam in ordine ad naturam rei, et ad operationem vel finem eius, secundum quod bene vel male aliquid ad hoc disponitur." *S.T.*, I-II, q. 49, art. 4, resp.

the will and directed by the intellect. When a potency is capable of being determined in different ways, then there is a need for a habit to make sure that the act can be performed consistently, without much thought, and pleasurably. Someone with the habit of geometry does not need to struggle when setting forth simple proofs. Similarly, it would be frustrating for a painter to relearn each day the basic principles of painting.

A habit not only produces a particular kind of act, it also causes the kind of act to be done in a particular way, namely pleasurably, readily, and easily.[54] Thomas often states that vice or virtue is natural in the sense that "custom is another nature."[55] These features of the act result from the fact that they are connatural to the habit that causes them. A habitual act's connaturality indicates an essential feature of habits, at least if the word "habit" is taken in the strictest sense. According to Thomas, there is a connection between the description of habit as another nature and Aristotle's description of a habit as a stable quality. Thomas writes:

> Truly [what is received] is retained in the mode of a habit when what is received is as it were made connatural to the one receiving: and thence it is that habit is called by the Philosopher "a quality difficult to change"; thence also it is that operations proceeding from a habit are pleasurable, ready at hand, and easily performed, since they are as it were connatural effects.[56]

The effects are connatural to the way in which the agent has been modified by the habit. Someone who habitually understands geometry is the kind of person who is able to construct geometrical proofs as if the activity were natural to him.

Thomas discusses habits along with dispositions, which can be either specifically distinct from habits or imperfect versions of them.[57] We will see that the virtues can be dispositions that are imperfect habits and that such

---

[54] Thomas, *In Sent.*, lib. 2, d. 27, q. 1, art. 2 (Mandonnet-Moos, 2, 695–696); *DV*, q. 1, art. 5, ad 12 (Leonine, 22, 20) *S.T.*, I, q. 89, art. 6, ad 3. The connection to pleasure is particularly addressed in *SLE*, lib. 2, lect. 5 (Leonine, 47.1, 83–84).

[55] "consuetudo est altera natura." Thomas, *DV*, q. 24, art. 10, resp. (Leonine, 22.3, 706). See also Thomas, *S.T.*, I, q. 63, art. 5. ad 2; I-II, q. 32, art. 2, ad 3; *DVC*, q. un., art. 8, ad 16; art. 9, resp. (Marietti, 729, 732). See Bonnie Kent, "Habits and Virtues," in *The Ethics of Aquinas*, 116–117.

[56] "Tunc vero recipitur per modum habitus quando illud receptum efficitur quasi connaturale recipienti et inde est quod habitus a Philosopho dicitur 'qualitas difficile mobilis'; inde est etiam quod operationes ex habitu procedentes delectabiles sunt et in promptu habentur et faciliter exercentur, quia sunt quasi connaturales effectae." Thomas, *DV*, q. 20. art. 2, resp. (Leonine, 22.2, 575). The definition is from Aristotle, *Categ.* 8.9a4.

[57] Miner, "Aquinas on Habitus," 68–75. For a full discussion of Thomas's texts in light of his Greek, Arabic, and Latin predecessors, see Santiago Ramirez, *De Habitibus in Communi: In I-II Summae Theologiae Divi Thomae Expositio (QQ. XLIX-LIV)* (Madrid: Instituto de Filosofia "Luis Vives," 1973), vol. 1, 60–93; vol. 2, 255–281.

dispositions can exist in those creatures that possess reason. In contrast, the other kind of dispositions, which are specifically distinct from habits, are common to nonrational creatures. Arabic, Latin, and Greek writers had generally understood all dispositions as members of the first species, namely as imperfect habits. Latin writers are in particular influenced by Boethius's presentation of this position in his commentary on Aristotle's *Categories*.[58] According to this explanation, disposition differs from habit even less than Socrates's humanity differs from Plato's humanity. Socrates and Plato are specifically the same, but they differ as persons. A disposition differs from a habit only in the way in which an older Socrates differs from Socrates as a child. A disposition itself becomes a habit when it becomes more permanent.[59] Disposition is distinct from habit because a disposition is unstable whereas a habit is lost only with difficulty. On this account, the formal characteristic of the disposition and habit is the same. The difference between them seems to be that the agent possesses a disposition imperfectly and a habit perfectly.

Thomas's most significant passage on habits in relation to dispositions is the *Summa Theologiae*, I-II, q. 49, art. 2, ad 3. In this passage, he makes a threefold distinction between 1) disposition as a genus of habit, 2) disposition as an imperfect habit, and 3) disposition as a distinct kind of quality from habit. The second and third kinds of disposition are both easily changed (*facile mobilis*). Thomas first distinguishes between that disposition which is a genus of habit and included in the definition of a habit and those dispositions which are distinct from habit. In this first sense a habit is a kind of disposition. The second and third kinds of disposition are distinct from habits. In these second and third senses of the term "disposition," a disposition is easy to lose whereas a habit is stable. These easily lost dispositions are divisible into the second sense of "disposition," which shares a common name with habits, and the third sense, which indicates dispositions that are distinct in kind from habits. The second sense is the same in kind as a habit but imperfect. It corresponds to the traditional usage, which Thomas usually follows in his other writings and later in the *Prima Secundae*.[60] In this sense justice or temperance might

---

[58] Boethius, *In Categoria Aristotelis Libri IV* (PL 64, col. 241).

[59] Thomas writes very little on the actual development of such habits. See Miner, "Aquinas on Habitus," 75–80; Tobias Hoffmann, "Aquinas on Moral Progress," in *Aquinas's Summa Theologiae: A Critical Guide*, ed. Jeffrey Hause (Cambridge: Cambridge University Press, 2018), 131–149.

[60] Thomas, *S.T.*, I-II, q. 88, art. 4, ad 4; *In Sent.*, lib. 3, d. 23, q. 1, art. 1, qc. 3 (Mandonnet-Moos, 3, 698); *In Sent.*, lib. 4, d. 4, q. 1, art. 1, resp. (Mandonnet-Moos, 4, 150); *DM*, q. 7, art. 2, ad 4 (Leonine, 23, 164); art. 3, ad 4, 11 (Leonine, 23, 168–169); art. 6, ad 5 (Leonine, 23, 175). Ramirez, *De Habitibus*, vol. 1, 63–93, argues that Thomas moves from an earlier "Aristotelian" understanding of dispositions to his own account of them as specifically distinct.

be a disposition and not a habit if it is imperfect. However, the passage
under discussion explicitly distinguishes between dispositions that are
unstable on account of their possession by the agent and dispositions that
are unstable on account of their species. This latter kind of disposition,
which is the third, includes sickness and health, which can easily be lost
on account of their formal characteristics. This third kind of disposition
is not operative, since it is concerned with the nature rather than with
operations. It changes when the relevant qualities change. Such specifically distinct dispositions are always unstable on account of their objects
even though they might be firmly possessed by some subjects. Such dispositions are essentially unstable, whereas the other kinds are only acci-
dentally unstable.

When discussing the way in which dispositions differ from habits on
account of their instability, it is important to consider the source of the
instability. Health and beauty are unstable because they are corporal dispositions.[61] They have changeable bodies as their subjects and therefore
are themselves easily changed. They always remain the kinds of things
that are unstable. In contrast, a virtue or science is stable because it is a
quality of the soul. The difference between a disposition and stable habit
in this context involves the way in which it is perfectly or imperfectly
possessed in the subject. The subject itself, namely the power in which
the habit inheres, presents no obstacle to the quality's stability. When perfectly acquired, the intellectual virtues acquired through acts of knowing
and the moral virtues are difficult to lose. Moral virtues are more difficult
to develop than demonstrative sciences are, since their possession requires
many more acts.[62]

This instability of bodily dispositions helps to explain why bodies cannot be the subjects of habits that are essentially stable.[63] Merely bodily
operations result from the nature of the body and do not need habits to
perfect them. In living substance, the soul is the principle of even those
vital operations that are carried out by means of the body. But the operations belong more to the soul insofar as they are less determined to occur
in only one way. Consequently, habitual dispositions such as beauty and
health primarily involve bodily options and consequently inhere in the
body. But habits more narrowly speaking are essentially stable dispositions that are ordered to operations of the soul. Consequently, essentially
stable habits such as virtues and sciences must exist in the soul, at least in

[61] Thomas, *S.T.*, I-II, q. 50, art. 1, ad 2.
[62] Thomas, *DVC*, q. un. art. 9, ad 11 (Marietti, 732).
[63] Thomas, *S.T.*, I-II, q. 50, art. 1.

a primary way. It is only in a secondary sense that habits can be said to be in the bodies insofar as the bodily composition of the animal helps the soul to act more quickly and easily. Moreover, even though such bodily dispositions might be stable on account of their individual subjects, they remain subject to change in a way that qualities of the soul are not.

The distinction between habits and specifically distinct dispositions indicates why moral virtues and sciences must belong to the soul's powers.[64] Broadly speaking, a habit or disposition can be in the soul in two ways. First, it can be present in the soul as a disposition to something higher. Thomas explains health and habitual grace in this way. Just as health is a disposition of the body as ordered to the soul, so habitual grace is a disposition of the soul in order to the divine nature. In this same way a habit or disposition can also be an inordinate disposition and lack of harmony. Thomas explains illness and original sin in this way.[65] Second, a habit can be present in a power. Such habits, since they involve operation, perfect those powers that are principles of operation. The operations are made better or worse by them.

Operative Habits

In I-II, q. 55, art. 2, Thomas argues that virtue is an operative habit. Although later writers would distinguish between operative and entitative habits, Thomas himself does not use the word "entitative." Nevertheless, he explicitly distinguishes between operative habits and habits that are not. The importance of this distinction between kinds of habits can be seen in light of its denial by later authors. For instance, Peter Aureol (d. 1322) and Durandus of Saint-Pourçain (d. 1334) hold that the powers and not the habits are causes of a human act.[66] According to their view, no habits would be essentially operative. In contrast, Francisco Suarez (1548–1617) argues that all habits are essentially operative.[67] Thomists in response to both groups defend the distinction between operative habits and nonoperative or entitative habits.[68]

---

[64] Thomas, *S.T.*, I-II, q. 50, art. 2.

[65] Thomas, *S.T.*, I-II, q. 82, art. 1, resp.

[66] Durandus of Saint-Pourçain, *In Sent.*, lib. 3, d. 23, q. 2, in *In Petri Lombardi Sententias Theologicas Commentariorum Libri IIII*, 2 vols. (Venice: Typographica Guerrae, 1571; repr. Ridgewood, NJ: Gregg Press, 1964), fol. 252v–253r; Peter Aureol, *In Sent.*, lib. 1, d. 17, 2, q. 4, in *Commentarium in Primum Librum Sententiarum, pars prima* (Rome: Zannetti, 1605), 422–423.

[67] Francisco Suarez, *Disputationes Metaphysicales*, d. 42, sect. 5, n. 19, in *Opera Omnia*, 26 vols. (Paris: Vives, 1856–1878), vol. 26, 620.

[68] Ramirez, *De Habitibus*, vol. 1, 94–117.

The position that all habits are essentially operative might seem to be similar to Thomas's position that all habits in some way involve an order to operation, which he defends in I-II, q. 49, art. 3. But Thomas distinguishes between two relevant kinds of order. The differences between the kinds of order reflect the definition of habit as a disposition with respect to a nature or with respect to an act or end. A habitual disposition such as health is in order to a nature. Consequently, it is directed to an act only insofar as nature is a principle of action. In contrast, an operative habit is directly concerned with the operation or end. Consequently, it can be denominated as "operative" in contrast with the kind of habit that is concerned with operation only by means of a nature. Thomas's distinction between habits that are operative and those that are not consequently depends on Aristotle's definition of "habit," which includes both nature and operation.

The main point is that such operative habits exist in order to modify actions. These actions need such modification because they are in some way undetermined. Animal actions, even though they might be similar to human actions, are ultimately explained by instinct. Human actions have their source in the intellect and in the will, which are to some extent indeterminate. Consequently, such properly human actions need to be perfected by habits. Properly speaking, habits can exist only in the possible intellect, the will, or the sense appetites. The possible intellect and the will can be determined to action by habits. Since human sense appetites are to some extent subject to reason, they can also be properly subject to habits. In contrast, the internal senses themselves are not principally subjects of habits, although, in a way, they can be modified to cooperate with the intellect.

The sensitive appetites can be the principal subjects of virtue, but the sense powers, including the inner senses, cannot.[69] The reason for this difference rests in the way that a good work is made complete. The perfection of human action often finishes with that of the sense appetite, but the perfection of knowledge starts with the senses and ends in the intellect. The activity of the will, which is the rational appetite, extends to that of the sense appetite when the will moves the sense appetite. The completion of virtue can be in the sense appetite. But the direction of influence is the other way for cognition. The works of the inner senses are ordered to intellectual knowledge. In this way the inner senses move the intellect. The completion of knowledge is not brought about in the inner senses.

---

[69] Thomas, *S. T.*, I-II, q. 56, art. 6, resp. et ad 1.

Thomas's understanding of the connection between habits and rationality is perhaps at odds with some later notions, according to which a habit is a kind of physical or mental conditioning that makes an act unthinking. According to such a view, habits could even be obstacles to human freedom. For Thomas, operative habits perfect the action of the intellect and the will either by directly inhering in these powers or by inhering in powers that participate somehow in their activity. A conditioned psychological response would not be habitual in this sense. A habit might cause such conditioning, but the conditioning would be distinct. Operative habits belong only to creatures that have an intellect and a will.

A Good Operative Habit

Both Thomas and Aristotle think that the ultimate end of humans is in one sense happiness and in another sense God, or the First Mover. They state that happiness consists in operations that are proper to humans. Happiness is consequently the ultimate end of human beings, and the ultimate end is the first principle of human action and ethics. They also hold that there is one final end of the universe, which Aristotle describes as the First Mover.[70] Thomas follows a long philosophical and theological tradition in identifying this First Mover with God.[71] He explains that God is the ultimate end of the entire universe and all human beings insofar as he is a thing that is to be attained, much in the same way that money is the final end of the miser.[72] But when we consider the human attainment of this end, the ultimate end is the good for the soul that is happiness. Virtue is part of the definition of this good of the soul.

Before looking at their description of the human good, it is worthwhile to consider the term "happiness," which is usually used to translate the Greek *eudaimonia* and the Latin *beatitude*. Other words are sometimes used, such as "flourishing" or "beatitude," but there seems to be no fully satisfactory translation in modern languages. Alasdair MacIntyre states that happiness is now generally understood as "a state of only positive

---

[70] Aristotle, *Met.* 12.10; Thomas, *In Met.*, lib. 12, lect. 12 (Marietti, 612–616).

[71] For the background in Neoplatonism, see Richard Sorabji, "Infinite Power Impressed: The Transformation of Aristotle's Physics and Theology," in *Aristotle Transformed: The Ancient Commentators and Their Influence*, ed. Richard Sorabji (Ithaca, NY: Cornell University Press, 1990), 181–198.

[72] Thomas, *S.T.*, I-II, q. 2, art. 7. See also Thomas, *S.T.*, I-II, q. 1, art. 8, and q. 3, art. 1. For a summary of Thomas's teaching on happiness, see Thomas M. Osborne Jr., *Aquinas's Ethics* (Cambridge: Cambridge University Press, 2020), 6–19.

feelings."[73] He notes that from the standpoint of a Thomistic Aristotelian, there might be good reasons to be unhappy in this sense.[74] For instance, one might have good feelings in a bad situation because of one's low expectations. Moreover, one might irrationally feel great in the face of terrible moral or physical evils. In contrast, for Aristotle and Thomas, happiness consists in leading what we might describe as a worthwhile life. It involves activities that are desirable for their own sake, although they may be desirable. Positive feelings have many internal and external causes, but the human end is there for us to discover and achieve. Consequently, there is a deep incompatibility between the happiness that is discussed by philosophers such as Aristotle and Thomas and the concept of happiness that is used by contemporary economists, political scientists, and indeed many ordinary persons. For lack of a better alternative, we will retain the term "happiness" for the attainment of the human end that is described by Aristotle and Thomas.

Aristotle and Thomas state that happiness is an operation in accordance with reason.[75] Aristotle writes, "the human good will be an operation according to virtue, but if there are many virtues, according to the most perfect and best."[76] A substance's perfection is connected with its proper function, which is based on the kind of substance that it is. For instance, dolphins, trees, and minerals all have different natures and consequently different proper functions. Minerals tend to stay what they are unless they are acted upon, and they have some determined sense qualities and weight. Trees share the inanimate qualities of their minerals and elements, but they also have properties that are proper to them, such as nutrition and growth. Generally speaking, a tree that stops growing upwards lacks perfection. Dolphins grow and have a certain weight, but their perfections consist in activities that involve sensation, desire, movement through water, and cooperative activity with members of their pod. When discussing the perfection of a species we look to its proper function. A dolphin's weight or growth is important only to the extent that it affects the dolphin's proper function. The animal's goodness is relative to such a function.

Having previously argued in q. 54, art. 3, that goodness and badness are specific differences of habits, it is unsurprising to see the use of "good"

---

[73] Alasdair MacIntyre, *Ethics in the Conflicts of Modernity: An Essay on Desire, Practical Reasoning, and Narrative* (Cambridge: Cambridge University Press, 2016), 196.

[74] MacIntyre, *Ethics in the Conflicts of Modernity*, 196–202.

[75] Aristotle, *EN* 1.7.1097b23-1098a21; Thomas, *SLE*, lib. 1, lect. 10 (Leonine, 47.1, 35–37).

[76] "humanum bonum operatio fit secundum virtutem, si autem plures virtutes, secundum perfectissimam et optimam." Aristotle, *EN* 1.7.1098a16-17, in Thomas, *SLE*, lib. 1, lect. 10 (Leonine, 47.1, 34).

as a specific difference that sets virtues apart from bad habits. The argument itself is based on the premise that virtue is a perfection of a power. Since evil is a defect and the good is perfect, the conclusion immediately follows. The only difficulty might be in the connection between the perfection of a power and goodness. Perhaps this connection is verbally more problematic in Latin, since *"virtus"* can be synonymous with *"vis,"* insofar as the latter word signifies strength or vigor. The first two objections note that there is a power to sin and that according to Scripture some are strong in the sense that they are able to drink large amounts of wine. Thomas easily responds to these objections by noting that virtue can be attributed to the bad in a metaphorical way. A thief can be called "virtuous" at stealing only to the extent that she is good at stealing. Such a thief is perfect as a thief, although imperfect as a human being. Similarly, a person might be strong in excessive drinking, but such virtue entails a defect of reason. This "virtue" is incompatible with human perfection.

Thomas's understanding of the virtues depends on the thesis that good and bad habits are specifically distinct. Earlier in the *Prima Secundae*, q. 18, art. 2, he argues that good and bad acts are specifically distinct on account of their objects. In his discussion of the specific difference between good and bad habits, Thomas draws attention not to the object or the active principle so much as to the nature to which the habit is suitable. There are two kinds of suitability. First, the habit might be suitable or unsuitable to the agent's own nature. Ordinary human virtues are concordant with human reason, whereas vices are discordant. But virtues can also make a subject suitable to a higher nature. Thomas argues that divine or heroic virtue is concerned with such suitability. We will return to Thomas's understanding of divine or heroic virtue in Chapters 3 and 4.

Thomas's position on the specific difference of good and evil habits draws attention to the way in which habits are principles of reasonable or unreasonable activity. An influential alternative to Thomas's view will eventually be formulated by John Duns Scotus (d. 1308), who will argue that the goodness of a habit is not essential but consists only in a habit's conformity to right reason.[77] Thomas and his followers claim that if the order to reason changes then the habit itself changes. This difference draws attention to a fundamental disagreement concerning the very nature of such habits. Both Thomas and Scotus agree that someone who abstains from food for bad reasons might learn to abstain for good reasons or that someone who habitually sins with his concubine will

---

[77] Scotus, *Ord.* I, d. 17, 1, qq. 1–2, nn. 62–66 (Vat. ed., vol. 5, 163–169).

cease to sin when he marries her. But for Thomas a habit is not a neutral quality that is made good or bad on the basis of an added order to reason. It is a kind of quality that has an essential conformity or lack of conformity to reason. The order of reason itself makes the habit what it is. Suppose that a person consistently performs reproductive acts with the same woman both before and after marriage. Although the natural species of the acts are the same, the human acts differ. Before marriage the agent commits fornication, and after marriage the agent renders the marriage debt. The habits consequently must change. The agent's habit of unchastity cannot change into a habit of temperance once he is married simply because the woman with whom he was unchaste has become his wife.

Thomas's discussion of habits provides the background for his general understanding of virtue as a good operative habit. Although Thomas's emphasis on habit is Aristotelian, his order of discussion is not. Some aspects of Thomas's treatment are clarified by considering that the Latin word for virtue differs in some respects from its English counterpart. Both the Latin "*virtus*" and the Greek "*aretē*" that it translates more generally signify any excellence and can consequently be easily applied to intellectual habits. Moreover, as we have seen, the Latin word is close to another Latin word, "*vis*," which can refer to a power of the soul or to strength. Many of his arguments presuppose this connection of virtue with a power or perfection. When Thomas first defines virtue generally in the I-II, q. 55, he explains how Augustine's definition of virtue includes the Aristotelian definition of virtue as a good operative habit. Only in subsequent questions does Thomas distinguish between moral virtues and intellectual virtues, including technical skill. The term "technical skill" is a possible but perhaps misleading, and to my ear awkward, translation of the Greek "*techne*" and Latin "*ars*." Other possible translations might include "craft," "art," or "productive art." These terms used in this way signify a habitual knowledge of how to make something. Horsemanship, bridle-making, and generalship are all "technical skills" in this sense. Since the term has a special meaning for Thomas and Aristotle, I will use "technical skill" for such knowledge.

It is at this point that we can see the way in which the Aristotelian definition of virtue allows Thomas to take into account how Aristotle's insights on the nature of virtue are compatible with the definitions that were given by Thomas's other sources, such as Cicero. It is important to consider Aristotle's own argument for the thesis that virtue is a kind of habit in light of Thomas's own commentary on it. Aristotle's definition of moral virtue as a habit occurs after he had already distinguished moral virtue from intellectual virtue. In his *Nicomachean Ethics*, Book II, chapters 1–4, Aristotle states that moral virtue comes from action whereas intellectual virtue comes from study and teaching. Moral virtue differs from technical skills because its acts must be done with knowledge, for their own sake, and from a firm and stable character. Aristotle's definition of virtue as a habit in the following chapters 5–6 is a definition of moral virtue and not of virtue in general.

According to Thomas, Aristotle gives in chapter 5 the genus of moral virtue as a habit and then in chapter 6 he provides the specific difference that distinguishes it from other habits. The argument for defining it as a habit depends on the premise that virtue, since it is a principle of operation in the soul, must be either a passion, a habit, or a power. Aristotelian passions include joy, sadness, love, and hate. Why is Aristotle so concerned with distinguishing habits from passions? Thomas gives comparatively less attention to this problem. Aristotle notes that virtues clearly involve passions. But by passion the agent is more moved than a source of action. The goodness of a virtuous action requires choice whereby the agent causes the act. We praise a person for what she does and not merely for what happens to her. Consequently, passions are in themselves neither good nor evil, whereas virtues are praised. Similarly, virtues cannot be powers of the soul, since we have the powers by nature. We do not acquire the powers of the soul through acting. If virtues are neither passions nor powers of the soul, then they must be habits. Aristotle's argument for the thesis that virtue is a habit therefore depends on the praiseworthiness of virtue and the fact that it is acquired rather than natural.

In Book II, chapter 6, Aristotle describes the specific difference that distinguishes moral virtues from other habits. Thomas combines Aristotle's statement here that virtue "perfects well the one having it, and renders his work well" with Aristotle's definition in the older Latin translation of the *De Caelo* that "virtue is the peak of a power."[78] Thomas writes:

> [T]he virtue of whatever thing is meant according to the peak of what it can do, for example in this, that someone is able to bring one hundred books, his virtue is determined not from the fact that he brings 500, but that he brings one hundred, as is said in Book I of the *De Caelo*: "now the peak to which the potency of something extends itself, is the good work." And therefore that which makes the work good pertains to the virtue of anything. And since the perfect operation proceeds only from a perfect

---

[78] Supra, note 18.

> agent, it follows that every single thing both is good and works well
> according to its own virtue.[79]

Aristotle himself illustrates this description with the examples of the virtue of an eye and of a horse. The eye's virtue enables it to see well and makes it a good eye. The virtuous horse runs well, carries the rider, and performs under battle. It enables the horse to be a good horse insofar as the horse fulfills its role. Similarly, moral virtue makes humans good and it perfects human actions. Both Aristotle and Thomas use the word "virtue" (*virtus, aretē*) in these contexts in a wide sense. They do not think that habits can perfect the power of sight or the nonrational powers of horses. Nevertheless, there is a strength or excellence by which the subjects and their acts are good. Human acts are produced by powers that need habits to act well. A virtue is a habit that perfects powers in their production of operations that are themselves good and make the agent good.

Since habits are defined through their acts, and the humans are praised or blamed on account of their choices, it follows that moral virtue must be defined through choice (*electio*). This choice must concern a mean, since error in virtue can involve excess or deficiency. This mean is relative to the agent and not fixed. For instance, the appropriate diet for a giant wrestler would be different from that for a small, inactive person. This mean is good insofar as it is determined by reason. Consequently, Aristotle states that "virtue is a habit of choice, existing in a mean relative to us, determined by reason." According to Thomas, Aristotle's definition of moral virtue therefore gives a genus ("a habit"), an act that defines the habit ("of choice"), an object of this act ("existing in a mean relative to us"), and that which makes the act good ("determined by reason"). Aristotle's definition of virtue was important for Thomas and his predecessors for understanding the way that all virtue is a habit, including intellectual virtue. But, as Thomas observes, Aristotle restricts this definition to moral virtue.

Habits Caused by God

After defining virtue in art. 1–3, Thomas follows his predecessors Philip and Albert in arguing for the superiority of the Augustinian definition of

---

[79] "virtus alicuius rei attenditur secundum ultimum id quod potest, puta in eo quod potest ferre centum libras, virtus eius determinatur non ex hoc quod fert quinquaginta, sed ex hoc quod fert centum, ut dicitur in I *De Caelo* : ultimum autem ad quod potentia alicuius rei se extendit est bonum opus, et ideo ad virtutem cuiuslibet rei pertinet quod reddat bonum opus; et quia perfecta operatio non procedit nisi a perfecto agente, consequens est quod secundum virtutem propriam unaquaeque et bona sit et bene operetur." Thomas, *SLE*, lib. 2, lect. 6 (Leonine, 47.1, 94).

virtue as "a good quality of the mind, by which we rightly live, which no one uses badly, which God works in us without us."[80] Thomas's discussion of this Augustinian definition can aid in thinking about the nature of the arguments in the previous three articles. Thomas states that Augustine's definition includes the whole nature (*ratio*) of virtue since it includes all four causes of virtues, namely the formal, material, final, and efficient. Thomas makes a similar but less developed argument in his early *In Sent.*, lib. 2, d. 27, q. un., art. 2.[81] But only in the *Prima Secundae*, q. 54, does he discuss this definition after having previously defined virtue as a good operative habit.

In the *Prima Secundae*, q, 55, art. 4, Thomas states that the definition is perfect because it mentions all four causes.[82] The formal cause of virtue is grasped in the genus and the specific difference. The definition's description of virtue as a "quality" does not give the more proximate genus, which is habit, although it lists the genus to which habit itself belongs. The specific difference "good" distinguishes virtues from other habits. According to Thomas, the Augustinian definition also includes matter in its definition, although a general definition of virtue must exclude that matter which is the object that specifies an individual virtue. The relevant matter is the subject in which virtue adheres, which is the "mind." The final cause of virtue must be operation, since virtue is an operative habit. Virtue's end is distinguished from other operative habits by the fact that it is that "by which we rightly live, which no one uses badly." Thomas follows Philip and Albert in holding that the stated efficient cause applies only to infused virtues, namely those "which God operates in us without us." If this last clause is removed, then the definition applies to any virtue.

The *Summa Theologiae* and to a lesser extent the *Commentary on the Sentences* explain Augustine's definition with reference to Aristotle's four causes. In the *De Virtutibus in Communi*, q. un., art. 2, Thomas provides an alternative account that is based on Aristotle's statement that virtue perfects the subject and the act.[83] According to Thomas, there are two features required for the act's perfection. First, the act that is produced must be good, and second the act's principle must be incapable of producing a bad act. These two features are taken into account by that part of the definition which states "by which we live rightly, which no one uses

---

[80] See supra, note 2.
[81] Thomas, *In Sent.*, lib. 2, d. 27, q. 1, art. 2 (Mandonnet-Moos, 2, 698).
[82] Austin, *Aquinas on Virtue*, 58–71; J. Budziszewski, *A Commentary on Thomas Aquinas's Virtue Ethics* (Cambridge: Cambridge University Press, 2017). 3–19.
[83] Thomas, *DVC*, q. un., art. 2 (Marietti, 711).

wrongly." This part of the definition refers to the act. The part of the definition that concerns the subject's perfection has three parts: the subject, the perfection, and the way in which the virtue inheres in the subject. The subject is the mind, and the virtue inheres in the mind as a quality rather than as a passion. The perfection is indicated by the fact that virtue is a good quality, and not a vice or a habit that can be used well or poorly. For example, opinion is not a virtue since it can be erroneous, but science is a virtue and it does not err. Consequently, the agent's perfection is taken into account by that part of the definition which states "a good quality of the mind." He argues that when the clause about God's work is removed, the Augustinian definition applies to acquired virtues, infused virtues, moral virtues, theological virtues, and even intellectual virtues.

Habits can be possessed naturally or be acquired through acts or be given by God. When discussing habits that are natural in the sense that they are possessed by nature, Thomas distinguishes first between the nature of the species and an individual nature.[84] For instance, Socrates and Plato are naturally both risible because of their human nature, although only Plato has naturally broad shoulders. There is no difficulty in describing bodily dispositions as natural. For instance, Socrates might be naturally less beautiful but healthier than Plato.

Some operative habits seem to be natural to the species and not only to the individual, such as the ability to make such judgments as "The whole is greater than the part." Thomas argues that these habits are only inchoately natural, since they require sense experience. For instance, without sense experience we would have no knowledge of what it is to be a whole and a part. On the other hand, the habit is natural to the extent that, once we possess the knowledge, we naturally and habitually make the judgment. The habit exists in the possible intellect that makes the judgment, but the developed habit presupposes the activity of the agent intellect whereby the intelligible species of the whole and the part are abstracted from phantasms.[85]

There is a parallel between the intellect's assent to first principles and the will's natural willing of happiness and the good in general, but the two acts differ to the extent that the will does not have in itself even inchoate virtue but a mere seed for acquiring virtue.[86] On account of his individual nature person might more easily acquire virtues such as chastity or

---

[84] Thomas, *S. T.*, I-II, q. 51, art. 1; see also q. 63, art. 1.
[85] Thomas, *SCG* 2.78 (Leonine, 13, 494).
[86] Thomas, *S. T.*, I-II, q. 51, art. 1, resp.

meekness, but the acquisition itself depends on free decision. This natural inclination that makes such acquisition easier resides in the individual's bodily nature and not in the soul. The inchoate natural operative habit of the intellect is directly present in the power that it perfects, but inchoate natural appetitive virtue is a bodily disposition to actions that are performed by another power of the soul.

Other habits are not natural but must be acquired through acts or directly infused by God. For instance, dispositions such as sickness or beauty in some cases can be easily removed or restored through acts.[87] Drinking poison might on its own take away health, and a powerful medicine on its own might restore it. Although the intellect has an inchoate natural habit of understanding first principles, other intellectual habits must be acquired. Strictly speaking, a habit of the possible intellect can be acquired through one act. For instance, by demonstrating the Pythagorean Theorem a scientific habit in the intellect can be engendered by which the agent firmly assents to it. But human reason relies on the inner senses, such as memory and the cogitative power. Insofar as they are in these lower apprehensive powers, such habits require multiple acts under normal circumstances and the assistance of other agents.[88] A proof is better known if it is repeated and impressed on the memory. However, even accounting for such repetition, the habit of knowing the Pythagorean Theorem can be acquired more quickly than the habits of acting justly or temperately. Habits that concern contingent actions under normal circumstances require multiple acts and the assistance of other agents.[89]

Only some kinds of virtue are essentially the kinds of virtue that must be caused by God alone. Since God can cause effects directly without the assistance of secondary causes, any habit can be caused by God. He could produce the ordinary habits recognized by Aristotle directly without any of the agent's own acts.[90] Such causation by itself would not make specifically distinct habits. These habits miraculously caused by God would be the same as habits that are produced through acts. Although such acquired virtues could miraculously be caused by God, there are other virtues that can be caused by God alone. These latter virtues are called infused virtues because they cannot be acquired through human acts. These infused virtues are essentially supernatural, such as the theological virtues and, as we will see, the infused moral virtues. These essentially supernatural

[87] Thomas, *S.T.*, I-II, q. 51, art. 2–3; *DVC*, q. un., art. 9 (Marietti, 729–733).
[88] Thomas, *DVC*, q. un. art. 9, ad 9, 11 (Marietti, 732).
[89] Thomas, *DVC*, q. un. art. 9, ad 9, 11 (Marietti, 732).
[90] Thomas, *S.T.*, I-II, q. 51, art. 4.

virtues dispose the agent to an end that exceeds human abilities. Only God can cause them. Human acts can dispose the agent to receive such an infused virtue and in some way aid in its increase, but they cannot cause an infused virtue.[91]

Acts cause not only the existence but also the growth and even decrease of acquired operative habits. Habits grow sometimes by addition to what is included in their formal object, as when a person knows more scientific truths, and they also can increase in the way that they are possessed by their subjects.[92] Even already stable habits can increase. Growth in science or in virtue does not involve a replacement of already existing habits but an increase in formally the same habit. These habits are greater and smaller according to the way in which the subject participates in them. Thomas to some extent responds to Simplicius's (d. 560) description of the Stoics in his own understanding of whether habits can be possessed in various degrees. According to the Stoics, some habits in themselves are capable of possessing degrees, such as the technical skills, whereas others are not, such as the virtues. On this account, a person might be more or less skillful at a task such as boatbuilding or farming, but everyone is equally just or temperate. Thomas addresses this thesis by drawing on the distinction between the habit's nature and its presence in a subject. Thomas agrees with the Stoics that there is a difference between the technical skills and sciences, on the one hand, and virtues, on the other. A person might be more or less grammatical insofar as she knows more or less. Similarly, a boat builder might know more about the hull than about relevant hardware. In contrast, virtues are concerned with objects that cannot be so easily divided. Someone who is temperate will possess temperance with respect to any food or drink. According to Thomas, the difference between virtues and such other habits is that virtues are not the kinds of things whose objects can be possessed more or less on account of the extension of their objects. Nevertheless, all of these habits, including virtues, are capable of being more or less possessed by their subject. The Stoics erred in identifying virtue with only that virtue which is possessed in the highest way.

---

[91] Thomas, *S.T.*, I-II, q. 92, art. 1, ad 1.

[92] Thomas, *S.T.*, I-II, q. 52, art. 1; see also Thomas, *DVCard.*, q. un., art. 3 (Marietti, 821–825); *In libros Physicorum*, lib. 7, lect. 5–6 (Leonine, 2, 337–345). For the acquisition of and growth in virtue, see Hoffmann, "Aquinas on Moral Progress," 131–149; Craig Steven Titus, "Moral Development and Connecting the Virtues: Aquinas, Porter, and the Flawed Saint," in *Ressourcement Thomism: Sacred Doctrine, the Sacraments, and the Moral Life: Essays in Honor of Romanus Cessario, O.P.*, ed. Reinhard Hütter and Matthew Levering (Washington, DC: The Catholic University of America Press, 2010), 330–352.

Some habits can increase by a kind of addition with respect to their object.[93] For instance, one can increase the science of geometry by proving conclusions other than the Pythagorean. The science extends to more conclusions. Other habits are made more intense and perfect through the performance of their own acts, if the acts are equal to or greater than the virtue's perfection. For example, by performing temperate acts the temperate agent disposes herself to temperance. Once a habit is acquired, it is stable. But a moral virtue's stability requires many acts. Thomas writes, "first it begins to be imperfectly in the subject; and gradually it is perfected."[94]

Some habits can be diminished or destroyed by contrary acts.[95] Natural habits that exist in an incorruptible subject cannot be lost, since there are no contrary acts to the habit of knowing first principles in theoretical or practical reason or to the intelligible species that have been abstracted by the agent intellect. However, acquired habits can be diminished and even lost by imperfect acts of the same species or by acts that are directly contrary to the specific habit. For instance, the habit of farming can be lost through farming poorly, and good opinions can be lost through bad arguments. Moral virtues are lost through bad judgments, ignorance, and bad decisions that directly oppose them. For example, temperance can be diminished and lost through repeated acts of gluttony or excessive drinking.

Insofar as habits depend on the operations of the inner senses, they need to be used in order to be retained.[96] For example, a science such as geometry is not diminished in the possible intellect over time, but it is diminished through disuse as it exists secondarily in the inner senses. It can also be diminished by an uncontrolled imagination. Furthermore, sciences and technical skills can be diminished or destroyed not only by contrary actions or disuse but also by damage or destruction to their subjects or even to subjects that they depend upon. For instance, sickness can take away science and technical skills insofar as they depend on the activity of the inner senses, including the particular reason. Even though science and technical skills are directly in the intellect, they are present in the inner senses in a secondary way, since they depend upon the cogitative power, imagination, and memory. If their sense organs are damaged or destroyed, these habits are in some way diminished or destroyed. To

---

[93] Thomas, *S.T.*, I-II, q. 52, art. 2–3.
[94] "imperfecte incipit esse in subiecto, et paulatim perficitur." Thomas, *S.T.*, I-II, q. 55, art. 1, ad 1. See also Thomas, *In Met.*, lib. 9, lect. 7, n. 1855 (Marietti, 445).
[95] Thomas, *S.T.*, I-II, q. 53, art. 1.
[96] Thomas, *S.T.*, I-II, q. 53, art. 3.

give an example, someone without the use of reason due to brain damage would be unable to exercise any intellectual habit. But not all habits depend on inner senses.

Only some virtues are of the kind that can be caused by God alone and not with the cooperation of secondary causes. Other virtues come from repeated acts. Moreover, acts preserve, increase, or weaken the habits. They are true efficient causes of some habits. Only certain habits are caused by God without secondary causes. Consequently, Lombard's full definition of virtue applies only to such habits. However, the other aspects of his definition, which indicate the formal, material, and final causes of virtue, apply to all virtue, including the virtue that Aristotle discussed. We will return to the problem of whether any intellectual or moral virtues are possessed simply by nature and the precise way in which the different kinds of virtue are caused.

In the *Primae Secundae*, Thomas emphasizes that habits in general, and even in particular, can be defined by their four causes. Habits are distinguished from each other by their causes and by their order to either a nature or an operation. Since they are accidental forms that belong to the genus of quality, they are individuated by their active principles. Similar principles cause similar effects. For instance, temperate acts cause the habit temperance, and acts of geometry cause the habit of geometry. Dispositions such as health and beauty are individuated by the natures to which they are ordered. Operative habits are individuated by the objects of their acts. For instance, physics differs from metaphysics because it is about being insofar as being is movable or changeable, whereas metaphysics is about being as such. The same habit can be about materially the same object so long as there is a formal difference. The Aristotelian astronomer and physicist both prove that the earth is a sphere, although they do so by means of different demonstrations. The astronomer demonstrates this conclusion through the figures of eclipses, whereas the physicist does so through the observation that heavy objects move towards the center of the Earth. The same conclusion is therefore known through distinct habits. Unlike many later figures, Thomas contends that sciences are distinguished and unified by their formal objects. They are not collections of various propositions or intellectual species.

In the *Summa Theologiae* and the *Commentary on the Sentences* Thomas explains the Augustinian definition in terms of Aristotle's doctrine of the four causes, and in the *De Virtutibus in Communi* he directly ties the Augustinian definition to Aristotle's statement that virtue perfects the agent and the act. In these two works Thomas relies on two different

Aristotelian texts. Nevertheless, in both he shows that when understood correctly, the Augustinian definition is compatible with both Aristotelian definitions. It is interesting that in these various texts Thomas approaches the definition from different angles without denying any of the assertions that are made in the parallel discussions.

Thomas's understanding of the Augustinian definition of virtue has deep roots in Aristotle and the previous scholastic tradition. His principal Augustinian definition itself is formulated not so much by Augustine as by Peter Lombard. His discussion of this definition is indebted to Philip the Chancellor and Albert the Great, who argued that Augustine's description of virtue as a quality is at bottom the same as Aristotle's description of virtue of a habit and that Augustine's description of virtue and its activity as caused by God applies only to infused virtues. They were among the first to show how both Aristotle and Christian writers such as Augustine could be helpful for moral philosophy and theology.

Thomas's contribution is to develop this moral tradition more systematically and convincingly. In the *Summa Theologiae*, his discussion of virtue follows a lengthy set of questions on habits. Thomas's discussion of habits incorporates newly available texts from Aristotle and arguably develops Aristotle's thought beyond what Aristotle himself was able to articulate. For instance, Thomas's distinction between the kinds of dispositions is not clearly stated by Aristotle although Thomas accurately describes a phenomenon that Aristotle recognized and needed to explain, namely the difference between dispositions such as health or beauty and dispositions that are imperfect virtues. Similarly, Thomas's description of virtue as a good operative habit applies to all Aristotelian virtues and not merely to moral virtue. He provides a definition that is Aristotelian even though Aristotle himself had not arrived at it. In general, Thomas's account is more developed than that of Aristotle even from an Aristotelian perspective. This enhanced Aristotelianism is able to take into account more clearly what Thomas inherits from his predecessors, such as the Augustinian definition of virtue.

CHAPTER 2

Intellectual and Moral Virtue

Both Aristotle and Thomas use the term "virtue" to signify more habits than we would normally do. For instance, they describe good humor (*eutrepelia*) as a moral virtue. Moreover, they think that in addition to moral virtues such as justice and courage, there are intellectual virtues such as the sciences and wisdom. Thomas's various definitions of "virtue" do not equally cover these different kinds of virtue. Aristotle distinguishes principally between intellectual and moral virtue. Thomas accepts this division and develops it in the context of his account of the relationship between the soul's powers. Although Thomas does not deny what Aristotle says about these virtues, his fuller theoretical framework requires and provides a means whereby he can more clearly distinguish between the ways in which these virtues have both different subjects and different formal objects.

Although Thomas already had argued that habits reside in either the power of reason or those powers that participate in reason in some way, his discussion was general and applied to both virtues and vices. His narrower and more detailed discussion of how virtues inhere in powers sheds more light on the way in which different kinds of virtues perfect their powers and acts. Since distinct powers have different formal objects, the distinction between the subjects of virtue will at least partially explain the difference between some virtues.

To a large extent, Thomas follows Aristotle's position that intellectual virtue perfects reason itself whereas moral virtue or virtue of character (*ēthikē aretē*) perfects that part of the soul which participates in reason, namely the appetite.[1] Among the apprehensive powers, Thomas thinks that only the intellect can be the principal subject of virtue.[2] The external sense powers cannot have habits or virtues since their acts are determined by

---

[1] Aristotle, *EN*, 1.13.1102b13–2.1.1103a18.
[2] Thomas, *S.T.*, I-II, q. 56, art. 5.

their objects. The inner senses such as the reminiscence and the cogitative power can be perfected by habits only insofar as they are directed to acts of the intellect. These two human sense powers are essentially connected to reason and consequently can be in some secondary sense subjects of virtue. As we have seen, Thomas divides the appetite into three distinct powers, namely the rational appetite or the will, the irascible sensitive appetite, and the concupiscible sense appetite. He discusses separately the way in which each of these powers can be the subject of virtue.

In this chapter we will see how human virtue is divided into two broad categories, namely intellectual and moral virtue, and then we will focus on intellectual virtue. Strictly speaking, intellectual virtues are higher than the moral virtues since they perfect the intellect, which is superior to the will. But the moral virtues are more perfectly virtues because of the way in which they make the agent good. We will first look carefully at all of the intellectual virtues, or at least the most general kinds of such virtue, but then we will focus more carefully on prudence, which is necessarily connected to moral virtue. Prudence depends on moral virtue because its commands presuppose that the agent is rightly ordered to the end of her action. But moral virtue depends on prudence in order to act.

Perfecting the Intellect and Appetites

Virtues, since they are habits, reside in powers of the soul.[3] The same power can be the subject of different habits because of the broadness of a power's formal object.[4] For instance, the intellect can be the subject of different skills, such as boatbuilding, bridle-making, or navigation. The intellect is concerned with truth, and each skill involves different truths concerning the kinds of things that can be made. However, any virtue must principally belong to only one power, since distinct powers have distinct formal objects and the formal object of a habit in some way includes the object of its power. Diversity in powers would entail diversity in the formal object of any inhering habits. Even though habits principally reside in one power, the perfection of one power might require perfection in another power.[5] For example, some perfections of the human intellect require corresponding perfections in the cogitative power or memory, which are inner senses

---

[3] Thomas, *S.T.*, I-II, q. 56, art. 1. See also Thomas, *In Sent.*, lib. 3, d. 33, q. 2, art. 4, sol. 1 (Mandonnet-Moos, 3, 1062–10633); *DVC*, q. un, art. 3 (Marietti, 707–710).

[4] Thomas, *S.T.*, I-II, q. 56, art. 2.

[5] See also Thomas, *DV*, q. 14, art. 5, ad 7 (Leonine, 22.2, 450).

that are necessarily connected with human reason. But strictly speaking a virtue will have a formal object that restricts it to only one power.

In his discussion of whether the intellect can be the subject of a virtue, Thomas in the *Summa Theologiae* uses Aristotle's description of virtue as that which makes the agent and the act good.[6] Intellectual virtues perfect the intellect although they do not, simply speaking, perfect the agent. When discussing intellectual perfection, Aristotle and Thomas do not focus on particular isolated acts of assent to true proposition or commands. They are concerned with the way in which such acts are produced by habits of knowing or thinking about action. It is clear that the intellect can acquire habits by which it can act well, such as a technical skill or a science. For example, the grammatical person is able to speak well and avoid barbarisms or solecisms. Such habits give an ability to act well and can consequently be described as virtues. The habit of grammar is not simply a collection of grammatically correct statements and judgments about grammar. It is an ability to form such sentences and to make such judgments.

Skills and sciences do not guarantee good use.[7] For instance, a good grammarian or a good builder might use her skills for a bad end. The good grammarian need only be good at grammar, and the good builder might only be good at building. Such intellectual virtues make the agent good only in a certain respect. In contrast to the other intellectual virtues, both the theological virtue of faith and the intellectual virtue of prudence presuppose an ordering by the will. Faith is a theological virtue whose act is intellectual. Nevertheless, this intellectual act depends on the will's choice. Prudence is a habit of right reason about what the agent should do. Since it is right reason about those things that are correctly desired, it depends on right appetite. Consequently, even though faith and prudence belong to the intellect and not to the will, they cannot be used badly by the will. Other intellectual virtues such as skills and sciences can be so used.

In the *Summa Theologiae*, the argument for the position that the intellect can be the subject of a virtue is based on the way in which virtue makes the act and agent good. In parallel passages in his *Commentary on the Sentences* and in his *De Virtutibus in Communi*, art. 7, Thomas gives slightly different explanations.[8] In these other texts he relies on the

---

[6] Thomas, *S.T.*, I-II, q. 56, art. 3.

[7] See also Thomas, *DVC*, q. un. art. 7, ad 2 (Marietti, 725).

[8] Thomas, *In Sent.*, lib. 3, d. 23, q. 1, art. 4, sol. 1 (Mandonnet-Moos, 3, 711–713); *DVC*, q. un., art. 7 (Marietti, 723–725).

distinction between the ways in which virtues might formally or only materially be ordered to the good. A formal ordering to the good is an order to the good taken precisely as good (*sub ratione boni*). A material ordering to the good is when this order is to something that is good, but not as good. Since only the appetitive parts are formally directed to the good, the intellect cannot have habits that are so ordered. The intellect is instead concerned with truth. Nevertheless, truth is good. Consequently, the intellect's habits are materially ordered to something that is good, namely truth, which is the good of the intellect. But they are not ordered to truth precisely as it is a good, or perhaps we could say that they are not ordered to truth "under the description" of good.[9] On the other hand, moral virtues that perfect the appetites are concerned with the good precisely as good.

In contrast to the intellect, the appetitive powers can be the subject of habits that are fully virtues in that they make both the act and the agent good. Such virtues are not only materially but also formally ordered to the good. Thomas applies his own classification of the appetites to Aristotle's claim that the virtues of character, or the moral virtues, can also belong to that irrational part of the soul that in some way participates in reason. He argues that even the two sense appetites can be subjects of virtue.

Since it might seem that the sense appetites are entirely nonrational, it can be difficult to see how they might be subjects of moral virtue.[10] These sense appetites are moved by sensible objects, and they are common to humans and to nonrational animals. Moreover, in humans these appetites often oppose reason. For instance, desire or anger can cause a person to judge falsely about whether an act of adultery or vengeance is good. The sense appetites can be subjects to virtue only if they are in some way rational.

Thomas follows Aristotle in stating that the soul rules the body despotically but reason rules the appetites politically and royally. This rule is political and royal because the appetites do not immediately follow reason. Since they are moved by what reason apprehends, they can be perfected by habits in such a way that they are able to conform habitually to reason. The will obeys the judgment of reason in its choices, and in some way

---

[9] Anscombe's usage for this general kind of scholastic distinction. See G. E. M. Anscombe, "Under a Description," *Nous* 13 (1979): 219–233; repr. in *Collected Philosophical Papers of G.E.M. Anscombe*, vol. 2: *Metaphysics and the Philosophy of Mind* (Oxford: Blackwell; Minneapolis: University of Minneapolis Press, 1981), 208–219.

[10] Thomas, *S.T.*, I-II, q. 56, art. 4. See also *DVC*, q. un., art. 4 (Marietti, 716–719).

its original intention of the particular end depends on the agent's moral character, which involves the good disposition of the sense appetites. If an agent has disordered sense appetites towards the end of action, she is likely to intend an inappropriate end and consequently to choose poorly. These appetites need to be perfected by habits that are ordered to the good.

This explanation of why the sense appetites need virtue presupposes that we can consider the sense appetites of humans in two different ways. First, the irascible and concupiscible appetites can be considered in themselves. Since the sense appetites are not themselves rational, they cannot be subjects of virtue in this way. Nonrational animals can have the same sense appetites but cannot have the virtues. Second, human sense appetites can be considered insofar as they are able to obey reason. As such, they are precisely human appetites. It is only as considered in this second sense that they participate in reason and consequently can be subjects of virtue.

If the sense appetites can be subjects of virtue, it is relatively easy to see why they would need virtue. Sense appetites need to be perfected by habits because of the distinction between reason and sense. But there is no comparable reason to posit habits in the rational appetite. The senses do not seem to directly interfere with the rational appetite. Moreover, the will's object is the good that is apprehended by reason. At first glance, the will might seem to be sufficient for its acts in the way that sensation is sufficient for its own acts. Apprehensive sense powers do not need habits in order to attain its proportionate object. The eye needs no habit to see color. Similarly, since the good is the object of the will, it seems that the will would not be helped by its own habit to will the good. However, Thomas argues that the will needs habits in order to perfect its action for goods that somehow exceed that good which is its proportionate object. Thomas writes:

> Whence since … the object of the will is the good of reason that is proportionate to the will; in respect of this the will does not need to be perfected by virtue. But if a good to be willed by a human is at hand that exceeds the proportion of the one willing (whether with respect to the whole human species, such as the divine good, which transcends the limits of human nature, or with respect to an individual, such as the good of one's neighbor), in that case the will needs virtue.[11]

---

[11] "Unde cum … obiectum voluntati sit bonum rationis voluntati proportionatum, quantum ad hoc non indiget voluntas virtute perficiente. Sed si quod bonum immineat homini volendum, quod excedat proportionem volentis; sive quantum ad totam speciem humanam, sicut bonum divinum, quod transcendit limites humanae naturae, sive quantum ad individuum, sicut bonum proximi; ibi voluntas indiget virtute." Thomas, *S. T.*, I-II, q. 56, art. 6, resp.

The proportionate object of the will is not simply any good but more narrowly the good of the agent. Consequently, Thomas argues that even though the will does not need a habit to will the agent's own good, it does need habits to will God's good or that of one's neighbor. Charity perfects the will principally with respect to the love of God over self. Justice perfects the will with respect to other humans and the common good.

Thomas does not think that a person forsakes his own good by dying for another. He agrees with Aristotle that by dying for a friend a person attains a great good for himself.[12] Moreover, he thinks that although it is good for a Christian to prefer another's bodily good to her own, the Christian should not and cannot prefer another's spiritual good to her own.[13] Perhaps more importantly, Thomas denies that there is a conflict between an individual's good and that of the common good. He thinks of the good citizen as a part of the civil whole in much the same way that the hand is part of the body.[14] Just as the hand is willing to expose itself to danger for the body's health, so the citizen should expose himself to death for the political community. The good citizen thereby loses his bodily goods but gains a greater spiritual good. Although the agent obtains a greater good by dying for a friend and preferring the political common good to her own good, by doing so she chooses a good that is in some way other than her own, even if it includes or entails her own.

Thomas's overall point is clear, namely that the will needs to be perfected by virtues that involve another's good. However, Thomists have disagreed significantly over the details of this argument and whether it is consistent with his earlier texts. One disagreement is over whether the will needs a virtue in order to will its own good when there is a difficulty or whether it ever needs such a virtue. According to Bartholomew Medina (1527–1581), Thomas's argument distinguishes between the agent's own good that is proportionate and the agent's own good that is difficult.[15] The will needs a habit for willing even its own good if there is an accompanying difficulty. In support of this interpretation, Medina mentions that according to Thomas the virtue of studiousness seems to be in the will. Studiousness primarily modifies an inordinate desire for knowledge, although it also overcomes difficulty in knowing

[12] Aristotle, *EN* 9.8.1169a18–29; Thomas, *SLE*, lib. 9, lect. 9 (Leonine, 47.2, 532).
[13] Thomas, *S.T.*, II-II, q. 26, art. 4–5.
[14] Thomas, *S.T.*, I, q. 60, art. 5, resp. For many other texts, a discussion, and references to the plentiful scholarly literature, see Thomas M. Osborne Jr., *Love of Self and Love of God in Thirteenth-Century Ethics* (Notre Dame, IN: University of Notre Dame Press, 2005), 70–94.
[15] Medina, *In I-II*, q. 56, art. 6, dub. 1, concl. 2, col. 784.

the more arduous truths.[16] Even though knowing such truths is clearly part of the agent's own good, the will needs the virtue of studiousness to attain such knowledge. In this context, some authors also mention that according to Thomas, continence and perseverance are both virtues of the will that are about the agent's own good. Continence is a habit of the will that enables the will to overcome a disordered desire for food, drink, and sexual pleasure. The habit of perseverance allows the will to overcome a disordered aversion to pain.

Other Thomists think that according to Thomas the will never needs a habit for willing its own good. On this account, the argument distinguishes only between the agent's proportionate good and another's good. There are at least two common ways of addressing the objection that continence belongs to the will and is concerned with the agent's own good. First, Thomists such as John Capreolus (d. 1444) noted that Thomas himself follows Aristotle in stating that continence is not fully a virtue.[17] Continence involves resisting disordered appetites and consequently disposes its subject to temperance. It is a habit of the will that ultimately in some way belongs to the sense appetite. Continence disappears when the agent correctly orders the sense appetites through the virtue of temperance. Moreover, it is reduced to temperance on account of its matter, which is sensible pleasure. Some Thomists think that this response is insufficient. Although they deny Medina's position that the will needs virtues for all difficulties that accompany the agent's good, they think that the will needs virtues to rectify disordered appetites that are contrary to the agent's good.[18] Those who hold this latter view in some ways are closer to Medina than to Capreolus.

Medina's primary example of studiousness poses a more significant difficulty for those who deny that virtues in the will can be concerned with the agent's proper good. The influential Thomist Thomas de Vio Cajetan (1469–1534) had previously argued that studiousness moderates the desire for truths that are supernatural or at least apart from nature (*praeter naturam*).[19] According to Cajetan's reading of what such truths

---

[16] Thomas, *S.T.*, II-II, q. 166, art. 2, ad 3.

[17] Thomas, *S.T.*, I-II, q. 58, art. 3, ad 2. Capreolus, *In Sent.*, lib. 3, d. 33, q. un., art. 3 (vol. 5, 400–402); translated in John Capreolus, *On the Virtues*, trans. Kevin White and Romanus Cessario (Washington, DC: The Catholic University of America Press, 2001), 273–274, 277. For a similar case of perseverance, see Thomas, *S.T.*, II-II, q. 137, art. 1, ad 1.

[18] Diego Alvarez, *In I-II*, disp. 99, q. 56, art. 6, n. 10, in *Disputationes Theologicae in Iam-IIae S. Thomae* (Trani, 1617), 267. See Cajetan, *In I-II*, q. 56, art. 6, n. 7 (Leonine, 6, 362–363).

[19] Cajetan, *In II-II*, q. 166, art. 1, n. 3 (Leonine, 10, 343).

are, the will needs studiousness not for its own proper good, which is proportionate to its nature, but for a good that is not proportionate to its nature. Cajetan's reading can be used to respond to Medina's argument, but it does not clearly correspond to anything that Thomas himself states.

The disagreement over Thomas's argument is understandable. On its own, his text in the *Prima Secundae*, q. 56, art. 6, is open to various interpretations. Thomas does not in this context address disordered appetites, and he merely asserts that the will needs a habit only with respect to another's good because one's own good is the will's proper object. The other texts in which he explicitly addresses the issue raise further questions about the assumptions that underlie the argument. These texts raise at least two problems.

The first problem is that this text seems to conflict with a text from Thomas's *Commentary on the Sentences*.[20] In this earlier text he implies that the will does not need a habit for willing the end that is another's good but merely the means to the end, whereas in the previously quoted text he seems to argue that the will needs a habit to properly will another's good precisely because it belongs to the other person. Thomas writes:

> For in the will, insofar as it is of the end, there cannot be some moral virtue, since the will has a natural inclination to the civil and natural good of the human just as to its proper object. But insofar as the will is of those things which are ordered to the end, thus there is moral virtue in the will, namely justice, just as prudence is in the cognitive reason.[21]

In this earlier text the proper object of the will includes not only the agent's own good but the civil good. The will has a natural inclination towards the civil good and consequently needs a habit only for the means of achieving this good, and not for the good end itself. This version of the argument is unique to the *Commentary on the Sentences*. Thomas had briefly referred to this position earlier in the same work, but it does not reappear in the same way in other texts.[22]

In the slightly later *De Veritate*, Thomas seems to give a position that is not entirely compatible with that of the earlier *Commentary on the Sentences* or the later *Summa Theologiae*. In a reply to an objection, he

---

[20] Thomas, *In Sent.*, lib. 3, d. 33, q. 2, art. 4, sol. 2, resp. (Mandonnet-Moos, 3, 1065).

[21] "In voluntate enim, secundum quod est finis, non potest esse aliqua virtus moralis, quia ad bonum civile et naturale hominis, voluntas naturalem inclinationem habet sicut in proprium objectum. Sed secundum quod voluntas est eorum quae sunt ordinata ad finem, sic in voluntate potest esse moralis virtus, scilicet justitia, sicut et prudentia in ratione cognitiva." Thomas, *In Sent.*, lib. 3, d. 33, q. 2, art. 4, sol. 2, resp. (Mandonnet-Moos, 3, 1065).

[22] Thomas, *In Sent.*, lib. 3, d. 27, q. 2, art. 3, ad 5 (Mandonnet-Moos, 3, 882).

states that philosophers do not think that the will is the subject of any acquired or natural habits, whereas theologians state that the will needs the habit of charity for meritorious acts.[23] Does Thomas think at this point that Aristotle would deny that the will could be the subject of a virtue such as justice? It is hard to reconcile this early text of the *De Veritate* with the other texts. On this account, there would be no need for acquired virtue in the will for either willing the end that is another's good or for willing the means to the civil good. This inconsistency would be unproblematic if we were to assume Thomas is in this text merely reporting positions with which he disagrees. But there are no clear textual grounds to think that he is doing so.

The *De Veritate* text raises a second problem, namely whether a virtue is needed to will God's good insofar as it is in some way proportionate to human nature. According to both this passage from the *De Veritate* and a text from the *Commentary on the Sentences*, theologians think that charity is needed to love God as a supernatural end because supernatural virtue makes possible supernatural merit.[24] These texts do not address whether, even apart from the wounds of original sin, a habit would be needed for the essentially distinct natural love of God over self. The *Commentary on the Sentences* perhaps implies that the will does not need a habit to will a good that does not exceed one's natural inclination. The obligation to naturally love God more than self is based on natural inclination, even apart from the elevation of human nature to a supernatural end.[25] Such love is based on the way in which God is the source of all natural goods. If the natural good of the human somehow includes such love, then it is unclear why the will if it were healed of original sin's effects through healing grace would need a habit to love God more than self. One criticism of Medina's view is that it would lead to the position that there would need to be a virtue even for such natural love.[26]

It may be that these early texts from the *Commentary on the Sentences* and the *De Veritate* contain opinions that are inconsistent with Thomas's later thought. For instance, in the *Summa Theologiae*, I, q. 60, art. 5, Thomas may attribute such natural love of God and the political community to

---

[23] Thomas, *DV*, q. 24, art. 5, ad 9 (Leonine, 22.3, 691–692).
[24] Thomas, *In Sent.*, lib. 3, d. 27, q. 2, art. 3, ad 5 (Mandonnet-Moos, 3, 882).
[25] For the many passages and an interpretation, see Osborne, *Love of Self and Love of God*, 69–112.
[26] Alvarez, *In I-II*, disp. 99, q. 56, art. 6, n. 5, 266. An anonymous reader points out that the inclination to sin, or the "tinder" of sin (*fomes*), remains even after the reception of sanctifying grace. Medina may hold the view that the healed agent remains wounded in such a way that although she can now love God more than self, she still needs the assistance of a habit of the will to do so.

virtuous habits. He compares the natural love of God over self with the love that the virtuous citizen has for the common good of the political community. In both cases the agent is a part who prefers the good of the whole to his own good. Although this rational preference follows a natural inclination of the part for the whole, Thomas states that the citizen is able to expose himself for the political community on account of his political virtue: "since reason imitates nature, we find an inclination of this sort in political virtue; for the virtuous citizen exposes himself to the danger of death for the conservation of the whole republic …."[27] He is not necessarily arguing that there needs to be a special virtue for willing the common good. Thomas may simply have in mind the political virtues of justice and courage. Consequently, this text does not clearly address the problem of whether the will needs the virtues in order to will the natural or civil good or just the means to this good. But the discussion of virtue in this context at least suggests that some such virtue is needed. A possible but not necessary implication could be that a virtue would be needed to love God naturally. A will unwounded by or healed of original sin and without virtue might be insufficient for willing either the common good or God as the source of natural goods.

These problems could easily be addressed by assuming that Thomas changed his mind concerning the relationship between the agent's own good and that of another. On this account, in the *Summa Theologiae* Thomas states that the will needs a habit with respect to another's good and consequently rejects his early positions. The two earlier texts might even show an evolution. In the *Commentary on the Sentences* he states that the will needs virtue only to will the ends, and in the *De Veritate* he perhaps holds from a philosophical perspective that there is no need for such virtue. On the other hand, the earlier passages might also be interpreted as compatible with the later ones. Or on even another interpretation, in the *Summa Theologiae* Thomas might have abandoned only the earlier view that he defended in the *Commentary on the Sentences*. The *De Veritate* text might after all simply be a mere report of different views.

On yet another interpretation, the *Summa Theologiae*'s discussion might not directly reject any of the earlier points. According to this fourth reading, perhaps Thomas at distinct times approaches the question in different but compatible ways. In the *Summa Theologiae* he might think that the

---

[27] "quia ratio imitatur naturam, huiusmodi inclinationem invenimus in virtutibus politicis: est enim virtuosi civis ut se exponat mortis periculo pro totius reipublicae conservatione" Thomas, *S.T.*, I, q. 60, art. 5.

discussion of the means and the end is superfluous. It could be the case that there needs to be a virtue to properly will the means to the ends of justice and charity precisely because the ends are not proportionate to the agent's own good. The end of justice is not one's own good. The end of charity is not proportionate or simply one's own good. This interpretation would make the earlier and later positions compatible, but it seems to me that it has no clear basis in these or other texts. It seems to me that there is an indeterminacy in Thomas's own treatment of the issue.

A review of the texts themselves leaves us at an impasse. Thomas's view on the need of the will for habits can be understood better not by focusing only on these texts that explicitly address the question but also by considering his wider understanding of the will.[28] According to Thomas, the will by nature has complete rectitude with respect to happiness and such goods as existence, living, and understanding without which happiness cannot be attained.[29] These three natural goods are all part of one's own good and are always apprehended by the intellect as good. The will can be described as free in its activity of choosing or not choosing such goods, but it lacks the freedom to reject such goods as evil. But since humans can misapprehend other goods as in some way evil, the will can be disordered with respect to the moral good. Nevertheless, many humans misjudge their own good as incompatible with God's good, whether considered as a supernatural end or a natural end, or that of the political community. Moreover, many humans err in thinking that by acting justly they would benefit another and harm themselves. Since they can judge another's good to be bad for themselves, they can reject another's good even if it is part of or includes one's own good. On the other hand, although one might misidentify one's own good, it is impossible to view one's own good as evil. Consequently, one can never reject one's own good when it is apprehended or even misapprehended as his own good. Therefore, the will needs a habit only for willing another's good and not for willing one's own.

This inability to will against one's own good is connected with Thomas's view that loving another for the other's own sake is based on some sort of unity with the loved object. Thomas explicitly relies on the Pseudo-Dionysius's claim that love is a "unitive power (*virtus*)" and Aristotle's

---

[28] My exposition partially follows John of St. Thomas, In I-II, disp. 15, art. 1, nn. 281–294 (Québec, 99–104); Collegium Salmanticense, *Cursus Theologicus*, 20 vols. (Paris: Palme, 1870–1883), tract. 12, disp. 2, dub. 3, n. 32, vol. 6, 252–268.
[29] Thomas, *DM*, q. 2, art. 3, ad 2; q. 6, resp. (Leonine, 23, 37, 250). See also Thomas, *S.T.*, I-II, q. 10, art. 1, resp.; art. 2, resp. and ad 3; *In Div. Nom.*, cap. 4, lect. 19, n. 541; lect. 23, n. 600 (Marietti, 197, 224).

claim that "the notes of friendship (*amicabilia*) which are for another come from those which are for oneself."[30] Aristotle lists several notes of friendship: showing one's good will to another, willing good to the other, spending time with the other, sharing choices with the other, and sharing passions with the other.[31] Each of these notes applies to one's relations with a friend, but they most of all apply to one's own self. For Aristotle and Thomas, self-love is necessary and in a way the root of love for other humans. Nevertheless, the will needs habits to will another's good, since willing such good depends on an understanding of the way in which the other's good is joined to or inclusive of the agent's own good. The command to love one's neighbor as oneself presupposes that the agent already wills his own good. Charity does not destroy but elevates and correctly orders such willing. The willing of one's own good should be ordered by charity in such a way that the agent loves God's good more than his own and his neighbor's good less than the good of his own soul.[32] Whereas charity perfects the will with respect to God, justice perfects the will with respect to others. There is no virtue that perfects self-love, since such love has a natural priority that makes any habit superfluous.

Speculative Virtue, Skill, and Prudence

After discussing the way in which the intellect and the appetites are subjects of virtue, Thomas considers separately the two kinds of virtue that perfect these powers, namely intellectual and moral virtue.[33] Every human virtue is included in these categories. Only those virtues that have God as their object fall outside of them. Thomas's argument for the sufficiency of this division for human virtue rests on the premise that human operations are produced either by the intellect or by the appetite. Since human virtues perfect the principle of operations, it follows that virtues either perfect the intellect and are thereby intellectual or that they perfect the appetite and are thereby moral.

---

[30] "amicabilia quae sunt ad alterum veniunt ex his quae sunt ad seipsum," Aristotle, *EN* 9.4.1166a1–2, in Thomas, *S.T.*, II-II, q. 25, art. 4. For Thomas's different interpretations of Aristotle's dictum and distinct interpretations of Thomas himself, see Osborne, *Love of Self and Love of God*, 108–110. For the unitive power of love, see Anthony T. Flood, *The Metaphysical Foundations of Love: Aquinas on Participation, Unity, and Union* (Washington, DC: The Catholic University of America Press, 2018), 1–24.

[31] Thomas, *SLE*, lib. 9, lect. 4 (Leonine, 47.2, 512–513).

[32] Thomas, *S.T.*, II-II, q. 25, art. 12; q. 44, art. 3, ad 1.

[33] Thomas, *S.T.*, I-II, q. 58, art. 3. For Thomas's understanding of Aristotle's division between rational and nonrational parts, see Thomas, *SLE*, lib. 1, lect. 20; lib. 6, lect. 1 (Leonine, 47.1, 73; 47.2, 333).

Like Aristotle, Thomas uses the word "virtue" both for moral virtues and more widely for speculative habits or genera of habits such as metaphysics, mathematics, and physics. Mathematics and physics are sciences that include other sciences. Metaphysics is a science of the highest causes and is consequently the intellectual virtue of wisdom. Speculative virtues are distinct habits or genera of habits by which the agent knows the world according to different kinds of abstraction. These speculative virtues, like the moral virtues, make the agent good, but unlike the moral virtues, they do not make the agent a good human being. For example, a criminal and a saint might be equally good at geometry. They are both in a qualified way better than someone who lacks geometry. But the criminal, although good as a geometer, is bad as a human being. Speculative intellectual virtues perfect the agent's intellect but not the whole agent. Moreover, the acts of geometry and the other sciences are not morally good on their own. The criminal might even use geometry to steal or murder better. The acts of the speculative intellectual virtues become morally good only through their use by a virtue.[34] For example, justice can command one to teach a science to his students, and charity can command that the one who has science use it to praise God.

In the *De Virtutibus in Communi*, art. 12, Thomas more clearly discusses the different ways in which intellectual and moral virtues are divided according to the two operations that are proper to humans, namely knowing the truth and acting.[35] The intellectual virtues perfect the intellectual part that knows the truth, whether it be of necessary truths or contingent truths. These virtues can consider the true and the false either in themselves or as in conformity with the right appetite. In contrast, moral virtue is concerned only with the good, which is the object of the appetite. Consequently, virtue, insofar as it makes the act and the agent good, more properly applies to moral virtue rather than intellectual virtue. However, since intellectual virtues perfect a higher part of the soul, namely reason, they are more noble perfections than the moral virtues are.

In the *Prima Secundae*, qq. 58–59, Thomas discusses the speculative intellectual virtues before he discusses the practical. Thomas accepts Aristotle's division of the intellectual virtues into understanding (*intellectus/nous*), science (*scientia/epistemē*), wisdom (*sapientia/sophia*), skill (*ars/technē*), and

---

34 R. Bernard, "Appendice I," in Thomas Aquinas, *Summe Théologique: La vertu*, 2 vols., trans. R. Bernard (Paris, Tournai, and Rome: Desclée, 1933), vol. 1, 357.

35 Thomas, *DVC*, q. un., art. 12, resp. (Marietti, 743–744). See also Thomas, *SLE*, lib. 6, lect. 2 (Leonine, 47.2, 336); *In Sent.*, lib. 3, d. 23, q. 1, art. 4, sol. 3 (Mandonnet-Moos, 3, 714).

prudence (*prudentia/phronēsis*).[36] The first three names can also signify gifts of the Holy Ghost, but we are concerned with their use to signify intellectual virtues.[37] All five virtues inhere in the intellect but have distinct formal objects. Strictly speaking, science and skill are genera of distinct virtues. As we will see, prudence is in at least one special way unitary, and it is unclear whether understanding is only one habit.

The speculative intellectual virtues are distinct from the practical because they are about necessary objects, which are those objects that cannot be otherwise.[38] For instance, speculative virtue considers the truths of mathematics or the motion of the heavenly bodies and not how to build a house or repay a debt. These necessary objects are either universal or particulars that are considered in a universal way. In his commentary on the *Nicomachean Ethics*, Thomas writes, "only practical sciences are about contingent objects insofar as they are contingent, namely in the particular; but speculative sciences are not about contingent objects except insofar as they are in accord with universal natures ...."[39] For example, a biological science considers trees that grow from saplings and eventually become dead wood. But it is not concerned with the life and death of any one tree insofar as it is an individual.

We have seen that according to Thomas virtues are most narrowly classified as good operative habits. If speculative virtues are not about those things that are subject to human action, in what sense are they operative habits? Thomas makes a distinction between two meanings of "operative" that is based on the difference between exterior and interior works.[40] The word "operative" can be understood in one way as divided from speculative. In this sense, a habit is operative insofar as it is directed to some exterior work. For example, boatbuilding is operative to the extent that the boat is external to the agent. A habit can be operative in a second way insofar as it is ordered to an interior work. Thinking about the truth is an interior work. Consequently, the speculative intellectual virtues are operative in and only in this second sense because they are ordered to knowing the truth.

Thomas follows Aristotle in holding that the speculative virtues can be divided into three virtues or perhaps genera of speculative virtue, namely

---

[36] Aristotle, *EN*, 6.3.
[37] For the gifts, see Thomas, *S.T.*, I-II, q. 68, art. 4.
[38] Thomas, *S.T.*, I-II, q. 57, art. 1; *DVC*, q. un., art. 7 (Marietti ed, vol. 2, 723–725).
[39] "solae scientiae practicae sunt circa contingentia in quantum contingentia sunt, scilicet in particulari; scientiae autem speculativae non sunt circa contingentia nisi secundum rationes universales ..." Thomas, *SLE*, lib. 6, lect. 3 (Leonine, 47.2, 342).
[40] Thomas, *S.T.*, I-II, q. 57, art. 1, ad 2.

understanding, science, and wisdom.[41] These three virtues, unlike prudence or technical skills, are about objects that cannot be changed by
human action. Thomas distinguishes the acts of these three intellectual
virtues from doubt, suspicion, and opinion.[42] Although these acts can be
about speculative objects, they do not belong to a habit of science about
the objects. Inquiry often begins with the suspicion that something is
true. This suspicion is frequently wrong. Opinion adheres to a proposition but lacks firmness on account of the fear that the opposite might be
true. According to Thomas, Aristotle discusses suspicion in the *Rhetoric*
and opinion in the *Topics*.[43] But through the three speculative virtues one
adheres to the truth with certitude. In English we might use "to know" to
describe the acts of these virtues. However, "knowledge" seems to be a better translation of the wider Latin term "*cognitio*," which applies not only to
some intellectual acts but also to some acts of the senses. For instance, we
might say that a dog knows that a squirrel has run behind a tree or that a
dolphin knows where its companions are. Dogs and dolphins lack intellects, but they do have knowledge (*cognitio*).

Understanding is distinct from the other speculative virtues because
it is concerned with truths that are known through themselves, whereas
science and wisdom are concerned with conclusions that are known
through first knowing distinct principles.[44] The virtue of understanding
knows the principles that are themselves indemonstrable and the basis
for demonstration. Such principles are known through their terms. For
instance, if someone knows what a whole is and what a part is, then
she immediately knows the truth that "every whole is greater than its
part."[45] The knowledge is not natural or innate in the sense that it is prior
to any sense experience.[46] In order to make the judgment, the knower
must have acquired the minimal relevant knowledge from the senses. But
given such sense experience, the knower grasps that it is true. It is natural
in the sense that it is at first inchoately in the knower on account of her
human nature.

---

[41] Thomas, *S.T.*, I-II, q. 57, art. 2. For the general distinction between these virtues, see also Thomas,
SLE, lib. 6, lect. 3 (Leonine, 47.2, 340–341); *DVC*, q. un., art. 1, resp. (Marietti, 744).

[42] Thomas, *S.T.*, I-II, q. 57, art. 2, ad 3. For suspicion and opinion, see especially Thomas, *S.T.*, I-II,
q. 67, art. 3, resp.; II-II, q. 4, art. 1, resp.

[43] Thomas, *In Post. An.*, proemium (Leonine, 1.2*, 6–7).

[44] Thomas, *SLE*, lib. 6, lect. 5 (Leonine, 47.2, 348–349).

[45] For the relevant texts in the context of the later scholastic debate over whether to know principles
we need to have experience of the terms or the complex of terms, see Petrus Hoenen, "De origine
primorum principiorum scientiae," *Gregorianum* 14 (1933): 153–184.

[46] Thomas, *S.T.*, I-II, q. 51, art. 2, resp.

Thomas uses the word "science" to describe the habit of demonstrating conclusions from principles in a way that satisfies the conditions that are set down in Aristotle's *Posterior Analytics*.[47] This habit of science involves much more than the truth of the propositions to which it assents. Aristotle and Thomas are concerned not only with true conclusions but also with the demonstration of such conclusions. Demonstrations do not proceed directly from sense experience. The mere sight of a tree or a fish does not give us principles. Demonstrations proceed from universals that are grasped by the intellect. Scientific demonstration is from such universal principles that are prior and causal. Principles are prior in the sense that they are known first and immediately rather than through other statements. If a conclusion is demonstrated from principles that are merely demonstrable and not yet demonstrated, the agent lacks scientific knowledge of this conclusion. Moreover, the premises must in some way cause the conclusion. The word "cause" in this context is used in a wide sense. The point of this condition is that the premises be better known and prior than their effects, which are the conclusions. There is a distinction between that which is better known in itself and that which is better known to us. For instance, God is prior to any other cause. Nevertheless, we know him very poorly and must arrive at the knowledge of his existence through his effects, which are better known to us. A demonstration is better as a demonstration if its principles are better known not only to us but also in themselves.

In one sense of the term, "wisdom" designates any science insofar as it makes judgments in light of the highest causes in the relevant area. More narrowly, wisdom is a distinct intellectual virtue. Although Thomas seems to think that there is only one speculative habit of understanding for all speculative principles, there are many sciences.[48] The most general division is between 1) physics, which considers being as abstracted from singular matter but still movable, 2) mathematics, which considers being as abstracted from sensible matter but still quantitative, and 3) metaphysics or first philosophy, which considers being as being and its principles.[49] Thomas identifies metaphysics with the speculative virtue of wisdom.

It may seen strange that wisdom is an intellectual virtue that is a science and yet is considered to be different from the sciences. Thomas notes

---

[47] Thomas, *In Post. An.*, lib. 1, lect. 4 (Leonine, 1.2*, 18–22).

[48] Thomas, *S.T.*, I, q. 79, art. 12; *DV*, q. 16, art. 1. See John of St. Thomas, *In I-II*, disp. 16, art. 2, nn. 688–698 (Québec, 221–225).

[49] Thomas, *SBT*, q. 5, art. 1 (Leonine, 50, 136–142); *In Met.*, lin. 6, lect. 1, nn. 1156–1166 (Marietti, 297–298).

that although in one way wisdom should be included among the sciences, in another way it should be considered separately.[50] Wisdom is a science simply to the extent that it demonstrates conclusions from principles in the way that is described in the *Posterior Analytics*.[51] It is more perfect than science or understanding in the same way that the rational soul is more perfect than the sensitive or the vegetative. There is an order among the three speculative habits of science, understanding, and wisdom. Science has the least perfection, since it depends on understanding for its principles. Wisdom is about the highest causes and judges and orders all effects including whatever is known in the sciences. Consequently, it is about both conclusions and first principles and more perfect than any science is. Moreover, since wisdom considers and judges the principles that are known through the virtue of understanding, it is even more perfect than understanding.

The practical intellectual virtues are more closely related to the moral virtues. In contrast to the speculative virtues, the practical virtues are concerned with contingent objects and particularly those that are essentially bound to human operations. In q. 57, art. 4, ad 2, Thomas states that both skill and prudence exist in the "opining part" (*pars opinativa*) of the soul because they are about such objects. What is this "opining part"? Is it the same as the practical intellect that Thomas describes as the subject of prudence in article 3? The intellect has only two powers, namely the possible intellect, which receives the known object, and the agent intellect, which makes the sense object intelligible. Thomas does distinguish between the practical and speculative intellects and at times he refers to them as separate intellects, but he denies that they are distinct powers.[52] Thomas several times quotes in this context the Aristotelian dictum "the speculative intellect through extension becomes practical."[53] The difference between the practical and speculative intellect is that the speculative is concerned with the truth in itself and the practical is concerned with the truth for the sake of another end. Since the formal object of the intellect is truth, such a distinction in their objects is accidental to the power of the intellect

[50] Thomas, *S.T.*, II-II, q. 9, art. 2, resp.
[51] Thomas, *S.T.*, I-II, q. 57, art. 2, ad 2–3.
[52] Thomas, *S.T.*, q. 79, art. 11. For possible development and many texts, see John Naus, *The Nature of the Practical Intellect according to Saint Thomas Aquinas* (Rome: Analecta Gregoriana, 1959), 17–34.
[53] "intellectus speculativus per extensionem fit practicus." Thomas, *In Sent.*, lib. 3, d. 23, q. 2, art. 3, sol. 2 (Marietti-Moos, vol. 3, 732); *S.T.*, I, q. 70, art. 11, s.c.; II-II, q. 4, art. 2, ad 3. For the widespread usage and source of this adage, see Naus, *Nature of the Practical Intellect*, 23–26.

itself. Other texts in the *Summa Theologiae* support this position that the speculative and the practical intellectual virtues have the same subject, namely the intellect.[54] Although the speculative and practical intellectual virtues inhere in the same power, they are essentially distinct from each other on account of their distinct formal objects. They are two distinct genera, which differ according to whether their objects are subject to human action.

Despite this textual evidence for Thomas's adherence to the position that all intellectual virtue, including practical virtue, inheres in the intellect, there are other texts that seem to assert the contrary. Also in his *Commentary on the Nicomachean Ethics*, Thomas states that prudence belongs to the "opining part."[55] But here it seems to be the cogitative power, which is an inner sense. Earlier he had stated that the part that is about contingents and that which is scientific belong to different genera, and he seems to be discussing the difference between reason and the cogitative power.[56] The identification of prudence with this inner sense is strengthened by his remark that even nonrational animals are called prudent since they have an estimative power.[57] Whereas in the *Commentary on the Nicomachean Ethics* Thomas states that prudence is in an opining power that is the cogitative sense, in the *Summa Theologiae* he states that prudence is in an opining power that appears to be the intellect. There seems to be a contradiction between the two texts.

There are ways of reconciling the seemingly different accounts. First, it could be that in the commentary Thomas is expounding Aristotle's position and in the *Summa Theologiae* he is giving his own position. One problem with this attempt to reconcile the texts is that in the *Prima Pars* he explicitly attributes to Aristotle the position that the opining power is the intellect.[58] Another approach is to accept Cajetan's argument that in the different works "opining power" is used in distinct ways to explain the same position that prudence belongs to the intellect insofar as it is joined to the cogitative sense in understanding singulars.[59] In the *Secunda Secundae*, Thomas himself states that Aristotle must be interpreted as holding that prudence

[54] Thomas, *S.T.*, I, q. 79, art. 9, ad 3; II-II, q. 47, art. 1.
[55] Thomas, *SLE*, lib. 6, lect. 4, 9 (Leonine, 47.2, 347, 368).
[56] Thomas, *SLE*, lib. 6, lect. 1 (Leonine, 47.2, 332–334).
[57] Thomas, *SLE*, lib. 6, lect. 7 (Leonine, 47.2, 359). For prudence in other animals, see Leo A. White, "Instinct and Custom," *The Thomist* 66 (2002): 597–602.
[58] Thomas, *S.T.*, I, q. 79, art. 9, ad 3.
[59] Cajetan, *In I-II*, q. 57, art. 5 (Leonine, 6, 368).

belongs to the intellect principally but is in the cogitative power secondarily.
Thomas writes:

> [J]ust as the Philosopher says in the Sixth Book of the *Ethics*, prudence does
> not consist in the exterior sense, by which we know the proper sensible,
> but in the interior sense, which is perfected by memory and experience for
> promptly judging concerning experienced particulars. However it is not
> that prudence is in the interior sense as in the principal subject: but princi-
> pally it is indeed in the reason, yet it reaches a sense of this kind through a
> sort of application.[60]

According to Cajetan's interpretation, in the commentary Thomas uses
"opining power" to signify the intellect with the connotation of the
adjoined cogitative power, and in the *Summa Theologiae* he uses "opining
power" to signify the principle of the operation, which is the intellect.
Although in the two works the meaning of "opining power" differs, there
is the same teaching that prudence is principally in the intellect and secondarily in the cogitative power.

Prudence is distinct from both the speculative intellectual virtues and
technical skills. Unlike speculative intellectual virtue, the practical virtue
of prudence is about human operations as such. Unlike technical skill,
prudence is concerned not with products of human activity but with
immanent acts.[61] Thomas divides human operations into doing (*agere*)
and making (*facere*), which are often called "transitive acts" and "immanent acts." Exterior acts of making are transitive because they pass into
exterior matter. For instance, building produces a house and weaving produces cloth. Immanent activity remains within the agent. The exercise of
the speculative intellectual virtues is immanent. All making is exterior
and transitive, even though it depends on a prior immanent activity. But

---

[60] "sicut Philosophus dicit, in VI *Ethic.*, prudentia non consistit in sensu exteriori, quo cognoscimus
sensibilia propria: sed in sensu interiori, qui perficitur per memoriam et experimentum ad prompte
iudicandum de particularibus expertis. Non tamen ita quod prudentia sit in sensu interiori sicut
in subiecto principali: sed principaliter quidem est in ratione, per quandam autem applicationem
pertingit ad huiusmodi sensum." Thomas, *S.T.*, II-II, q. 47, art. 3, ad 3. Cf. Thomas, *QDA*, q. 8,
resp. (Leonine, 24.1, 68). For an important discussion of prudence and the cogitative power,
see Maureen Bielinski, "At the Crossroads of Epistemology and Ethics: Aquinas and the Impact
of Moral Perception on Prudence and the Moral Virtues," PhD diss. (University of St. Thomas
(Houston)), 2021.

[61] Thomas, *S.T.*, I-II, q. 57, art. 4, resp.; *DVC*, q. un., art. 12, ad 17 (Marietti, 745); *SLE*, lib. 6,
lect. 3 (Leonine, 47.2, 341–342); *DV*, q. 5, art. 1, resp. (Leonine, 22.1, 139). *In Met.*, lib. 9, lect. 8,
bb. 1862–1865 (Marietti, 447–448). For the distinction between transitive and immanent action,
see especially Johm F. Wippel, *The Metaphysical Thought of Thomas Aquinas: From Finite Being to
Uncreated Being* (Washington, DC: The Catholic University of America Press, 2000), 226–228;
Marianne Therese Miller, "The Problem of Action in the Commentary of St. Thomas Aquinas on
the *Physics* of Aristotle," *The Modern Schoolman* 23 (1945–46): 135–167.

willing is itself immanent even though it can be a part of an act that at the
same time has interior and exterior components.

The immanent act of willing, unlike the immanent act of understanding, directly leads to transitive acts such as an act of production or the
exterior component of a moral act.[62] In this context, an act is "exterior"
in the sense that it is commanded by the intellect as a means of carrying
out the will's choice. This exterior act might be observable and transitive, such as handing over change to a customer. The choice to provide
change is an interior act and the exterior act is the resulting movement
of the hands. The hand's movement is itself a transitive act, as is its effect
on the change. In Thomas's usage, although not in that of later scholastics and even later Thomists, an immanent act such as thinking can be
commanded and therefore an "exterior" act.[63] For instance, one might
decide to pass some free time by thinking about geometry. Such thinking is an exterior act. Production is always exterior not only in the sense
that it is commanded by an act of choice but also in the wider sense
that its effect passes into exterior matter. An immanent act of choosing to build might cause a transitive act of building that involves the
arrangement of matter as a building. The immanent act of choosing to
build might itself perfect the agent insofar as it is an act of justice. But
the transitive act of building perfects only the object that is produced,
namely the house.

Both skill and prudence are concerned with contingent objects, namely
those objects that can otherwise be and consequently are subject to human
action. Skill is about production, which is a transitive act, and prudence is
about action, which can but need not lead to transitive acts. Skill is right
reason with respect to those things that can be made or produced (*recta
ratio factibilium*).[64] Such skill is good merely on account of the product.
For instance, someone who makes a good bridle is a good bridle maker,
and someone who guides a ship safely to its port is a good navigator. One
can possess such a skill without using it well. For instance, a bridle maker
might make a good bridle for an unjust soldier or a navigator might guide
well a pirate ship. Cajetan notes that one might blaspheme well with perfect grammar.[65] The difference between the good and the bad grammarian

[62] Stephen L. Brock, *Action and Conduct: Thomas Aquinas and the Theory of Action* (Edinburgh: T&T Clark, 1998), 171–196.

[63] For the change in terminology, see Thomas M. Osborne Jr., "The Separation of Interior and Exterior Acts in Scotus and Ockham," *Mediaeval Studies* 69 (2008): 111–139.

[64] Thomas, *S.T.*, I-II, q. 57, art. 3; *DVC*, q. un, art. 7, resp. (Marietti, 724); *SLE*, lib. 6, lect. 3 (Leonine, 47.2, 342–343).

[65] Cajetan, *In I-II*, q. 57, art. 3 (Leonine, 6, 367).

is not in whether they blaspheme or pray but in whether they do either activity in a grammatically correct way. A good human will not blaspheme, whether it be done well or poorly. Moral virtue is necessary for the good use of a skill.

Prudence is right reason with respect to action (*recta ratio agibilium*).[66] It is concerned with the immanent act that perfects the agent. In order for such action to be correct, the agent must be disposed correctly to the end through moral virtue.[67] Consequently, prudence involves good use of the faculty. It is distinguished from skill precisely because skill does not presuppose moral virtue. For instance, a good builder might be able to fulfill an obligation she has contracted to build a house and yet refuse to do so due to her disordered desire for revenge. But if the builder is prudent, she will use her skill to build the house when justice requires that she do so.

Thomas accepts Aristotle's observation that if someone errs with respect to a skill, it is better from the perspective of the skill to err knowingly.[68] For instance, a bad builder will make a shoddy house because she lacks the necessary skill. A good builder will build a shoddy house only if she wants to. She is able to build a good house but might choose to build a shoddy house in order to obtain revenge on the one who will live in it. On the other hand, a prudent person errs only out of involuntary ignorance. For instance, an imprudent person might knowingly accept too much money for a contract. She voluntarily or willingly acts for a bad end. In contrast, a prudent person only would be mistaken involuntary, perhaps concerning the amount of money that is given or the nature of the product that she has provided. Someone with prudence will not knowingly perform a bad action but an agent with a disordered appetite might knowingly misuse a skill that she possesses.

An important consequence of the Aristotelian distinction between prudence and skill is that prudence is the only practical virtue that is concerned with the good life as a whole, whereas skill is concerned merely with a good product.[69] Thomas writes:

> Prudence involves good deliberation concerning these things which pertain to the whole life of the human and to the last end of human life. But in some arts there is deliberation about those things which pertain to the

---

[66] Thomas, *S.T.*, I-II, q. 57, art. 4; *DVC*, q. un., art. 7, resp. (Marietti, 744); *SLE*, lib. 6, lect. 4 (Leonine, 47.2, 345–346).

[67] Thomas, *DVC*, art. 7, ad 5; *SLE*, lib. 6, lect. 4, 11 (Leonine, 47.2, 346–347).

[68] Aristotle, *EN*, 6.5.1140b23–25. See Thomas *SLE*, lib. 6, lect. 3 (Leonine, 47, 347).

[69] Thomas, *SLE*, lib. 6, lect. 4; lect. 8 (Leonine, 47.2, 345, 363).

proper ends of those skills. Therefore some, insofar as they have good coun-
sel in war or nautical matters, are called prudent leaders or pilots, but not
prudent simply speaking; but those who have good deliberation concerning
what makes up a whole life are prudent.[70]

This concern with the good life as a whole not only distinguishes prudence from such skills but it also indicates how the matter of prudence
includes the matter of the various moral virtues.[71] Different moral virtues are concerned with different kinds of goods. But the intellect is concerned with the truth concerning action. Although such human actions
belong to specifically distinct kinds, the practical truth about them does
not. Consequently, prudence differs from the arts and the moral virtues
because it is concerned not with the truth about a particular exterior or
even moral good but with the truth about an entire good life.

Unlike speculative truth, practical truth requires conformity with
correct appetite. This conformity exists in the context of both skill and
prudence. Nevertheless, there is a stark difference in these two kinds of
conformity.[72] Skill is concerned with practical truth concerning a desired
or needed product. For instance, a sculptor exercises her skill by performing a sculpture with proportions that satisfy the artist, or at least her
clients. Her skill is measured by the desired goal that is a product. But
prudence is concerned with the correct use of the means to an end that is
set by moral virtue.

The distinction between practical truth and speculative truth indicates a way in which prudence, unlike the speculative virtues, is in one
respect fallible.[73] In general, the intellectual virtues exclude falsehood.
Insofar as one acts in accordance with them, one will make correct judgments. The truth of such judgments is measured by their conformity
to the world. But since human prudence must judge singular events, it
can err in many ways. One might without negligence be ignorant of the
fact that a cloak belongs to someone who needs it or that his purported

---

[70] "prudentia est bene consiliativa de his quae pertinent ad totam vitam hominis et ad ultimum finem
vitae humanae. Sed in artibus aliquibus est consilium de his quae pertinent ad fines proprios illarum
artium. Unde aliqui, inquantum sunt bene consiliativi in rebus bellicis vel nauticis, dicuntur prudentes duces vel gubernatores, non autem prudentes simpliciter; sed illi solum qui bene consiliantur
de his quae conferunt ad totam vitam." Thomas, *S.T.*, I-II, q. 57, art. 4, ad 3. See also Thomas, *S.T.*,
II-II, q. 47, art. 13, resp.

[71] Thomas, *S.T.*, I-II, q. 65, art. 2, ad 3–4; *DVC*, art. 12, ad 21, 23 (Marietti, 746).

[72] Thomas, *S.T.*, I-II, q. 57, art. 5, ad 3.

[73] Thomas, *S.T.*, I-II, q. 57, art. 5, ad 3; II-II, q. 1, art. 4; II-II, q. 47, art. 3, ad 2. See T.-H. Deman,
"Appendice II," in Thomas Aquinas, *Somme Théologique: La Prudence*, trans. T.-H. Deman (Paris,
Tournai, and Rome: Desclée, 1949), 459–478; Réginald Garrigou-Lagrange, "La prudence: sa place
dans l'organisme des vertus," *Revue Thomiste* 31 (1926): 420–426.

wife is married to someone else. Prudence's judgment is correct in this way only for the most part. But practical truth in ethics is measured both by its conformity to the world and by its conformity to the end of virtue, which is set by nature.[74] Prudence measures the correctness of an action. Consequently, the truth of prudential judgments depends not only on the correct assessment of particulars but also on right appetite. The prudent person who makes a mistake will not with her prudence choose to act for a vicious end or in a disordered way with respect to the end. Prudence cannot err in directing action. On the other hand, the imprudent person who lacks moral virtue will err not only with respect to the relevant singulars but also with respect to this end to which action will be directed. He will knowingly steal a cloak or have relations with someone who is not his wife. His judgments are erroneous on account of his disordered end.

Prudence is necessary for a good life more than skill is necessary for a good product.[75] Someone who lacks skill might produce a good product, and a skillful person might knowingly produce a bad product. But in order to live a good life the agent must do the correct action in a correct way. For instance, one might repay a debt well or poorly. Virtue requires that this debt be paid for justice. If one uses money set aside to feed his parents in order to pay a debt, she will be acting poorly. Such an agent does not correctly deliberate concerning the proper way to repay her debt. The repayment does not contribute to acting well. Moral virtues dispose the agent to have the correct end. But in order to knowingly deliberate about and choose the means to the end, the agent must also have prudence.

When Thomas first discusses prudence in I-II, q. 57, art. 5, he mentions the different acts of deliberation, judgment, and command. Here he speaks of prudence more broadly. But in art. 6 he restricts the proper act of prudence to command. Deliberation and judgment belong to other virtues, which he describes as virtues that are potential parts of the virtue of prudence. In his account of how a virtue such as prudence has other virtues as parts, he follows a tradition whereby many virtues are categorized by joining them to four principal virtues. Given the importance of such parts for Thomas's understanding of the virtues, it is important to understand the distinction between these parts.

---

[74] Thomas, *S.T.*, I-II, q. 64, art. 3, resp.; *SLE*, lib. 6, lect (Leonine, vol 47.2, 336–337). See especially Cajetan, *In I-II*, q. 57, art. 5 (Leonine, 6, 369–370).

[75] Thomas, *S.T.*, I-II, q. 57, art. 5; *DVC*, q. un. art. 6, resp. (Marietti, 722–723).

The principal virtues have other virtues that are integral, subjective, and potential parts.[76] Generally speaking and apart from the moral context, integral parts can be separated from an integral whole. For instance, the roof and the foundation are integral parts of the house, and the head and the neck are integral parts of a human. They are parts according to our most ordinary English usage. Subjective parts are distinct from each other although they fully participate in the whole. For example, a cow and a human are different parts of the genus "animal," and yet they are each fully "animal." Potential parts are usually powers or abilities. For example, the human soul is a whole that has distinct rational, sensitive, and vegetative potential parts. Potential parts are most different from what we normally describe as parts. Although they can be distinguished from each other, they cannot be separated from one another and from the whole.

In the *Prima Secundae*, Thomas devotes a full article to only the three virtues that are joined to prudence as potential parts. The discussion of all the parts is much more developed in the *Secunda Secundae*.[77] Thomas finds eight integral parts of prudence in the writings of Macrobius, Cicero, and Aristotle.[78] Five such parts pertain to the purely cognitive aspect of prudence, namely the memory of relevant experiences, the understanding of relevant particulars, docility to instruction, promptness in making the necessary judgments, and reasoning well about actions. Three parts pertain to the application of knowledge to the work to be done, namely foresight, circumspection concerning the relevant circumstances, and caution concerning danger. These eight virtues are integral parts in the sense that prudence can act perfectly only when it is accompanied by them. Prudence depends on these virtues in the way that a house depends on its foundation, walls, and roof.

Prudence does have subjective parts, but they are not distinct from each other in the way that the moral virtues might be. For instance, there is not a subjective prudence that is concerned with the matter of justice and another that is about the matter of courage. There are four subjective parts of prudence, namely individual prudence, "economic" or

---

[76] Lottin, *PM*, 191–194, mistakenly attributes the origin of this kind of classification to Albert the Great. It seems to have its source in the twelfth century and perhaps ultimately in Stoicism. See René-Antoine Gauthier, "Comptes Rendus," *Bulletin Thomiste* 8 (1947–1953), 60, note 1; Th. Graf, *De subiecto psychico gratiae et virtutum*, 2 vols. (Rome: Herder, 1934), vol. 1, 88, note 38. For a discussion of these parts, see Thomas, *In Sent.*, lib. 3, d. 33, q. 3, art. 1, sol. 1, resp. (Mandonnet-Moos, 3, 1073); *S.T.*, q. 48, art. un., resp.

[77] Thomas, *S.T.*, I-II, q. 57, art. 6, ad 4; II-II, q. 48, art. un.

[78] Thomas devotes a full article to each of these integral parts in *S.T.*, II-II, q. 49. For some of these parts, see Thomas, *In Sent.*, lib. 3, d. 33, q. 3, art. 1, sol. 2 (Mandonnet-Moos, 3, 1074–1075).

family prudence, ruling prudence, and military prudence.[79] Each of these kinds of prudence is a distinct species that belongs to the wider genus of prudence, which is right reason in human action. Since prudence is concerned with commanding acts that are part of the good life as a whole, the different subjective parts cannot be specified on account of the matter that is commanded. For example, the prudence that is concerned with food and drink is the same prudence that is concerned with courageous action. The subjective parts of prudence are instead specified by the individual or group that is commanded. Individual prudence is about the individual's own good. "Economic" prudence is about the good life as achieved by a family, and ruling prudence is about the good life of a political community. Individual, economic, and ruling prudence are all concerned with the good life as a whole and not with any particular affair. Military prudence is an exception to the extent that it is concerned about a particular area, namely success in war. Nevertheless, even such an apparent exception exists only on account of the way in which military prudence is necessary for the protection of the whole common good. Such military prudence is presumably distinct from a mere skill in warfare. There is no such thing as "shoemaking prudence" or "boatbuilding prudence." Nonmilitary affairs are concerned with mere parts of the common good.

The potential parts of a virtue are virtues that do not fully correspond to the virtue in which they participate. They somehow are joined to the virtue by sharing in its matter or having an order to its proper act. Thomas and the translators keep the Greek names that Aristotle gives to the potential parts of prudence, presumably because there are no obvious counterparts in Latin.[80] In order to command an act, prudence depends on previous inquiry about the way in which an end can be instantiated or achieved. The virtue of *eubulia* perfects such deliberation concerning the means to or instantiation of an end. After discovering such a means or instantiation, the prudent agent must make a judgment about such means. The virtues of *synesis* and *gnome* both perfect these judgments about acts, although they are used in different situations. *Synesis* is about

---

[79] In addition to the brief discussion in Thomas, *S.T.*, II-II, q. 48, art. un., resp., see q. 50, art. 1–4; *SLE*, lib. 6, lect. 7 (Leonine, 47.2, 356–358). Thomas gives a slightly different account in *In Sent.*, lib. 3, d. 33, q. 3, art. 1, sol. 4, resp. and ad 3–5 (Mandonnet-Moos, 3, 1077–1079).

[80] In addition to the brief discussion in Thomas, *S.T.*, II-II, q. 48, art. un., resp., see q. 51, art. 1–4; *SLE*, lib. 6, lect. 8–9 (Leonine, 47.2, 360–367); *In Sent.*, lib. 3, d. 33, q. 3, art. 1, sol. 3 (Mandonnet-Moos, 1075–1076). See especially Steven Jensen, "Of Gnome and Gnomes: The Virtue of Higher Discernment and the Production of Monsters," *American Catholic Philosophical Quarterly* 82 (2008): 411–428; Risto Saarinen, "The Parts of Prudence: Buridan, Odonis, Aquinas," *Dialogue* 42 (2003): 755–759.

judgments concerning ordinary cases, whereas *gnome* perfects judgments about those cases that do not fall under the general rule. These three potential parts of prudence are ordered to the proper act of prudence, which is command.

Usually Thomists identify these three virtues of prudence with three distinct stages in Thomas's understanding of human action, namely deliberation, the judgment of choice, and command. *Eubulia* perfects deliberation, *synesis* and *gnome* perfect judgment, and prudence perfects command (*imperium*). In the twentieth century, René-Antonin Gauthier strongly objected to this identification.[81] Part of his argument is that Thomas uses two different words for "command," namely "*praeceptum*" and "*imperium*." According to Gauthier, neither Aristotle nor Thomas understands the command of prudence to be posterior to choice. For Thomas, the "*praeceptum*" that is the proper act of prudence is the same as the judgment of choice and consequently prior and distinct from the "*imperium*" that Thomas teaches is posterior to choice. Nevertheless, despite Gauthier's demur, there remain good reasons for identifying "*imperium*" with "*praeceptum*" in the context of prudence.[82] For example, Thomas himself refers to an earlier discussion of reason's *imperium*.[83] Moreover, he seems to interpret Aristotle as having an understanding of *praeceptum* that is similar to his own understanding of *imperium* in that it involves the final perfection and completion of the act.[84] Whether the traditional identification of the potential parts of prudence with the three intellectual acts is correct or not, these parts are specifically distinct from each other and from prudence, and they have their own proper acts.

Moral Virtue and Prudence

Thomas' discussion of prudence leads to a discussion of moral virtue, to which prudence is closely related. He notes that prudence is included in the definition of moral virtue, since this definition contains "the mean that

---

[81] Gauthier, "Comptes Rendus," 64–71; "Saint Maxime le Confesseur et la psychologie de l'acte humain," *Recherches de théologie ancienne et médiévale* 21 (1954): 82–88. For an overview and defense of Gauthier, see Paul Morriset, "Prudence et fin selon Saint Thomas," *Sciences ecclésiastiques* 15 (1963): 439–449.

[82] T.-H. Deman, "Le 'précepte' de la prudence chez Saint Thomas d'Aquin," *Recherches de Théologie ancienne et médiévale* 20 (1953): 40–59; Servais Pinckaers, "Comptes Rendus – Deman et Gauthier," *Bulletin Thomiste* 9 (1955), 345–362; Daniel Westberg, *Right Practical Reason: Aristotle, Action and Prudence in Aquinas* (Oxford: Clarendon Press, 1994), 191–197.

[83] Thomas, *S.T.*, II-II, q. 47, art. 8, ad 3.

[84] Thomas, *SLE*, lib. 6, lect. 9 (Leonine, 47.2, 356).

is determined by reason."[85] Moreover, there is a way in which prudence
can be included with both the intellectual and moral virtues.[86] Thomas
distinguishes between prudence's essence and its matter. According to its
essence, prudence is an intellectual virtue and not a moral virtue, since it
perfects the practical intellect. But prudence has the same matter as the
moral virtues do, since it is concerned with right reason with respect to
human action. This identical matter makes it possible for prudence to be
in a way counted among the moral virtues.

Thomas first considers moral virtue's nominal or etymological definition, which is based on the Latin word "*mos*," from which "*moralis*" is
derived.[87] He remarks that it has two meanings that are covered by distinct but related words in Greek. First, "*mos*" can mean a custom. Second,
"*mos*" can mean a certain natural or quasi-natural inclination. According
to Thomas, a virtue is "*moralis*" primarily according to this second sense,
although this meaning is in some way related to the first. Custom can
become an inclination that is similar to natural inclination. Such custom
involves the appetite and consequently is relevant to moral virtue. Custom
brings about inclination, and the inclination to act properly belongs to
the appetitive power. Such an inclination plays a role in the agent's choice.
Choice is the proper act of moral virtue. An agent can choose to exercise
the intellectual virtues, but the moral virtues are exercised by choosing.
Consequently, such virtue is called moral because of the way that it perfects this appetitive power by inclining an agent's choice. Moral virtue
can move the will and, in relation to the will, the other appetites and all
powers that are subject to appetite. For this reason, Aristotle defines moral
virtue as habit of choosing.

In order to distinguish between intellectual and moral virtue, Thomas
discusses Socrates's thesis that prudence is the only virtue.[88] Socrates's
view is at first glance plausible because reason is a principle of all human
works. Even the appetite causes action by means of its obedience to reason. According to Thomas, if every human power obeyed reason in the
way that the bodily members do, then Socrates would be entirely correct.
A perfected reason would be sufficient for acting well. All sin would be

---

[85] Thomas, *S.T.*, I-II, q. 58, art. 2, obj. 1 and ad 1.
[86] Thomas, *S.T.*, I-II, q. 58, art. 3, ad 1. Robert Miner, "Non-Aristotelian Prudence in the *Prima Secundae*," *The Thomist* 64 (2000): 401–422, at 407–411.
[87] Thomas, *S.T.*, I-II, q. 58, art. 1; *SLE*, lib. 2, lect. 1 (Leonine, 47.1, 77); *In Sent.*, lib. 3, d. 23, q. 2, art. 4, sol. 2, resp. (Mandonnet-Moos, 3, 713). For the sources of Thomas's remarks about the Greek, see the Leonine editor's notes on vol. 47.1, 77.
[88] Thomas, *S.T.*, I-II, q. 58, art. 2

caused by ignorance. But, as Aristotle notes, reason has only a political and royal rule over the passions and habits of the appetitive parts, and not a despotic rule.[89] They sometimes oppose reason. Passion and bad habits can impede correct reasoning about particular action. Consequently, Thomas states that Socrates is correct only to the extent that at the time that the agent acts wrongly, she does not know what the right action is.[90] All sin involves at least some particular ignorance about the malice of the act. Moral virtue disposes the appetitive parts in such a way that they no longer bring about this particular ignorance. Therefore, acting well depends not only on habits that perfect reason but also on those habits that perfect the appetitive parts so that they obey reason.

Thomas follows Aristotle in distinguishing between perfected virtue and virtues that are "natural" in the sense that they are nonrational inclinations.[91] For instance, some individuals might from birth have a tendency towards gentleness, temperance, or courage. Nevertheless, without knowledge these natural virtues do not cause good actions and can even be misused. For example, a naturally courageous human might use his ability to overcome fear to carry out a cruel crime. Thomas states that such natural virtues are never fully virtues because they can be used badly. Unlike such natural virtue, moral virtue depends on prudence for its choice of the right means to an end. In his defense of this thesis, Thomas seems to discuss prudence not narrowly as the moral virtue whose proper act is command but more generally as including the potential parts of *eubulia*, *synesis*, and *gnome*. He notes that moral virtue guarantees rectitude towards the end and its proper act is the choice of the means towards this end. But this choice of a means depends on the intellectual acts of deliberation, judgment, and choice. These intellectual acts depend for their perfection on prudence and the virtues that are joined to it. Both prudence and science ultimately depend on principles that they do not themselves grasp.

Prudence is the only human intellectual virtue that depends on moral virtue. Prudence requires moral virtue for its rectitude to the end, and moral virtue itself needs general moral knowledge.[92] In contrast, science,

---

[89] See Chapter 1.

[90] See also Aristotle, *EN*, 6.13.1144b19–21; Thomas, *SLE*, lib. 6, lect. 11 (Leonine, 47.2, 376). An overview of the kinds and relevance of ignorance for action can be found in Joseph Caulfield, "Practical Ignorance in Moral Actions," *Laval théologique et philosophique* 7 (1951): 69–122.

[91] Thomas, *S.T.*, I-II, q. 58, art. 4. See also Thomas, *SLE*, lib. 6, lect. 11 (Leonine, 47.2, 375–377); *DVCard.*, q. un., art. 2, resp. (Marietti, 818). For a translation of art. 4–5 and an introduction to the terminology, see J. Budziszewski, *A Commentary on Thomas Aquinas's Virtue Ethics* (Cambridge: Cambridge University Press, 2017), 20–42.

[92] In addition to the texts cited below, see Thomas, *DVC*, q. un, art. 7, resp. (Marietti, 724–725).

wisdom, and skill depend on the will only for their good or evil use. They
give the agent the ability to perform certain acts, but they do not perfect
the agent. Although moral virtue causes the appetite to be well ordered
to the end, it does not directly cause knowledge of this end. In order to
desire the end one must first grasp general moral principles through the
understanding of principles or through practical science. Thomas writes:

> Just as through natural understanding or through the habit of science a hu-
> man is rightly in relation to universal principles, so in order for him to be
> correctly related to particular principles of acts, which are ends, he must be
> perfected through some habits whereby it becomes in some way connatural
> for the human to judge rightly concerning the end. And this comes about
> through moral virtue, for the virtuous human rightly judges concerning the
> end of virtue, since "Such as a human is, so does the end appear to him," as
> is said in Book III of the *Ethics*.[93]

In this text the judgment concerning this end itself is not the act of moral
virtue. But moral virtue orders the individual in such a way that she can
make the judgment about the end that allows her to pursue the appropriate means. Such virtue makes such her judgment connatural, or as if by
second nature.

Since prudence is broadly speaking right reason about human action,
it might seem that prudence should be concerned with ends as well as
means. In subsequent years, John Duns Scotus argued for the rival position and interpretation of Aristotle that moral virtue depends on prudence both for knowledge of the end and knowledge of the means to the
end.[94] He stated that since an agent develops moral virtue by acting in
accordance with right reason, she must be able to judge rightly before she
acquires moral virtue. Thomas, on the other hand, in some texts seems to
make this judgment generally posterior to moral virtue.

One objection to Thomas's view is that agents often deliberate about
ends. For instance, one might deliberate about the best medicine to take

---

[93] "Et ideo, sicut homo disponitur ad recte se habendum circa principia universalia, per intellectum
naturalem vel per habitum scientiae; ita ad hoc quod recte se habeat circa principia particularia
agibilium, quae sunt fines, oportet quod perficiatur per aliquos habitus secundum quos fiat quo-
dammodo homini connaturale recte iudicare de fine. Et hoc fit per virtutem moralem, virtuosus
enim recte iudicat de fine virtutis, quia qualis unusquisque est, talis finis videtur ei, ut dicitur in III
Ethic." Thomas, *S.T.*, I-II, q. 58, art. 5, resp. See also Thomas, *SLE*, lib. 6, lect. 10 (Leonine, 47.2,
373), and even *Super I Cor.*, c. 2, lect. 3, n. 118 (Marietti, vol. 1, 255). For Thomas's understanding of
connaturality, see especially Rafael Tomás Caldera, *Le jugement par inclination chez Saint Thomas
d'Aquin* (Paris: Vrin, 1980), 97–116; Taki Suto, "Virtue and Knowledge: Connatural Knowledge
according to Thomas Aquinas," *The Review of Metaphysics* 58 (2004): 61–79
[94] John Duns Scotus, *Ord.* 3, d. 36, nn. 86–92 (Vatican ed., vol. 10, 255–256).

in order to attain health. But if somebody else needs the medicine, or it is harmful in some way to obtain the medicine, then this end of attaining health itself should be rejected. In such a case it seems that prudence is concerned both with the means of attaining health and with the end of health.

Terence Irwin attributes to Thomas a distinction between "macro-prudence" and "micro-prudence."[95] This distinction is based on the difference between the universal end and more particular ends. He writes, "Virtues sets the specifically virtuous end for micro-prudence and *synderesis* sets the universal end for macro-prudence."[96] There is little justification for such a distinction in Thomas's own text. Moreover, there is no need to posit such a distinction in order to correct the misunderstanding of those who object to Thomas's view by noting that prudence can be about some ends. Thomas clearly states that only the knowledge of and order to the most general ends are set by nature. The many other ends are intermediate. Such ends can be principles of practical reason in comparison to particular conclusions drawn from them, but they can also be derived from more general ends and principles.

Thomas notes that since the conclusion in one chain of reasoning is often the principle to another chain, the conclusion of one chain of deliberation, which is a means to an end, can be the principle or end of another chain.[97] For instance, if we conclude that it is unjust to spend money on medicine rather than food, then we will deliberate differently concerning how to restore our health. Or if we conclude that someone needs to be provided a warm coat even if it risks our health, we can then deliberate over whether giving our own coat is the best means. The general ends are set by nature. But the intermediate ends are subject to deliberation and choice and, consequently, prudence. Insofar as they are ends, the agent is rightly ordered to them through moral virtue. But these intermediate ends are chosen and commanded by prudence not insofar as they are ends but insofar as they help to attain a further end.

According to Thomas, *synderesis* is the natural habit whereby we know such first practical principles that make it possible to know the ends of the

[95] Terence Irwin, "Practical Reason Divided: Aquinas and His Critics," in *Ethics and Practical Reason*, ed. Garrit Cullity and Berys Gaut (Clarendon: Oxford, 1997), 204–208.

[96] Irwin, "Practical Reason Divided," 205.

[97] Thomas, *S.T.*, I-II, q. 14, art. 2; Thomas M. Osborne Jr., *Human Action in Thomas Aquinas, John Duns Scotus, and William of Ockham* (Washington, DC: The Catholic University of America Press, 2014), 123–124; Westberg, *Right Practical Reason*, 165–167.

moral virtue.[98] Prudence is related to *synderesis* in the way that science is related to understanding. Right reason in speculative matters depends on the knowledge of speculative principles through the virtue of understanding. Similarly, prudence, since it is a kind of right reasoning, depends on the understanding of practical principles.

Thomas discusses these principles more fully later in his discussion of natural law in q. 94, art. 2, of the same *Prima Secundae* of the *Summa Theologiae*. He states there that there is a first principle that is supposed in all practical knowledge, namely that "good is to be done and pursued, and evil is to be avoided."[99] This first practical principle has the same role in practical knowledge that the principle of noncontradiction has in speculative knowledge. There are other principles as well that are known to everyone, such as the substance of the Ten Commandments and the commandments to love God and neighbor.[100] Knowledge of such general principles does not depend on prudence. Although such principles are distinct from speculative principles, it is unclear whether Thomas thinks that they are known by an intellectual habit distinct from that of knowing first practical principles. In the *Prima Secundae*, q. 57, art. 2, Thomas identifies the virtue of understanding with the knowledge of speculative first principles. In q. 58, art. 4, he states that moral virtue is dependent not only on prudence but also on the virtue of understanding, and consequently he seems to ascribe the knowledge of such principles to this intellectual virtue. Perhaps a more general virtue of understanding includes distinct habits for knowing speculative and practical principles.

Thomists have historically disagreed over this question of whether or not *synderesis* is the same as the habit of understanding of first speculative principles.[101] In the *Summa Theologiae*, I-II, q. 58, art. 4, Thomas states, "for through the understanding are known the principles that are naturally known, in speculative matters as well as in practical matters."[102] In

---

[98] Thomas, *S.T.*, II-II, q. 47, art. 7, ad 3; *In Sent.*, lib. 3, d. 33, q. 2, art. 3, resp. (Mandonnet-Moos, 3, 1057). For Thomas's understanding of *synderesis* and scholarly literature, see Westberg, *Right Practical Reason*, 100–106.

[99] "bonum est faciendum et prosequendum, et malum vitandum." Thomas, *S.T.*, I-II, q. 94, art. 2, resp. See also Vernon J. Bourke, "The Background of Aquinas's Synderesis Principle," in *Graceful Reason: Essays in Ancient and Medieval Philosophy Presented to Joseph Owens, CSSR*, ed. Lloyd Gerson (Toronto: Pontifical Institute of Mediaeval Studies, 1983), 345–360.

[100] Thomas, *S.T.*, I-II, q. 100, art. 3. Thomas considers the precept to avoid evil alongside other commands such as that against theft in *SLE*, lib. 5, lect. 12 (Leonine, 47.2, 305).

[101] John of St. Thomas, *In I-II*, disp. 16, art. 2, nn. 215–225, 669–671, 699–704 (Québec, 76–80, 215–216, 225–227).

[102] "Per intellectum enim cognoscuntur principia naturaliter nota, tam in speculativis quam in operativis." Thomas, *S.T.*, I-II, q. 58, art. 4, resp. See also Thomas, *S.T.*, II-II, q. 49, art. 2.

this text understanding seems to be one habit of knowing both kinds of principles, although it could perhaps be a genus that contains two correspondingly specifically distinct habits. Evidence for this latter reading can be found in the *De Veritate*, in which Thomas states, "this name *synderesis* either names absolutely a natural habit similar to the habit of [knowing] principles, or it names the same power of reason with such a habit."[103] In this earlier text *synderesis* is a natural habit that is similar to and therefore distinct from understanding, which is the habit of knowing principles. It is not clear why if Thomas later continues to hold this view he does not include *synderesis* in his list of the intellectual virtues. If *synderesis* is a distinct natural habit, it should probably be added as a sixth intellectual virtue to the five Aristotelian intellectual virtues. On the other hand, perhaps Thomas reads Aristotle's virtue of understanding as a genus in the way that Aristotle's science is a genus. If this is the case, it is not clear why in the *Summa Theologiae* Thomas describes the intellectual virtue of understanding as the habit by which we know speculative first principles. The source of the difficulty might simply be that Thomas's understanding of intellectual virtue comes from Aristotle but his understanding of *synderesis* is his own adaptation of a notion that he inherited from the previous scholastic tradition.

Some general principles of human action are known not by *synderesis*, or perhaps not only by *synderesis*, but by moral science. Such practical science produces universal judgments such as "fornication is bad" and "theft should not be done."[104] Vice is fully compatible with such moral science, although it can corrupt the application of the general judgments in a particular judgment. For instance, someone who generally knows that fornication is bad might make a judgment that fornicating in the present context is good. But prudence produces a judgment about a particular present situation, such as that taking this money would be an act of theft. Disordered passion causes a person to falsely judge. Such ignorance is opposed to prudence and never excuses an act. But vice by itself does not cause ignorance of the general principle that theft is bad, although one might be mistaken about such general principles through negligence or a directly willed ignorance.[105] For this reason Thomas states that sins that

---

[103] "hoc nomen *synderesis* vel nominet absolute habitum naturalem similem habitui principiorum, vel nominet ipsam potentiam rationis cum tali habitu …" Thomas, *DV*, q. 16, art. 1, resp. (Leonine, 33.3, 504).

[104] Thomas, *DVC*, q. un. art. 6, ad 1, 3 (Marietti, 723).

[105] For such ignorance, see Thomas, *S.T.*, I-II, q. 19, art. 6. For other passages and a discussion, see Lottin, *PM*, 3.1, 44–46, 88–90.

come about through the use of vice are due to malice, which is a disordered will, rather than to ignorance or weakness.[106]

Up until this point we have primarily considered those texts that state that prudence is about the means and not about the end of virtue. In these texts Thomas denies that prudence prescribes the end. But several texts seem to contradict this point. For instance, in a reply from the *Prima Secundae*, Thomas writes:

> [P]rudence not only guides moral virtues in choosing those things that are for the sake of the end, but even in prescribing the end. Nevertheless, it is the end of any moral virtue to attain the mean in its proper matter; but such a mean is determined according to the right reason of prudence, as is said in Book II and Book VI of the *Ethics*.[107]

In this text Thomas explicitly states that prudence prescribes the end, but he also illustrates how this end differs from the end that is its principle. Prudence prescribes the proximate end of the action, which is chosen by virtue. This proximate end is the means that is determined by prudence. Thomas clearly distinguishes between two ends, namely an end that is chosen and a further end that is intended. The very end that prudence prescribes, namely the end that is chosen by moral virtue, is itself a means towards the further end that it presupposes. Moral virtue rectifies the appetite with respect to this presupposed end and ultimately moves prudence to command the end that is a mean of moral virtue. In this way prudence is concerned with particular goods that are part of or lead to the ultimate end.

The distinction between the two different usages of the term "end" is seen in that question of the *Summa Theologiae* in which Thomas distinguishes between two different virtues that are both called "understanding" (*intellectus*).[108] The first virtue is that by which first principles are known, and the second is that by which the singular minor proposition in a prudential syllogism is known. Prudence depends on the first and has the second as an integral part. According to the first virtue of understanding, a person by nature knows not only universal speculative principles

---

[106] Thomas, *S.T., I-II*, q. 78, art. 2. Steven Jensen, *Sin: A Thomistic Psychology* (Washington, DC: The Catholic University of America Press, 2018), 158–184; Colleen McCluskey, *Thomas Aquinas on Moral Wrongdoing* (Cambridge: Cambridge University Press, 2017), 116–147.

[107] "prudentia non solum dirigit virtutes morales in eligendo ea quae sunt ad finem, sed etiam in praestituendo finem. Est autem finis uniuscuiusque virtutis moralis attingere medium in propria materia: quod quidem medium determinatur secundum rectam rationem prudentiae, ut dicitur in II et VI Ethic." Thomas, *S.T., I-II*, q. 66, art. 3, ad 3.

[108] Thomas, *S.T., II-II*, q. 49, art. 2.

but also universal practical principles, such as "Crime should be done to no one."[109] The second virtue of understanding might identify a particular act of theft as a crime. Thomas writes, "the intellect that is held to be a part of prudence is a certain right estimation of some particular end."[110] This second virtue is an integral part of prudence, since the prudent agent needs such particular judgments in order to conclude his reasoning. The proper act of prudence is the conclusion, which is the command that the crime not be done. The separate virtue of understanding is concerned with the end that is identified in the major premise of a practical syllogism. The virtue of understanding that is part of prudence is concerned with the end that is identified in the minor premise. It belongs to the cogitative power.[111] Both virtues are called "understanding" because they are in some way about statements that are known in themselves.

Thomas more clearly distinguishes between such ends in his *Commentary on the Sentences*.[112] He explains that the perfection of virtue requires the prescription of the end, the inclination to this end, and the choice of the means to this end. The first end is the good of reason in common. Natural reason, in the sense of reason without science or prudence, is sufficient with respect to this end. For this reason, it precedes prudence, which determines the good of reason more particularly as a mean of a specific virtue. Therefore, prudence prescribes the end to the extent that it prescribes the end as made present in a particular act. But the inclination to this act and its resulting choice are due to moral virtue. He states that this inclination of moral virtue follows prudence in the way that natural inclination follows from natural reason. In the context of this early text Thomas does not discuss the dependence of prudence on moral virtue. Consequently, this text does not entirely correspond to Thomas's later discussions. Nevertheless, it importantly indicates how prudence depends upon a different end than the end that it prescribes, which is the mean of virtue.

These various texts show that the word "end" can be used in ways that apply both to the universal end of action and to the particular end that is introduced in the minor term and then commanded or chosen. Prudence depends on a separate virtue of understanding or *synderesis* to know the universal end and on moral virtue to correctly desire it. Both such general knowledge and correct desire are necessary for the deliberation.

---

109 "nulli esse malifaciendum." Thomas, *S.T.*, II-II, q. 49, art. 2, ad 1.
110 "intellectus qui ponitur pars prudentiae est quaedam recta aestimatio de aliquo particulari fine." Thomas, *S.T.*, II-II, q. 49, art. 2, ad 1.
111 Thomas, *S.T.*, II-II, q. 49, art. 2, ad 3.
112 Thomas, *In Sent.*, lib. 3, d. 33, q. 2, art. 3 (Mandonnet-Moos, 3, 1057).

The importance of this judgment concerning the proximate end can be seen in the way that moral vice corrupts prudence. Although Thomas states that intemperance can in some instances corrupt even scientific knowledge, the corruption of universal knowledge is different from that of particular knowledge.[113] Intemperance in food and to a greater degree sexual pleasure can corrupt universal knowledge by focusing the mind on bodily objects in a way that impedes the knowledge of spiritual objects. Moreover, sexual pleasure and drunkenness hinder reason from intellectual pursuits while the pleasure is experienced. Nevertheless, despite such hindrance, the vice of intemperance is generally compatible with intellectual virtue. For example, both the temperate and the intemperate can know that a triangle has three angles that are equal to two right angles.

Aristotle notes that the vice of intemperance corrupts prudence because it corrupts the principle of action.[114] This principle is not that which is grasped through science or understanding but instead that through which the more particular end of moral virtue is known. In commenting on this passage, Thomas notes that intemperance does not corrupt the speculative sciences, which are not about human operations.[115] For example, pleasure and pain do not take away our knowledge of the Pythagorean Theorem. But since human operations are motivated by the appetites, and especially vehement pleasure and pain, our knowledge of human actions is corrupted by them. Humans judge the pleasurable to be good and the painful as something to be avoided. Because an intemperate person will find good actions painful and bad actions pleasurable, he will view the painful good end as bad and the pleasurable bad end as good. Correct judgment concerning the end is the principle of the act and is presupposed by prudence, although it does not belong to prudence.

Thomas's understanding of the dependence of virtues of prudence sheds light on the way in which prudence can be more accessible than sciences, wisdom, and skill. In particular, science and wisdom seem practically impossible for unintelligent persons, although even the unintelligent can possess moral virtue. Consequently, even unintelligent humans who have moral virtue will be prudent. Thomas admits that prudence guarantees the correct use of reason only with respect to the matter of the virtues and not to other aspects of life. Nevertheless, simplicity in such other matters

---

[113] Thomas, *S.T.*, I-II, q. 33, art. 3; II-II, q. 15, art. 3; q. 53, art. 6. See Mary William, "The Relationships of the Intellectual Virtue of Science and Moral Virtue," *New Scholasticism* 36 (1962): 475–505, at 499–505.

[114] Aristotle, *EN* 6.5.1140b1–21.

[115] Thomas, *SLE*, lib. 6. lect. 4 (Leonine, 47.2, 346).

can be combined with a kind of prudence. Thomas writes, "those who seem simple, by the fact that they lack worldly astuteness, are able to be prudent, according to Matthew 10:16: 'Be prudent as serpents, and simple as doves.'"[116] Perhaps such unintelligent persons will particularly need the virtue of docility, which we have seen is the integral virtue of prudence by which the agent listens to the advice of others.[117]

Moral virtue can also help those without moral science to make correct judgments about general moral matters. Thomas does not state that such knowledge requires moral virtue. As we have seen, the original apprehension of the end seems to come from *synderesis* and perhaps other learned or derived moral knowledge. This knowledge does not depend on moral virtue, since the agent knows first principles through *synderesis*, which sets the end of the moral virtues and moves prudence.[118] In such passages moral virtue seems to assist only in rectifying the appetite towards the end on which prudence depends. However, Thomas also suggests that moral virtue assists in some kind of general knowledge that is described as either connatural as by inclination.

Moral virtue without science can help to supply knowledge that would otherwise be learned through moral science. Thomas compares moral virtue to the intellectual light by which speculative first principles are understood. He writes, "just as a human assents to principles through the natural light of the human intellect, so the virtuous human through the habit of virtue has right judgement about those things that befit that virtue."[119] Although at times Thomas suggests that this intellectual light is the agent intellect, his overall account can be unclear.[120] The relevant point for us is that the intellectual light makes its object knowable in the same way that physical light makes color visible. Similarly, moral virtue makes some moral knowledge possible. This moral knowledge is distinct from that given by *synderesis* because it is available only to the virtuous, whereas

---

[116] "etiam qui videntur simplices, eo quod carent mundana astutia, possunt esse prudentes; secundum illud Mt. 10, 16: 'Estote prudentes sicut serpentes, et simplices sicut columbae.'" Thomas, *S.T.*, I-II, q. 58, art. 4, ad 2.

[117] Thomas, *S.T.*, II-II, q. 49, art. 3.

[118] Thomas, *S.T.*, II-II, q. 47, art. 6, ad 1, 3.

[119] "sicut homo per naturale lumen intellectus assentit principiis, ita homo virtuosus per habitum virtutis habet rectum iudicium de his quae conveniunt virtuti illi." Thomas, *S.T.*, II-II, q. 2, art. 3, ad 2.

[120] Thomas, *S.T.*, I, q. 79, art. 3, ad 2; q. 84, art. 5, resp. For additional texts and a discussion of this natural light, see Bernard Lonergan, *Verbum: Word and Idea in Aquinas*, ed. David B. Burrell (Notre Dame, IN: University of Notre Dame Press, 1967), 79–84; Robert Pasnau, *Aquinas on Human Nature: A Philosophical Study of Summa Theologia 1a 75–89* (Cambridge: Cambridge University Press, 2002), 302–310.

synderesis is equally present in the good and in the bad. Although the passage does not go into sufficient detail to be certain, this moral knowledge seems to be distinct from that which belongs to prudence because it is about that which is generally fitting and consequently not limited to the particular judgments that belong to prudence and its parts.

In other passages Thomas clearly states that someone without moral knowledge has a quasi-natural or connatural knowledge of the same matters that can be learned through moral science.[121] For instance, he writes, "someone who has learned moral science through the inquiry of reason judges correctly concerning that which pertains to chastity, but he who has the habit of chastity rightly judges them through some connaturality."[122] There is fittingness between the virtuous agent and the objects of virtue that makes not only particular judgments but also general judgments practical. The chaste individual makes the same judgments as the one who possesses moral science but lacks chastity. On Thomas's view, even though moral vice attacks primarily the particular judgments of a practical moral syllogism and not general propositions, moral virtue gives an ability to make the same correct general judgments that moral science makes. Although moral virtue is unnecessary for such knowledge, it seems sufficient for those who lack moral science and yet possess moral virtue. Such connatural knowledge is distinct from both the *synderesis* on which it depends for its principles and the particular knowledge that is made possible by prudence and it parts.

In general, Thomas thinks that moral virtue depends on the intellectual virtues of prudence and understanding or *synderesis* and that prudence is the only intellectual virtue that depends on moral virtue. This interdependence does not exhaustively account for the relationship between the intellectual and moral virtues. For instance, he states that virtues such as temperance can assist the speculative sciences and that moral virtue makes possible through connaturality a kind of knowledge that is learned in moral science. But most of Thomas's texts are on the connection between moral virtue, prudence, and *synderesis*. Prudence depends on natural reason or *synderesis* in a manner that resembles the dependence of science on

---

[121] Thomas, *S.T.*, I, q. 1, art. 6, ad 3; II-II, q. 45, art. 2, resp. For a slightly different interpretation, see Tobias Hoffmann, "Prudence and Practical Principles," in *Aquinas and the Nicomachean Ethics*, ed. Tobias Hoffmann, Jörn Müller, and Matthias Perkams (Cambridge: Cambridge University Press, 2013), 174–182.

[122] "de his quae ad castitatem pertinent per rationis inquisitionem recte iudicat ille qui didicit scientiam moralem; sed per quandam connaturalitatem ad ipsa recte iudicat de eis ille qui habet habitum castitatis." Thomas, *S.T.*, II-II, q. 45, art. 2.

the understanding of speculative principles. But unlike science, prudence depends not only on knowledge of the end but also on the right appetite concerning the end, which is due to moral virtue. Prudence is about the command of a particular means and presupposes for deliberation a correct desire for the end. This desire itself presupposes a judgment about the end that is made either through *synderesis*, moral science, or connatural knowledge.

By the end of q. 58 of the *Treatise on Virtue*, Thomas has distinguished between the two kinds of human virtue, namely moral and intellectual, and he has shown that the definition of virtue more completely applies to moral virtue. The virtue of prudence particularly stands out as belonging in some way to both categories. It is principally an intellectual virtue because it perfects the intellect, but it can be counted among the moral virtue because it perfects the intellect with respect to the practical truth about human action. Prudence depends on the intellectual virtue of understanding or *synderesis* for its general principles concerning the end, although it also relies on moral virtue for its rectitude concerning the end. Its own acts establish a mean that forms part of Aristotle's very definition of moral virtue.

Unlike prudence, the other intellectual virtues fade into the background for the rest of the Treatise. Thomas is concerned primarily with moral virtue, since it makes the agent good simply speaking. But these intellectual virtues do play a necessary role in his moral philosophy and theology. They truly perfect human acts of knowing and they even perfect the agent in a qualified way. Moreover, the *Summa Theologiae* itself introduces the reader to the science of theology. Although this science is not a human science, it to some extent shares the features of science as described by Aristotle's *Posterior Analytics*, and it directly concerns the highest principle of being, which is God. It is the highest kind of science. The *Treatise on Virtue* is part of moral theology, which is part of this speculative science, and also uses or subsumes moral philosophy. Consequently, the attentive reader should to some extent develop a habit of moral science. Such a habit presumably has some practical value, although unlike prudence it can be possessed by the wicked, who do not make proper use of it.

CHAPTER 3

Divisions of Moral Virtue

Whereas prudence is the sole intellectual virtue that directs human action, the various moral virtues assist and perfect the choice of such action. In contrast to the intellectual virtues, which belong to the intellect, the moral virtues belong to the appetitive parts. Some moral virtues perfect the rational appetite, which is the will, while other moral virtues perfect the sense appetites. These latter moral virtues are about the passions that are the proper acts of the sense appetites, such as desire, fear, and anger. In qq. 59–61 of the *Prima Secundae*, Thomas distinguishes between many moral virtues by considering them in relation to the passions. Thomas first distinguishes moral virtue from the passions, and then he distinguishes between those moral virtues that are directly about the passions from those that are not. This discussion of the passions allows him to explain Aristotle's list of the moral virtues and prepares the way for his discussion of what are traditionally known as the four cardinal virtues, namely prudence, temperance, courage, and justice.

Thomas's account draws on a variety of disparate sources, such as Aristotle, Stoics, Church Fathers, and Neoplatonists. He combines these elements in a way that often shows an underlying compatibility between apparently conflicting accounts, and he situates the older theses in his own philosophical framework. For instance, Thomas develops and extends Aristotle's account of the moral virtues in the context of his own more precise moral psychology in which the moral virtues must belong to one of three appetitive powers. In doing so he also takes into account the debate between Aristotelians and Stoics over whether the virtuous person even has passions. Thomas then uses this developed account of moral virtue to shed light on the common patristic doctrine of the "cardinal virtues," which has ultimate roots in Plato's *Republic* and Stoicism. These cardinal virtues include the intellectual virtue of prudence along with the three moral virtues of justice, courage or fortitude, and temperance. Thomas uses his sources in such a way that we can see how Aristotle and early Christian writers shed light on this classification.

In this chapter we will look at the way in which the moral virtues are distinguished from each other. The first division is between those moral virtues that are about operations and those that are about passions. Before addressing this issue, we need to look at how Thomas addresses a central disagreement on the passions between the Peripatetics, who are followers of Aristotle, and the Stoics. After establishing that some moral virtues are about the passions, we will consider how Thomas assimilates different descriptions of the kinds of moral virtue. First, we will see how he tries to show that Aristotle's distinction between eleven moral virtues is reasonable, with justice assigned to the will and the other virtues assigned to the sense appetites. Then we will look at how he emphasizes the traditional Stoic and Platonic tradition of four cardinal virtues, which he inherited from the Christian tradition. These cardinal virtues provide him with a framework for organizing the various virtues that were recognized not only by Aristotle but also by subsequent philosophical traditions. Last, we will look at how he uses the Neoplatonic division between political, purgative, purged, and exemplar virtue. This Neoplatonic division does not need to indicate different kinds of habits but instead can situate the virtues in relation to political life and in the agent's assimilation to God.

Passion and Virtue, Peripatetics and Stoics

Q. 59 of the *Prima Secundae* is about the relationship between moral virtue and the passions. Thomas first argues that the moral virtues are not passions even though they moderate the passions and even have them as their matter. He repeats and develops more systematically Aristotle's own arguments from the *Nicomachean Ethics*, which were used by Aristotle to show that virtue is a habit. But Thomas has already in q. 55 established that virtue is a habit. Consequently, he does not use these arguments in the same context. The reader already knows that virtue is a habit, and yet the relationship of the habit to the passions needs clarification. Thomas, like Augustine, is concerned with the Stoic thesis that the passions as such are bad. To some extent Thomas draws on Aristotle's text as a preparation for his criticism of this Stoic understanding of passion, as well as for his own description of how some moral virtues moderate the passions. Thomas' comparison of moral virtues with the passions in this question (q. 59) has no parallels in his other work, even though some particular issues are discussed in his *Commentary on the Nicomachean Ethics*.

In the *Nicomachean Ethics*, Book II, Ch. 5, Aristotle states that there is an obvious link between the passions of the sense appetites and human action. We can say that someone acts on account of passions such as pity or anger.[1] In several texts Thomas notes that confusion can arise because some passions share names with virtues and vices.[2] The names themselves are ambiguous. Consider the two passions that were mentioned in the context of Aristotle's text, namely pity and anger. Mercy or pity (*misericordia*) can refer to either the feeling of sadness for another's misery or the virtue by which someone acts to relieve another's misery. Similarly, anger can name either the passion that moves one to right a wrongful injury, or it can refer to a vice that produces unreasonable anger. Thomas maintains that among both virtues and vices there is a clear distinction between the habit and the similarly named passion.

Thomas distinguishes between passions and habits by remarking that "the passions come to us without choice, because sometimes they precede the deliberation of reason which is required for choice."[3] This connection between passions and choice will explain how certain passions come under the influence of reason and the will and are thereby subject to moral evaluation.

Even though the virtues and vices can both be about passions, only some vices seem to have passions as their proper acts in the narrowest sense.[4] For instance, the vice of anger is a habit by which one desires vengeance

---

[1] Thomas, *SLE*, lib. 2, lect. 5 (Leonine, 47.1, 91–92).

[2] Thomas, *S.T.*, I-II, q. 59, art. 1, ad 2–3. See also Thomas, *S.T.*, II-II, q. 158, art. 2; *DM*, q. 12, art. 1, ad 9 (Leonine, 23, 236). For scholarly disagreement over whether the passions can improve deliberation, see Steven Jensen, "Virtuous Deliberation and the Passions," *The Thomist* 77 (2013): 193–227; Daniel De Haan, "Moral Perception and the Function of the *Vis Cogitativa* in Thomas Aquinas's Doctrine of Antecedent and Consequent Passions," *Documenti e studi sulla tradizione filosofica medievale* 25 (2014): 289–330; Nicholas Kahm, *Aquinas on Emotion's Participation in Reason* (Washington, DC: The Catholic University of America Press, 2019), 237–266.

[3] "Passiones autem adveniunt nobis sine electione, quia interdum praeveniunt deliberationem rationis quae ad electionem requiritur." Thomas, *SLE*, lib. 2, lect. 5 (Leonine, 47.1, 92). For Thomas's general distinction between antecedent passions, which precede willing, and consequent passions, which follow willing, see especially Simo Knuuttila, *Emotions in Ancient and Medieval Philosophy* (Oxford: Clarendon, 2004), 253–254; Nicholas Lombardo, *The Logic of Desire: Aquinas on Emotion* (Washington, DC: The Catholic University of America Press, 2010), 109–111; Richard K. Mansfield, "Antecedent Passion and the Moral Quality of Human Acts," *Proceedings of the American Catholic Philosophical Association* 71 (1997): 221–231. For virtue and the passions, see Nicholas Austin, *Aquinas on Virtue: A Causal Reading* (Washington, DC: Georgetown University Press, 2017), 130–149.

[4] For a less proper way according to which passion can be said to be an act of virtue, see Thomas, *S.T.*, I-II, q. 59, art. 5, ad 1. For the ways in which passion can impede moral reasoning, see Steven Jensen, "The Error of the Passions," *The Thomist* 73 (2009): 349–379.

apart from the order of reason. In this case the disordered act of the irascible appetite is at the same time an act of a bad habit. In general, the passions can have a bad influence insofar as they impede reason. In contrast, passions merely concur with virtuous acts. They are themselves not the proper act of virtue, which belongs to the will. Although Thomas denies that passions cause virtuous acts, he does think it of prime importance that they can be regulated by virtue. Some moral virtues cause more moderate passions. For example, the temperate person has different passions concerning food and drink than the intemperate person does. Although such passions do not cause the good acts, they assist the will in following the correct judgments of reason more promptly and easily.[5]

The dispute between the Stoics and the Peripatetics on this issue was well known in the Hellenistic and Latin world. Stoics held the at least initially implausible view that the sage or virtuous person does not have any passions.[6] Thomas's account of this disagreement between Stoics and Peripatetics is heavily indebted to Augustine's *City of God*, in which Augustine partially follows Cicero in holding that the dispute is more about words than about things, which was also the opinion of Seneca and some other Hellenistic philosophers. Contemporary scholarship suggests weaknesses in Augustine's account of Stoicism and in particular his claim that the dispute is merely verbal.[7] This book is not the place to address such a point. Whether or not their historical accounts are accurate, Augustine and Thomas discuss Stoic views in a way that sheds wider light on the importance of the passions for moral virtue. Moreover, not only do they generally oppose the Stoic account of the sage as without passion, they criticize separately and in particular the Stoic belief that virtue is incompatible with sadness. Thomas relies heavily on Augustine, who defends as Christian the view that the virtuous truly suffer evil and consequently experience painful passions.

In his account of the dispute between the Peripatetics and the Stoics Thomas does not focus on Aristotle's texts or on any particular Aristotelian

---

[5] Thomas, *DV*, q. 26, art. 7, resp. (Leonine, 22.3, 773).
[6] For a sympathetic account, see Michael Frede, "The Stoic Doctrine of the Affections of the Soul," in *The Norms of Nature: Studies in Hellenistic Ethics*, ed. Malcolm Schofield and Gisela Striker (Cambridge: Cambridge University Press, 1986), 93–110.
[7] Richard Sorabji, *Emotion and Peace of Mind: From Stoic Agitation to Christian Temptation* (Oxford and New York: Oxford University Press, 2000), 206–210; Knuuttila, *Emotions in Ancient and Late Medieval Philosophy*, 153–159. For Augustine's account in itself, see Gerard O'Daly, *Augustine's Philosophy of Mind* (Berkeley, CA: University of California Press, 1987), 48–54. For Thomas, see also Thomas, *DM*, q. 12, art. 1 (Leonine, 23, 233–237).

philosopher. He relies on Augustine's *City of God*, Book IX, chapter 4, even for his account of the Peripatetic position. Thomas states that the disagreement between the schools does not seem to directly involve Aristotle so much as those who belong to the tradition that Aristotle established. According to the Stoics, the virtuous, whom Stoics call the wise, do not have any passions of the soul. In contrast, the Peripatetics hold that "the passions are able to exist at the same time with moral virtue, but are reduced to a mean."[8] Augustine states that the Peripatetics follow the Platonists on this issue and notes that Aristotle himself was a student of Plato.[9] Thomas does not mention Augustine's identification of the Peripatetic view with the Platonic one.

Although Thomas agrees with Augustine that the dispute is mostly verbal, he provides a more detailed account of its source in light of his own understanding of the divisions between the intellectual and sense appetites, which he also attributes to the Peripatetics. According to Thomas, the Stoics call "passions" only those movements of the sense appetite that are repugnant to reason. On the other hand, the Peripatetics use the word "passion" for movements of the sense appetite. On the Peripatetic account, a passion is any movement of the sense appetite, whether are not it is repugnant to reason. Consequently, the difference is largely verbal. When the Aristotelians state that the virtuous experience passions, they mean that the virtuous have movements of the sense appetite that are not repugnant to reason. Stoics do not describe such movements as passions. According to the Stoic understanding, all passions are unreasonable. Consequently, they think that since such passions are unreasonable, they cannot deliberately arise in the virtuous. The Stoics think that the virtuous might experience such passions only in a way that precedes any deliberation.

Augustine himself states that the Stoics allow for something like passions in the sage. He repeats an account of Aulus Gellius, whom he describes as eloquent but perhaps longwinded. Gellius was on a sea voyage with a philosopher who showed great fear in a storm. When the philosopher was asked about his fear, he read a passage from a book by the Stoic philosopher Epictetus. Thomas quotes *verbatim* Augustine's description of the passage's contents:

> With the soul having seen what they call "sense images" (*phantasiae*), it is not in our power whether they ever incite the soul; and when they come

---

[8] "passiones simul cum virtute morali esse possunt, se ad medium rei reductae." Thomas, *S.T.*, I-II, q. 59, art. 2, resp.

[9] "Hoc qui sentiunt, Platonici sunt siue Arisotelici, cum Aristoteles discipulus Platonis fuerit, qui sectam Peripateticam condidit." Augustine, *De Civ. Dei*, lib. 9, cap. 4 (CCSL 47, 251).

from terrible things, it is necessary that they move the soul of the sage, such that for a little while either he trembles with fear, or he is drawn down with sadness, insofar as these passions have preceded the work of reason; but he does not approve of them or consent to them.[10]

Augustine in this passage is describing a distinction that late Stoics make between propassions (*propatheai* in Greek; *propassiones* or *antepassiones* in Latin) and passions.[11] The propassions result from sudden experiences, whereas the passions properly speaking involve a mistaken judgment. The sage can have propassions but not passions. According to Augustine's account of Stoicism, these propassions are immediate responses to sense information that precede the exercise of reason.

According to Richard Sorabji, Augustine's account is inaccurate in part because Gellius explains Epictetus in such a way as to obscure the original point.[12] Whereas Epictetus states that the sage can "grow pale" (*pallescere*), Gellius states that he can "grow jittery" (*pavescere*). In contrast to Augustine, the Stoics think that these propassions differ in kind from passions. Epictetus in fact taught that the sage suffers a first movement but does not experience fear. Sorabji states that Augustine misreads Gellius as holding that there is one fear that precedes reason and a different fear that follows it. Augustine's distinction between passions that precede and follow reason is rooted in Augustine's own Platonic moral psychology

Whether Augustine's reading of this Stoic view is plausible or not, Thomas depends on it for his own account of the relationship between moral virtue and the passions. Thomas thinks that the Stoic denial of passions to the sage is based on their description of passions as inordinate. On such an interpretation, the Stoics merely hold that the virtuous do not after deliberation consent to disordered movements of the appetite. This purported Stoic understanding of virtue corresponds to a view that Aristotle attributes to some of his own contemporaries. Thomas writes:

Whence Aristotle states in Book II of the *Ethics* that someone does not well describe the virtues as certain impassible and quiet things, because they speak in an unqualified way: but they must say that they are quiet

---

[10] "eo quod animi visa quae appellant phantasias, non est in potestate nostra utrum aliquando incidant animo; et cum veniunt ex terribilibus rebus, necesse est ut sapientis animum moveant, ita ut paulisper vel pavescat metu, vel tristitia contrahatur, tanquam his passionibus praevenientibus rationis officium; nec tamen approbant ista, eisque consentiunt." Augustine, *De Civ. Dei*, lib. IX, cap. 4, cited in Thomas, *S. T.*, I-II, q. 59, art. 2, resp. For the contemporary critical text, see CCSL 47, 252.

[11] Knuuttila, *Emotions in Ancient and Late Medieval Philosophy*, 63–67; Sorabji, *Emotion and Peace of Mind*, 121–132.

[12] Sorabji, *Emotion and Peace of Mind*, 372–384. For Augustine's account, see also Knuuttila, *Emotions in Ancient and Late Medieval Philosophy*, 152–160.

from the passions that are as they should not be, and when they should not be.[13]

The virtuous person is free only from disordered passions. In his discussion of this same passage in his *Commentary on the Nicomachean Ethics*, Thomas similarly situates the Stoic understanding of virtue as freedom from passion in the context of Aristotle's discussion of the relationship of virtue to pleasure and pain.[14] Aristotle notes that many become evil or are evil due to the pleasures or pains that they experience. He gives this ability of passions to mislead reason as an explanation of why some might say that the virtuous do not experience pleasure and pain. But Aristotle states that this view is correct only if we speak of pleasures or pains in a qualified way as those that are inordinate.

In his *Commentary*, Thomas mentions that the view criticized by Aristotle is the same as that of the Stoics. He never states that Aristotle is responding to the Stoics. His point is that the Stoics and those criticized by Aristotle make the same mistake. They erroneously reason from the premise that pleasures and pains can be harmful to the conclusion that the virtuous experience rest and impassibility rather than pleasure and pain. Neither Aristotle nor Thomas finds this inference plausible. Nevertheless, the similarity between the Stoics and the earlier group is important because it shows how an error can be based on widely held true beliefs that there is a close connection between moral virtue and passion and that disordered passion is incompatible with such virtue.

Thomas's thesis that even the virtuous experience passions finds support not only in Aristotle but also in the Christian tradition. In particular, there are two theological issues that both Augustine and Thomas addressed.[15] First, Jesus Christ was fully human and had no vice, and yet he experienced passions such as sadness. Second, on account of the way that original sin has wounded human nature, even virtuous persons can feel passions that are in some way disordered. With respect to this second point, Thomas notes that St. Paul provides an account of his own struggles

[13] "Unde Aristoteles dicit, in II Ethic. quod non bene quidam determinant virtutes impassibilitates quasdam et quietes, quoniam simpliciter dicunt, sed deberent dicere quod sunt quietes a passionibus quae sunt ut non oportet, et quando non oportet." Thomas, *S.T.*, I-II, q. 59, art. 3. Aristotle *EN* 2.3.1104b.23–27.

[14] Thomas, *SLE*, lib. 2, lect. 3 (Leonine, 47.1, 84–85).

[15] Paul Gondreau, *The Passions of Christ's Soul in the Theology of St. Thomas Aquinas* (Scranton, PA: University of Scranton Press, 2009), 288–317; Lombardo, *Logic of Desire*, 118–124, 201–223. For Christ, see also Craig Steven Titus, "Passions in Christ: Spontaneity, Development, and Virtue," *The Thomist* 73 (2009): 53–87.

with concupiscence. Does the fact that St. Paul struggled indicate that he lacked virtue? Thomas writes:

> [I]t does not belong to the nature of temperance that it excludes all improper sensual desires, but that the temperate human does not suffer some such vehement and strong sensual desires, such as they who do not strive to restrain sensual desires suffer. Therefore Paul suffered inordinate sensual desires because of the corruption of the human on account of evil desire (*corruptio fomitis*): however neither strong nor vehement [sensual desires], because he strived to repress them in castigating his body, and in reducing it to servitude; whence he was truly temperate.[16]

Both the temperate and the intemperate experience evil desires even though they do not experience them in the same way. The habit of restraining such desires also moderates them. In another passage Thomas mentions that virtue does not take away such desire, unless it is accompanied by a miracle.[17] God might in an extraordinary fashion take away someone's lust or fear. But under normal conditions even the temperance that Aristotle describes only makes improper desires less vehement.

Since Jesus Christ did not contract original sin and its attendant disorders, he never experienced such repugnant passions. Nevertheless, he did experience passions which in some way preceded reason. However, his passions were never disordered or vehement so as to influence reason.[18] In this context Latin theology had invoked the previously mentioned Stoic distinction between propassions and passions. Jerome borrowed the word "propassion" from Stoicism, and Latin scholastics sometimes connect Christ's propassions with the first movements of the sense appetite that are shared by other humans.[19] This view perhaps reflects Augustine's identification of the propassions with the Neoplatonic and Peripatetic account of passions that precede reason. Thomas himself does not use the term "propassion" in this way

---

[16] "non est de ratione temperantiae quod omnes pravas concupiscentias excludat, sed quod temperatus non patiatur aliquas tales concupiscentias vehementes et fortes, sicut patiuntur illi qui non studuerunt concupiscentias refrenare. Paulus igitur patiebatur concupiscentias inordinatas propter fomitis corruptionem: non tamen fortes neque vehementes, quia studebat eas reprimere castigando corpus suum, et in servitutem redigendo; unde vere temperatus erat." Thomas, *DVCard.*, q. un. art. 1, ad 6 (Marietti, 816). See also Thomas, *S.T.*, III, q. 69, art. 4, ad 3.

[17] Thomas, *DVC*, art. 10, ad. 14 (Marietti, 737).

[18] Gondreau, *Passions of Christ's Soul*, 362–337; Lombardo, *Logic of Desire*, 210–211. It is interesting that Thomas in the *S.T.* states that sensible pain (*dolor sensibilis*) is a passion of the sense appetite, which he had denied in his earlier works. See Gondreau, *Passions of Christ's Soul*, 380–383; Capreolus, *In Sent.*, lib. 3, d. 15, art. 3, ad secundum argumentum Scoti (vol. 5, 250); Bartholomew Medina, *Expositio in Tertiam Divi Thomae Partem*, q.15, art. 5 (Renaut: Salamanca, 1596), 333.

[19] For the reference to Jerome and earlier uses in Origen and Didymus the Blind, see Gondreau, *Passions of Christ's Soul*, 68, 366–367.

but instead uses it in a limited number of texts to describe the affectivity of Christ's soul and not that of other humans. He does not limit the term to describe that which precedes human reason. When he discusses propassions, Thomas has in mind not only first movements but instead Christ's general affectivity, which is fully human even if it differs significantly from ours.

Thomas uses this account of Christ's propassions to criticize the wider Stoic account of the passionless sage.[20] Whereas Stoics thought that the sage could not be saddened by secondary goods, Christ himself was saddened by them and also felt fear. Christ's sadness and fear are "propassions" and not "passions" because they do not disturb reason. But they are acts of the sense appetite in response even to his own bodily evil. Christ's propassion of sadness resembles our own passion of sadness more than any experience of the sage would. The legitimacy of Christ's sadness in part indicates that virtuous human beings can also experience such a passion.

Although Augustine and Thomas accept partially the Stoic view that the virtuous are free from disordered emotion, they reject what they think is the Stoic view that sadness is always disordered. The question of whether the virtuous person experiences sadness is distinct because although the Stoics denied that the sage experiences passions, at least some held that the sage experiences some dispositions that correspond to these passions. Each of the passions except for sadness has a corresponding disposition in the sage. We have already seen that in q. 59, art. 2, Thomas is concerned with whether the virtuous experience any passions at all. The root of the discussion is in the Stoic discussion of the way in which the sage is subject to first movements, which Augustine and Thomas to some extent identify with passions that precede reason. In art. 3, Thomas is concerned with the somewhat different late Stoic thesis that even though the sage experiences dispositions that correspond to most of the passions, the sage experiences no disposition that corresponds to sadness.

Thomas draws heavily on Augustine's *The City of God*, Book XIV, Chapter 8, in which Augustine explicitly explains and rejects a Stoic distinction between the "dispositions" (*eupatheiai* in Greek/*constantiae* in Latin) of the sage and the passions or disturbances (*pathe* in Greek/*pertubationes* or *passiones* in Latin) that belong to fools.[21] These dispositions differ from propassions in that they do not precede reason. They differ from both passions and propassions in that they are present only in the sage. In this passage Augustine recognizes that for Cicero and other Stoics dispositions

---

[20] Thomas, *S.T.*, III, q. 15, art. 6, ad 2; art. 7, ad 2.
[21] For Thomas's frequent use of this passage, see Gondreau, *Passions of Christ's Soul*, 53–55.

are distinct in kind from the passions even though they correspond to them in some way.

Fools experience the passions of desire, joy, fear, and grief. Although these passions are unreasonable, there are corresponding dispositions that are not and consequently can be felt by the wise. For instance, although the wise human does not fear, she avoids evil, and although she does not desire, she pursues the good. Moreover, the wise human enjoys the good that she achieves. Consequently, Cicero and some other Stoics hold that the sage experiences caution (*cautio*) rather than fear (*metus*), will (*voluntas*) rather than desire (*cupiditas*), and gladness (*gaudium*) rather than joy (*laetitia*).[22] But the sage can have no disposition that corresponds to sadness (*tristitia*), since sadness is concerned with an evil that has occurred, and no evil can befall the sage. The thesis that the sage cannot experience evil results from the thesis that virtue is the only good. Since the sage is virtuous, there is no present evil to which she could be subject.

Augustine criticizes this Stoic account of the three dispositions of the sage in two ways. First, he states that Cicero's distinction between dispositions and passions is merely verbal. Augustine notes that there is some fluidity in language, but desires and wills can both be described as good or bad. He writes, "Then both the good and the bad will, experience caution, and are glad; and as we might express with different words, both the good and the bad desire, fear, and have joy; but those well, these badly, just as the will of humans is right or perverse."[23] His second criticism of this Stoic view is that sadness for sins is praised in Scripture, although he notes that the Stoics have a reply to this objection in that on their account the sage is sinless. He recalls Cicero's account of how Alcibiades was saddened when he was admonished by Socrates for his foolishness. It was appropriate for Alcibiades to experience sadness, but it was appropriate only because he was not virtuous. In the next chapter (nine), Augustine notes that in the Scriptures the good experience the same passions as the evil. They both feel pain and sadness, but the good do so only for good reasons. Moreover, even Christ felt sadness in particular for the sins of others, whereas the Stoic sage seems immune even to the spiritual evils that are suffered by others. On Augustine's view, the Stoics praise a dispassion that is in fact

---

[22] Augustine, *De Civ. Dei*, lib. XIV, cap. 8 (CCSL 47, 423). See Cicero, *Tusculanae disputationes*, 4.10–14. For Cicero's context and sources, see the commentary in Margaret Graver, trans., *Cicero on the Emotions: Tusculan Disputations 3 and 4* (Chicago: University of Chicago Press, 2014), 134–139.

[23] "Proinde volunt cauvent gaudent et boni et mali; atque ut eadem aliis uerbis enuntiemus, cupiunt timent laetantur et boni et mali; sed illi bene, isti male, sicut hominibus seu recta seu peruersa voluntas est." Augustine, *De Civ. Dei*, lib. XIV, cap. 8 (CCSL 47, 425).

vicious, since it does not indicate a proper response to real goods and evils. The sage's lack of sadness for another's sin is inhumane.

Thomas has these passages from Augustine in mind when he criticizes the Stoic thesis that the virtuous person cannot undergo sadness. But Thomas surpasses Augustine by more clearly developing two arguments for the Stoic position and an adequate response to these arguments. We will see how Thomas's response to the first argument undermines the Stoic thesis that virtue is the only good for humans, and his response to the second is against the Stoic belief that even though for the sage caution about future evils might be useful, there is no need to be sad about present evils. Even though Thomas's presentation is to some extent rooted in Augustine's discussion, it brings out fundamental aspects of his own view of the connection between moral virtue and the passions.

The first argument that Thomas attributes to the Stoics is that since the sage is virtuous, he is not subject to any evil.[24] Thomas begins his reply to this argument by stating that the error of the Stoic position concerning bodily evil is incompatible with the fact that humans have both souls and bodies. If bodies are part of the human being, then in addition to spiritual evil there is also such a thing as a bodily evil, which, even if it is not supreme in the way that spiritual evil is, remains truly bad and consequently a proper object of sadness. Thomas finishes his reply to this first argument by criticizing the notion that the virtuous person must have reached a state that makes unnecessary sadness for past or present sins. There is no such perfect sage. Even the most just sin lightly, and they may have sinned more seriously in the past. Consequently, it is appropriate for them to be sorrowful for their own present and past sins. Moreover, the virtuous person should be sorrowful for the sins of others. He is not concerned with his own spiritual good alone. In all of these cases the sadness must be moderated by reason. But even so moderated it remains sadness.

The second argument that Thomas attributes to the Stoics is that the sage cannot experience sadness because he is concerned only with avoiding future evil rather than with any present evil. Even though such Stoics admit that the sage can experience a caution that is akin to the fear experienced by the foolish, they deny that the sage needs sadness over any present evils. In his response to this point Thomas to some extent repeats his previous rejection of the position that the virtuous person has no appropriate objects of sadness. But he also emphasizes the usefulness of sadness for right action. Stoics seem to think that caution alone is sufficient for

---

[24] Thomas, *S. T.*, I-II, q. 59, art. 2, resp.

dealing with evil. Thomas states that as a passion of the sense appetite, sadness can also help the virtuous person. On this point, Thomas draws not so much on Augustine as on Aristotle, who holds the view that the virtuous person is moderately sad about the appropriate matters.[25] Not only fear but also sadness can help the virtuous person avoid that which is contrary to virtue. Thomas explains, "Just as the good is more promptly sought on account of pleasure, so evil is more strongly avoided on account of sadness."[26] He is not saying that the operation of virtue itself is sad, but that the virtuous person feels sad in a moderate way.

In general, Thomas holds that the passions are not inherently bad, even if they need to be moderated by reason. In these first three articles of q. 59, he shows that although virtue is not a passion it is compatible with the passions. In the final two articles he argues that only some virtues are directly about the passions and that those virtues that are not about passions might even be possessed without any passions of the sense appetite. In these last articles, Augustine's criticism of Stoicism remains in the background of the discussion. However, Thomas is primarily concerned here with Aristotle's account of moral virtue. First, Aristotle states that "moral virtue is about pleasures and pains."[27] This statement might seem to imply that all moral virtues are about the passions. Second, according to Aristotle, the just person differs from the unjust at least in part because he enjoys acting justly.[28] The exercise of virtue is itself pleasant.[29] Third, Aristotle holds that moral virtue differs from intellectual virtue precisely in that it perfects not reason but the appetites that participate in reason.[30] Aristotle explicitly states that some virtues are about the passions. For example, courage is about fear and temperance about the pleasure of touch.

Thomas notes that moral virtue is that kind of virtue which perfects the entire appetite, which includes both the sense appetites and the

---

[25] Aristotle, *EN* 2.6.1106b19–24. See also Thomas's commentary in *SLE*, lib. 2, lect. 6 (Leonine, 47.1, 96).

[26] "Sicut enim bona propter delectationem promptius quaeruntur, ita mala propter tristitiam fortius fugiuntur." Thomas, *S.T.*, I-II, q. 59, art. 3, resp. See Robert Miner: *Thomas Aquinas on the Passions: A Study of Summa Theologiae 1a2ae 22–48* (Cambridge: Cambridge University Press, 2009), 199–203, 207–211.

[27] "circa voluptates et tristitias est moralis virtus." Aristotle, *EN* 2.2.1104b8, cited in Thomas, *S.T.*, I-II, q. 59, art. 4, obj. 1. See Thomas, *SLE*, lib. 2, lect. 3 (Leonine, 47.1, 83–84).

[28] Aristotle, *EN* 1.8.1099a17–19, cited in Thomas, *S.T.*, I-II, q. 59, art. 5, sc. See Thomas, *SLE*, lib. 1, lect. 13 (Leonine, 47.1), 47

[29] See especially Aristotle, *EN* 7.13; Thomas, *SLE*, lib. 7, lect. 13 (Leonine, 47.1, 431–433).

[30] Aristotle, *EN* 1.13.1103a1–9, cited in Thomas, *S.T.*, I-II, q. 59, art. 5, obj 2. See Thomas, *SLE*, lib. 1, lect. 20 (Leonine, 47.1, 73).

rational or intellectual appetite, which is the will.[31] All three appetites in
some way participate in reason. This division between the will or rational appetite and the sense appetites will be the basis for distinguishing
between those moral virtues that are about passions and those that are
not. Strictly speaking passions are acts only of the sense appetites and
not of the will. As we have seen in Chapter 1, Thomas had argued earlier
in the same part of the *Summa Theologiae* that passions are properly in
the sense appetite rather than in the will, since changes in the sense
appetites involve a bodily change that can most properly be described as
a "passion."[32] For instance, the passions of love and joy are most properly in the sense appetite and involve certain bodily changes and belong
to both humans and other animals. These sense passions correspond
to affections, or passions broadly speaking, that are acts of the will.
Although God and the angels may be said to love or be joyful, their
affections or passions of love and joy are not the same as those of animals. Spiritual affections or passions share the same names as the animal
passions because the effects of the affections or passions of the will are
the same as the corresponding passions of the sense appetite. Although
they have no bodily passions, the angels are able to will goods, rest in
them, and consequently have spiritual joy about them. Since humans
have both sense appetites and the will, we have both the passions of the
sense appetites and the passions or affections of the will.

Some moral virtues, such as courage and temperance, are about passions in the proper sense, since they involve bodily changes in response
to goods that are perceived by the senses.[33] Such moral virtues moderate
and order such passions. These moral virtues that are about the passions
are consequently inseparable from the passions, since they are defined
by them. The effect of such virtues is a mean between two extremes of
passion, such as excessive and deficient fear or excessive and deficient
desire for physical pleasure.[34] Angels lack such moral virtues because
they do not have such passions. Nonhuman animals lack such moral
virtues because even though they experience passions, they lack reason
and will.

Since the will is not a subject of passions taken in their narrow sense,
the moral virtues that perfect the will are about operations rather than

---

[31] Thomas, *S. T.*, I-II, q. 59, art. 4.
[32] In addition to Thomas, *S. T.*, I-II, q. 22, art. 3, see also *SLE*, lib. 2, lect. 5 (Leonine, 47.1, 91–92).
[33] Thomas, *S. T.*, I-II, q. 59, art. 5.
[34] Thomas, *S. T.*, I-II, q. 59, art. 1, ad 1.

passions.[35] For instance, justice is not about passions such as fear or the desire for physical pleasure but about the operation of rendering another his due. Because such moral virtue is not about the passions, it is separable from them in a way that virtues such as courage and temperance are not. But Thomas does not wish to entirely sever the connection between the passions and such virtues. He writes, "For every virtuous person rejoices in the act of virtue, and is saddened in its contrary."[36] The just person finds pleasure in acting justly even though the act of justice is not about pleasure. In this way passions of the sense appetite can be involved in perfecting the act even though they do not define what the act is.[37]

There are two particularly significant ways in which such virtue might be related to the passions.[38] First, Thomas describes the way in which the will can have an effect on even the sense passions as an "overflowing" (*redundancia*).[39] Since the sense appetite and the rational appetite both belong to the same agent, when the agent is moved by the rational appetite to a good, the sense appetite is brought along. If the will renders another his due, the sense appetite should correspondingly find pleasure in such an act of justice. When an act is done virtuously it is by that fact also done pleasurably. This pleasure is not only spiritual joy but also a pleasure in the sense appetite. Such pleasure in the act of virtue is a sign of an already generated habit even when the habit is itself not about bodily pleasures and pains. Second, such pleasure perfects the act by making it more prompt. A just person will act more justly precisely because of the pleasure of the sense appetite that is taken in her just acts.

On account of this connection between virtue and pleasure, all moral virtues have some passions as their effects. Thomas carefully follows Aristotle and not the Stoics when he states that a virtuous act is done with pleasure. Even virtues that are not about pleasures or pains involve pleasure and pain. For instance, the fact that someone finds just acts unpleasant shows that she has not yet acquired the virtue of justice. Passions of the sensitive appetite can flow from and indicate habits of the will.

---

[35] For virtues of the will, see especially Bonnie Kent, *Virtues of the Will: The Transformation of Ethics in the Late Thirteenth Century* (Washington, DC: The Catholic University of America Press, 1995), 216–224; Jean Porter, *The Perfection of Desire: Habit, Reason, and Virtue in Aquinas's Summa Theologiae* (Milwaukee, WI: Marquette University Press, 2018), 91–138.

[36] "Omnis enim virtuosus delectatur in actu virtutis, et tristatur in contrario." Thomas, *S.T.*, q. 59, art. 4, ad 1.

[37] Thomas, *S.T.*, I-II, q. 24, art. 3.

[38] Thomas, *S.T.*, I-II, q. 24, art. 3, ad 1. See also Thomas, *SLE*, lib. 2, lect. 3 (Leonine, 47.1, 83); *DVC*, art. 9, ad 13 (Marietti, 732); *S.T.*, I-II, 1. 100, art. 9, ad 3. For more texts and discussion, see Gondreau, *Passions of Christ's Soul*, 264–286; Miner, *Thomas Aquinas on the Passions*, 88–93.

[39] For this influence of the will on the passions, see especially Lombardo, *Logic of Desire*, 89–93.

Virtues Concerning Passions and Concerning Operations

Although all moral virtues involve the passions at least to the extent that their exercise is pleasant and unimpeded by passion, only some moral virtues are about the passions. In q. 60 of the *Prima Secundae*, which is about the distinction between the moral virtues, Thomas relies on his earlier account of the relationship between the virtues and the passions. The fundamental difference is between those moral virtues that are about passions and those that are about operations. There are distinct moral virtues about the passions. In his account of these virtues, he draws attention to how moral virtues are distinguished by their formal objects. This emphasis on the formal objects allows him to explain how there are many moral virtues even though there is only one intellectual virtue that covers the matter of the entire moral life, namely prudence. Moreover, it gives him a way of accounting for Aristotle's list of ten distinct virtues that are about the passions. This emphasis on Aristotle's list of moral virtues distinguishes the division of virtue in q. 60 of the *Prima Secundae* from the more complicated divisions in the *Secunda Secundae*.[40] Thomas's discussion here in the *Prima Secundae*, q. 60, is closely related to that of his *Commentary on the Nicomachean Ethics*. This simpler division reflects his interpretation of Aristotle and, it seems to me, gives an overview of his general philosophical account of moral virtue. The more complex division of the *Secunda Secundae* allows him to give an orderly account of all the particular issues surrounding the moral virtues that needed to be discussed in moral theology.

In this q. 60 of the *Prima Secundae*, and in his account of the various moral virtues in the early *Commentary on the Sentences*, Thomas first establishes that there is more than one moral virtue.[41] In both texts he considers the objection that just as there is only one intellectual virtue concerning human action, so there should be only one moral virtue. Both the "on the contrary" arguments briefly mention that the moral virtues must be distinct because some moral virtues belong to distinct powers, such as the will, the irascible appetite, and the concupiscible appetite. Similarly, in the responses of both texts Thomas focuses more carefully on the formal differences between the moral virtues than on the differences between the subjects of the moral virtues. But the earlier *Commentary on the Sentences* focuses on the different goods involved, whereas the question

---

[40] Thomas, *S.T.*, II-II, qq. 48, 61, 79–80, 128, 143.
[41] Thomas, *S.T.*, I-II, q. 60, art. 1; *In Sent.*, lib. 3, d. 33, q. 1, art. 1, qctla. 1 et sol. 1 (Mandonnet-Moos, 3, 1016, 1018–1020).

of the *Summa Theologiae* considers more carefully the way that the moral object depends on the order of reason.

The earlier text gives a summary account of the way in which objects specify powers and acts and then uses the diversity of the human good to argue for the diversity of moral virtue. Thomas notes that moral virtue is distinguished from vice because it is about the good of reason. Although this good of reason is known by the one intellectual habit of prudence, the diversity of this good requires diverse virtues.[42] We have seen in the previous chapter how prudence presupposes the distinct ends that are established by these virtues, which are concerned not directly with the ultimate end that is happiness but with the particular goods that are parts of or means to happiness.

In the *Summa Theologiae*, I-II, q. 60, art. 1, Thomas emphasizes the way in which the moral virtues as habits of the appetitive parts are specified by the formal species that are given by reason. This discussion of the diversity of moral virtue depends on the description of moral virtue as a perfection of those powers that participate in reason. His explanation is based on the way in which reason has different effects on the appetite and ultimately on the distinction between univocal and equivocal causes, which are two kinds or modes of efficient cause.[43] A univocal cause is a cause that produces an effect that belongs to the same kind. For instance, a rabbit generates other rabbits, and fire generates fire. Equivocal causes have effects that participate unequally in the agent's power. For instance, fire might cause heat in water. Thomas most frequently gives the sun as an example. He thinks that it is responsible alongside other causes for the generation of plants and animals. The sun is an equivocal cause because it has one action that is received by terrestrial matter in different ways. Whatever the truth of Thomas's account of the role of the sun in generation, its use as an explanation in this context is clear. Sometimes a cause is univocal in that it produces a particular effect that belongs to the same species, and sometimes it is equivocal and consequently has diverse effects. Thomas perhaps most commonly uses equivocal causality to explain God's diverse causal effects among creatures and the correspondingly different ways in which

---

[42] For Thomas's account of the good of reason, see especially Dominic Farrell, *The Ends of the Moral Virtues and the First Principles of Practical Reason in Thomas Aquinas* (Rome: Gregorian & Biblical Press, 2012), 122–127.

[43] For the roots of this distinction in Aristotle, see Thomas, *In Phys.*, lib. 2, lect. 11 (Leonine, 2, 88). For some texts and an interesting discussion, see Gyula Klima, "What Ever Happened to Efficient Causes?," in *Skepticism, Causality and Skepticism about Causality*, ed. Gyula Klima and Alexander W. Hall, Proceedings of the Society for Medieval Logic and Metaphysics 10 (Newcastle upon Tyne: Cambridge Scholars Publishing, 2013), 41.

creatures participate in God.[44] In the context of moral virtue, he uses it to explain how the one power of reason has diverse effects on the appetite.

Thomas's account of reason as an equivocal cause is based on reason's commanding and moving of the appetitive powers.[45] Just as the sun does, reason produces effects that are distinct in kind from itself. The intellect not only causes intellectual acts, but it also causes those acts of the appetitive powers that follow the way in which reason presents the good. It should again be remembered that although the nonrational animals have sense appetites, such appetites are not rational even by participation, since the animals to which they belong lack reason. But human sense appetites are rational because they are informed and directed by reason. Their acts are or can be effects of reason. In contrast to the sense appetites, the will, since it is a rational appetite, is inseparable from reason. The will and its acts depend on reason in much the same way that the sense appetites and their acts depend on sensation.

Even though the will differs from the sense appetites in that it is necessarily connected with reason, like them it is rational only by participation, since it is an appetitive and not a cognitive power. The distinction between the ways in which the various appetitive powers participate in reason explains some of the variety among the moral virtues. There is only one virtue of prudence because there are not distinctions between truths about human action in the way that there are distinctions between truths concerning different sciences such as mathematics, physics, and metaphysics, which, as the science of the highest cause, is the intellectual virtue of wisdom. These distinctions are based on formal differences in the objects that are known. But the same one truth concerning human action is related to the distinct human appetites in many ways, which makes necessary the existence of various moral virtues.[46] It should be kept in mind that in this context Thomas is denying only that there is a distinct matter for prudence that corresponds to the matter of the different moral virtues. He is not thinking of the other ways in which there might be different parts of prudence, such as individual, household, and political prudence, and even military prudence.

In his *Commentary on the Nicomachean Ethics*, Thomas distinguishes between moral virtues that direct passions and those that direct actions

---

[44] Johm F. Wippel, *The Metaphysical Thought of Thomas Aquinas: From Finite Being to Uncreated Being* (Washington, DC: The Catholic University of America Press, 2000), 117, 517–518, 525.
[45] Thomas, *S.T.*, I-II, q. 60, art. 1, resp.
[46] Thomas, *S.T.*, I-II, q. 60, art. 1, ad 1.

by emphasizing that actions such as buying and selling do not in themselves resist reason by desiring good or avoiding evil.[47] On account of this resistance, some moral virtues must restrain passions such as desire, hope, and wrath, and other moral virtues must overcome passions such as fear and hatred. In general, such moral virtues are concerned with passions that involve either the corporal life of human beings, exterior goods, or human acts. A moral virtue such as justice establishes an external mean. Unlike moral virtues that are concerned with the rectitude of the passions, a virtue such as justice is concerned with the action itself.

In the rest of the *Prima Secundae*, q. 60, Thomas provides an overview of the way in which the various moral virtues are distinguished according to the different kinds of matter that they are concerned with. This matter is the "matter concerning which" (*materia circa quam*).[48] Thomas's list in this part of the *Summa* follows Aristotle's list of virtues in the *Nicomachean Ethics*, Book II, chapters 8. First, Thomas distinguishes those moral virtues that are about operations from those that are about passions.[49] This division should not lead us to think that some virtues do not involve operations at all and that other virtues have nothing to do with passions. Since every virtue has been defined as a "good operative habit," even the virtues that are about the passions must have operations as their proper acts. Moreover, as we have seen, every moral virtue involves passion, at least to the extent that it makes virtuous actions pleasurable and is indicated by appropriate passions. Consequently, all virtue produces operations and has passions at least broadly considered as effects and signs. But Thomas here is considering the way in which moral virtue might be about operations or passions considered in the narrow sense, and not about both. In this context Thomas is reserving "operation" to acts of the will that involve some sort of external good or operation, and as opposed to the passions of the sense appetite.[50]

Typical examples of such operations would be acts such as buying and selling, which are about what is due to another.[51] Their reasonableness is not determined by the agent's own passions. For instance, if someone pays me three dollars for a two-dollar cup of coffee, then I owe him one dollar in return unless she indicates that the dollar is a tip. There is a precise fee

---

[47] Thomas, *SLE*, lib. 2, lect. 8 (Leonine, 47.1, 101–103).

[48] Miner, *Thomas Aquinas on the Passions*, 287–295. For *materia circa quam*, see Thomas M. Osborne Jr., *Human Action in Thomas Aquinas, John Duns Scotus, and William of Ockham* (Washington, DC: The Catholic University of America Press, 2014), 155–156, 163–164.

[49] Thomas, *S.T.*, I-II, q. 60, art. 2.

[50] Cajetan, *I-II*, q. 60, art. 2, n. 1 (Leonine, 6, 388).

[51] Thomas, *S.T.*, I-II, q. 60, art. 2, resp.

and the change can either be too little or too much. Similarly, if someone agrees to work for a certain wage, then that wage is owed to him. One might argue whether the amount charged for the coffee is a just price or the amount offered to the worker is a just wage, but the argument is still over what is external to the agent. It is mostly irrelevant to consider whether paying the money makes the agent or even the recipient sad, fearful, or even glad. When determining the mean in operations, the relevant questions that need to be asked are not about passions. What is the price of the coffee related to other goods and to the costs of the materials and production? What are the laborer's needs, and typically what are such laborers paid? In such cases there is something "due" that is independent to some extent of the passions. In contrast, virtues such as courage and gentleness are primarily about passions. The courageous person overcomes fear and a lack of confidence, whereas the gentle person restrains anger.

Unlike in the *Commentary on the Nicomachean Ethics*, Thomas in the *Summa* emphasizes not so much the passion's resistance to reason but the distinction between the fittingness of an act considered in itself and the agent's own affectivity.[52] In this text, he states that operations are reasonable or not according to some exterior measurement of the work performed. The moral virtue of justice and associate virtues are directly concerned with the work itself. In contrast, other moral virtues are concerned with the agent's subjective affectivity. Since passions are good insofar as the agent experiences them in a reasonable way, some moral virtues are directly concerned with rectifying these passions. The kinds of virtue differ according to whether they are about the external measurement of an operation or the agent's subjective passions. Although Thomas states that the agent's affectivity is regulated by a distinct group of moral virtues, he admits that this affectivity is important even for those other moral virtues that are concerned with external operations. For instance, an angry person might unjustly strike another. Such an act fails in two ways. The injury against another is in itself an offense against justice and shows that the agent lacks rectitude in external operations. But the unjust act has its root in the agent's inability to control her own anger. The failure in justice is also a failure in gentleness. The act can be considered as disordered both with respect to what is due to one's neighbor and with respect to the agent's anger.

Every moral virtue that is concerned with operations is either justice or a virtue closely associated with justice, and every other moral virtue is about the passions. The virtues concerning operations are all connected with justice

---

[52] Thomas, *S. T.*, I-II, q. 60, art. 3, resp; art. 4, resp.

insofar as they are about that which is owed to another, but they are distinct according to the nature and way in which something is owed.[53] Thomas here and in other passages adopts Aristotle's distinction between general, distributive, and commutative justice, although in this text he focuses on commutative justice.[54] In the *Secunda Secundae*, Thomas uses the three possible relationships among citizens and a political community to explain these three kinds of justice, namely that of the citizen to the community, that of the community to the citizen, and that of one citizen to another.

First, the individual is related to the common good of the political community as a part is related to the whole.[55] Acts of other virtues, including those of temperance, can and should be ordered to this common good.[56] General or legal justice is the kind of justice that commands acts of the other virtues so that they are directed to this common good. This "general justice" indicates a wider use of the term "just" to describe not just a particular virtue involving another's good but the general ordering of the just person. Even virtues that are primarily concerned with the passions can be directed by such general justice.

The particular species of justice are distributive and commutative.[57] Distributive justice is concerned with the second possible relationship, namely that of the political community to the citizen. It is about the disposal of honors or commonly held goods to citizens who have merited such goods. It considers the correct amount of the good to be distributed and the worth of the one to whom the good is distributed. The typical sin against distributive justice is the "respect of persons" by which someone is rewarded not according to merit but according to some irrelevant quality.[58] In contrast, commutative justice concerns the notion of what is due between two citizens. Such justice requires that the members be equally private citizens and that there be some stricter notion of what is owed. Commutative justice is the kind of justice that regulates operations such as buying and selling. Murder, theft, insult, fraud, and usury are typical sins against commutative justice.[59]

Other virtues concerned with external operations fall short of the notion of justice only insofar as they involve some notion of the due that does not

---

[53] Thomas, *S.T.*, I-II, q. 60, art. 3.
[54] For this division, see Aristotle, *EN*, 5.1–2; Thomas, *SLE*, lib. 5, lect. 2–3 (Leonine, 47.2, 268–274).
[55] See, for instance, Thomas, *S.T.*, I-II, q. 92, art. 1, ad 3; q. 94, art. 3, ad 1; II-II, q. 47, art. 10, ad 2.
[56] Thomas, *S.T.*, I-II, q. 96, art. 3; II-II, q. 47, art. 10, ad 3.
[57] Thomas, *S.T.*, II-II, q. 61, art. 1. See also Thomas, *S.T.*, I, q. 21, art. 1, resp.; *In Sent.*, lib. 3, d. 33, q. 3, art. 4, qcla. 5 ad 2 (Mandonnet-Moos, 3, 1101); *SLE*, lib. 5, lect. 4–6 (Leonine, 47.2, 276–285).
[58] Thomas, *S.T.*, II-II, q. 63.
[59] Thomas, *S.T.*, II-II, qq. 64, 66, 72, 77–78.

involve a strict debt or there is a lack of equality between the persons that makes it impossible to give to another what is due.[60] For instance, friendship or affability makes someone pleasant in his dealing with others. As a virtue it is connected to justice insofar as it involves others, but it falls short of the notion of justice because such pleasantness is not strictly owed in the way that money is owed in a commercial exchange. Similarly, one does not give others what is strictly owed to them when she gives money out of liberality or gratitude. We can say precisely whether or not someone has been given the precise change when coffee has been bought. We cannot say in precisely the same way whether a tip is too much or too little. Some virtues fall short of the notion of justice because it is impossible to give too much in a particular context. For instance, religion governs one's worship of God, and piety requires that one give one's country and parents their due. But even Aristotle recognized that there is no equality between us and the Gods or a child and his parents.[61] Whatever is given will in some way fall short of what has been received.

Although these various moral virtues that are associated with justice differ from each other and from justice, they are similar in that they are about operations and not about the agent's affectivity. They differ from each other insofar as the operations themselves differ specifically according to what is owed. For instance, what is due to one's parents out of piety is different from what one gives to the poor out of liberality.

The virtues that are connected with justice are distinguished from those virtues that are about the passions. In both the *Commentary on the Nicomachean Ethics* and in q. 60 of the *Prima Secundae* of the *Summa Theologiae*, Thomas provides a justification for Aristotle's list of ten such virtues. In the latter text, he writes

> Thus therefore is apparent that according to Aristotle there are ten moral virtues concerning passions: namely courage, temperance, liberality, magnificence, magnanimity, love of honor (*philotimia*), gentleness, friendship, truth, and playfulness (*eutrapelia*). And they are distinguished according to diverse matter; or according to diverse passions; or according to diverse objects. If therefore justice is added, which is about operations, there will be eleven.[62]

---

[60] Thomas, *S.T.*, I-II, q. 60, art. 3, resp.; II-II, q. 80, art. 1.

[61] Aristotle, *EN* 8.14.1163b17, cited in Thomas, *S.T.*, II-II, q. 80, art. 1, resp.

[62] "Sic igitur patet quod, secundum Aristotelem, sunt decem virtutes morales circa passiones, scilicet fortitudo, temperantia, liberalitas, magnificentia, magnanimitas, philotimia, mansuetudo, amicitia, veritas et eutrapelia. Et distinguuntur secundum diversas materias vel secundum diversas passiones; vel secundum diversa obiecta. Si igitur addatur iustitia, quae est circa operationes, erunt omnes undecim." Thomas, *S.T.*, I-II, q. 60, art. 5, resp.

Aristotle himself introduces this list of ten moral virtues in Book II, Ch. 7, in order to provide a more particular account of the general notion of virtue than he had previously developed. He does not provide a justification of the number of distinct virtues but instead uses them to illustrate how in different ways moral virtue involves a mean that is between excess and deficiency. In his *Commentary* on this chapter, Thomas argues that Aristotle's list of moral virtues follows the different objects of the passions. In the *Summa Theologiae,* he provides a related but more comprehensive account of the way in which these moral virtues are specified.

In his *Commentary,* Thomas uses the distinction between the objects of passion to distinguish between the different moral virtues that either restrain or overcome the passions.[63] The passions themselves are concerned either with bodily life, exterior goods, or exterior acts. In each of these cases the virtue governs a passion that has a distinct object. With respect to the first object, namely bodily life, courage is concerned with the danger to life itself and temperance is about that which serves life, namely food, drink, and reproduction. Thomas follows Aristotle in showing how each virtue falls between two extremes. For instance, courage lies between vices such as cowardice and rashness. Sometimes a virtue or vice is so rare that it is unnamed. For example, temperance lies between gluttony and an unnamed insensitivity to bodily pleasure.

With respect to bodily goods, some virtues are concerned with money and others are concerned with honor. Each of these goods has a corresponding virtue that either involves great objects or smaller ones. For instance, liberality is the moral virtue that is concerned with ordinary amounts of money, whereas magnificence is concerned with giving large amounts. The difference between these virtues can to some extent be seen by their correspondingly distinct vices. The excess with respect to giving ordinary amounts of money is wastefulness, but the excess in giving large amounts is vulgarity. Similarly, magnanimity, the virtue that is concerned with great honors, differs in kind from that moral virtue which orders the desire for small honors. In both Aristotle's text and in Thomas's *Commentary* on it, the virtue that corresponds to small honors is unnamed. According to Thomas, Aristotle describes a virtue that is concerned with exterior evils which are opposed to such external goods. Such evils evoke wrath, which is moderated by gentleness.

The three remaining virtues are concerned with passions that have human acts as their objects. They are about the ways in which humans

---

[63] Thomas, *SLE,* lib. 2, lect. 8–9 (Leonine, 47.2, 103–109).

speak and act with each other. Truthfulness is concerned with manifesting the truth to another in words and deeds. Playfulness (*eutrapelia*) regulates enjoyments, and affability regulates one's ordinary relations with
others. The affable person is neither quarrelsome nor flattering. Although
Thomas thinks that these three virtues are similar to the preceding virtues
in that they regulate the passions, his scheme might seem artificial and
does not clearly represent Aristotle's intention.

Whatever the plausibility of Thomas's account of how Aristotle distinguishes between these moral virtues, Thomas does not contradict
Aristotle, and his *Commentary* provides a helpful context for reading
Thomas' description of the moral virtues in the *Summa Theologiae*, I-II,
q. 60. In the last two articles of this question Thomas argues that there
are many moral virtues concerning the passions (art. 4) and that these
moral virtues are themselves distinguished according to the objects of
the passions (art. 5). This account differs in some ways from that of the
Commentary in its order and detailed argumentation, but it resembles it
in general outline.

In art. 5, Thomas establishes that the moral virtues that are about the
passions are diversified not only according to the diverse subjects of the
passions but also according to the way in which their objects are related to
reason.[64] Since Thomas had already established that different powers have
different habits, he straightforwardly makes his first point that the habits
that belong to the concupiscible appetite must be distinct from those that
belong to the irascible. His second point is that a distinction between the
passions themselves does not entail a distinction between the moral virtues that perfect them. For example, since moral virtue establishes a mean
that is between two extremes, a moral virtue can involve two opposite
passions. Thomas draws an analogy with natural things about the way
in which one mean is between two opposed extremes, such as the way in
which grey is between white and black.

Thomas notes that even though sometimes the passions are repugnant
to reason in only one way, there can be an additional repugnance. For
instance, temperance restrains all of the desires of the sense appetite for
bodily pleasure. There is only one mean between excess and deficiency.
But the irascible passions, since they involve an element of difficulty,
imply additional kinds of disorder that need to be corrected by distinct
moral virtues. For instance, fear and daring are both concerned with a

---

[64] Thomas discusses fortitude and gentleness in the ad 2. The other eight virtues concerning the passions are delineated in the resp.

great evil, namely death, whereas hope and despair are concerned with the difficult good. Courage is concerned with the first pair, namely fear and daring, but not with hope and despair, which are moderated instead by magnanimity. Wrath, which is concerned with injury, must be restrained by the distinct moral virtue of gentleness.

The objects of the passions not only specify the passions themselves but insofar as they involve an order to reason they specify the moral virtues as well. There are different ways in which the human good can be the object of a passion. Thomas in this text states that this good can be considered in itself as either bodily or spiritual, or not in itself but insofar as it is ordered to others. Moreover, the human good can be considered insofar as it is apprehended by the external or internal senses or as apprehended through these senses by reason. Both the goods themselves and the ways in which the good is apprehended will help to distinguish between moral virtues.

The virtue of temperance perfects the bodily good as perceived by the senses. This bodily good either belongs to the individual and is concerned with food and drink or to the preservation of the species and is concerned with reproduction. In contrast to temperance, which is about bodily pleasures that are shared with other animals, other moral virtues regulate goods such as wealth and honor, which are perceived interiorly and not by other animals. There is an order among these goods. Even though money involves reason, it is ordered to bodily life. In contrast, honor is distinct in kind because it is apprehended only by the soul and not by the body. The moral virtues concerning these goods not only differ according to whether or not they are about money or honor but also according to whether they perfect concupiscible or irascible passions. Liberality is a virtue that perfects the ordinary desire for money, whereas magnificence is concerned with large amounts of money, which are objects of the irascible appetite because such amounts imply difficulty. Similarly, Thomas distinguishes between *philotimia*, which is about the ordinary desire for honor and magnanimity, which involves honor considered as a great and therefore difficult good.

Thomas's use of *philotimia* is a noteworthy departure from Aristotle, who stated that the virtue concerning small honors is nameless and that *philotimia* is a vice.[65] This departure seems to be unique to this passage. In his *Commentary on the Nicomachean Ethics*, Thomas recognizes Aristotle's

---

[65] Aristotle, *EN* 2.7.1107b28–30.

description of the honor-lover (*philotimus*) as vicious.[66] In the *Secunda Secundae* Thomas also adopts Aristotle's usage.[67]

Thomas distinguishes between the rest of the moral virtues by distinguishing between the different objects of concupiscible passion. Playfulness, for which Thomas retains the Greek word "*eutrapelia*," is about pleasantness insofar as it is for its own sake. Truthfulness and affability are both about serious actions. Affability involves pleasantness in this common action, and truthfulness is concerned with words and deeds. The division of goods has accounted for eight of Aristotle's ten moral virtues that are about the passions. The remaining two virtues are concerned with avoiding evil, namely courage and gentleness. Just as there is only one virtue concerning the fear of bodily evil, namely courage, so there is only one virtue concerning wrath, namely gentleness.

By the end of q. 60 Thomas has accounted for eleven moral virtues that belong to three different subjects. Justice and its associated virtues are the moral virtues that belong to the will. Temperance, liberality, the love of honor all belong to the concupiscible appetite, as well as the three virtues that involve the human good in relation to another, namely playfulness (*eutrapelia*), truthfulness, and affability. Courage, meekness, magnificence, and magnanimity belong to the irascible appetite. They all are distinct moral virtues that have distinct moral objects.

Why in the text quoted above does Thomas state that these virtues are distinguished from each other "according to diverse matter; or according to diverse passions; or according to diverse objects"? Thomas usually states that the virtues are distinguished formally according to their objects, whereas here he apparently mentions two other distinguishing features, namely matter and passions. Perhaps by "object" Thomas here does not mean the formal object of the virtues but more generally what things these virtues might be about. Or possibly he is stating that some differ according to formal objects and these other characteristics that can be included in them, whereas some differ only by their formal objects. Cajetan provides one solution to this difficulty by using this threefold distinction to show how moral virtues might differ in one or more of each of these three ways.[68] First, love of honor and magnanimity are distinct on account of their matter from liberality and magnificence. The first pair share honor as their matter, whereas the second pair have money as their matter. Second,

---

[66] Thomas recognizes Aristotle's description of the honor-lover "*philotimus*" as vicious in his *SLE*, lib. 2, lect. 9 (Leonine, 47.1, 107).

[67] *S. T.*, II-II, q. 129, art. 2, resp.

[68] Cajetan. *In I-II*, q. 60, art. 5, n. 3 (Leonine, 6, 392).

sometimes the passions alone seem to distinguish two virtues. Both courage and gentleness perfect the irascible appetite, but courage is about confidence and fear, whereas gentleness is about anger. Third, truthfulness and playfulness (*eutrapelia*) seem to differ only in their objects and not in their shared matter, which is ordinary human intercourse. Moreover, they both involve the passions of love and enjoyment. But they differ only in their objects in the sense that the first is about manifesting the truth in human interaction and the second is about the pleasure that accompanies such. The difference between these virtues is narrower than that between temperance and courage, which differ in each of these three ways even when understood broadly.

Another peculiar feature of the vision of the moral virtues in this text is that it contradicts Thomas's earlier accounts of liberality and magnificence.[69] Whereas in this text liberality and magnificence are about passions, in the *Commentary on the Sentences* Thomas states that they belong to the will and are about operations rather than passions.[70] Moreover, in the *Summa Contra Gentiles* and in the *Prima Pars* of the *Summa Theologiae*, Thomas states that liberality (and in the *Prima Pars* also magnificence) is about actions rather than passions and consequently can in a way be attributed to God.[71]

An appealing explanation for these divergent accounts is simply that Thomas changed his mind on the issue. The *Commentary on the Sentences*, the *Summa Contra Gentiles*, and the *Prima Pars* of the *Summa Theologiae* are all earlier works in which liberality (and magnificence in three cases) is a habit that belongs to the will and is about operations. On the other hand, in the *Secunda Secundae* of the *Summa Theologiae*, Thomas clearly states that although justice is about operations in themselves, "liberality and magnificence consider operations taken as they are compared to the passions of the soul."[72] He repeats what he had said in the *Prima Secundae*, namely that liberality and magnificence belong to the concupiscible appetite and are about passions concerning money. Similarly, in his *Commentary on the Nicomachean Ethics*, Thomas also states that these virtues are about the passions. It seems likely that Thomas changed his mind by reflecting on the way in which Aristotle distinguishes between the virtues in the *Nicomachean Ethics*, Book II, Ch. 7. One objection to

[69] Cajetan. *In I-II*, q. 60, art. 5, nn. 1–2 (Leonine, 6, 392).

[70] Thomas, *In Sent.*, lib. 3, d. 33, q. 2, art. 4, sol. 3 (Mandonnet-Moos, 3, 1065).

[71] Thomas, *Summa contra Gentiles*, lib. 1, cap. 93 (Leonine, 13, 254); *S.T.*, I, q. 21, art. 1, ad 1.

[72] "liberalitas et magnificentia considerant operationes sumptuum secundum quod comparantur ad passiones animae." Thomas, *S.T.*, II-II, q. 134, art. 4, ad 1.

the developmental thesis is that Thomas assigns liberality to the will in his *De Virtutibus in Communi*, art. 5, which was written perhaps at the same time as the *Secunda Secundae* and the *Commentary on the Nicomachean Ethics*.[73] Perhaps the *De Virtutibus in Communi* merely reflects his earlier view. No explanation of these differences seems entirely satisfying to me.

Cardinal Virtues

Thomas's account of why Aristotle mentions eleven distinct moral virtues is significant for understanding Thomas's use of Aristotle and even his own account of the relationship between virtue and the passions. Nevertheless, it is not particularly significant in light of Thomas's account of moral virtue as a whole. Even though Thomas never rejects Aristotle's list of eleven moral virtues and reasserts it in the text under discussion, in the rest of the *Summa Theologiae* he supplements it greatly with divisions of moral virtues taken from later authors. In particular, in the *Secunda Secundae*, he organizes all the moral virtues around the mostly non-Aristotelian doctrine of the four cardinal virtues, which Thomas inherits from Plato and the Stoics through Church Fathers such as St. Ambrose, who may have been the first to describe them as "cardinal."[74] These cardinal virtues are prudence and the moral virtues of temperance, courage, and justice. This use of the cardinal virtues as an organizing principle explains why in the *Prima Secundae* Thomas devotes an entire question (q. 61) to the cardinal virtues immediately after he discusses the division between justice and the ten moral virtues that are about the passions. Although the *Summa Theologiae* makes special use of the cardinal virtues, they also play a central role in Thomas's earlier moral teaching. He discusses them at length in his early *Commentary on the Sentences*. More importantly, while writing the *Secunda Secundae* of the *Summa Theologiae* he also devoted an entire disputed question to them, namely the *De Virtutibus Cardinalibus*.

---

[73] Thomas, *DVC*, art. 5 (Marietti, 720)

[74] Lottin, *PM*, 3.1, 153–194; Rollen Edward Houser, trans and ed., introduction to *The Cardinal Virtues: Aquinas, Albert, and Philip the Chancellor* (Toronto: Pontifical Institute for Mediaeval Studies, 2004), 1–82. For different ways of using these virtues as an organizational schema, see Istvan Bejcvy, "The Cardinal Virtues in the Medieval Commentaries on the Nicomachean Ethics, 1250–1350," in *Virtue Ethics in the Middle Ages: Commentaries on Aristotle's Nicomachean Ethics, 1200–1500*, ed. Istvan Bejcvy (Leiden: Brill, 2007), 199–221; Stanley Cunningham, *Reclaiming Moral Agency: The Moral Philosophy of Albert the Great* (Washington, DC: The Catholic University of America Press, 2008), 179–198. For a translation of and introduction to the *S.T.*, I-II, q. 61, art. 2–3, see J. Budziszewski, *A Commentary on Thomas Aquinas's Virtue Ethics* (Cambridge: Cambridge University Press, 2017), 43–63. For Aristotle's recognition of these four virtues, see *Pol.* 7.1.1023a26–30.

Thomas's account not only is influenced by patristic and ancient philosophical sources but also incorporates elements from his contemporaries and predecessors at the University of Paris. Before Thomas's generation, scholastic philosophers did not have access to the later books of the *Nicomachean Ethics* in which Aristotle discusses at length the distinct virtues. Philosophers and theologians were largely concerned with the cardinal virtues and the Stoic thesis that the virtues are united. On the other hand, they knew many texts in which these virtues are considered to be distinct habits or qualities. Scholastic theologians needed to account for the difference between these authorities. In this context, Philip the Chancellor distinguished between the cardinal virtues considered as concerned with the good life as a whole and considered as distinct virtues with separate matter.[75] In one way, the cardinal virtues are present in the features of every virtuous act. In the second way, each of the cardinal virtues produces acts that are distinct from those that are produced by the other cardinal virtues. Philip thinks that the former use of the term "cardinal virtue" explains the Stoic and patristic description of cardinal virtues as unified. If they are present in every virtuous act they would have to be inseparable. Philip's approach was widely adopted.[76] For instance, it was transmitted among Franciscans through the influence of theologians such as Odo Rigaud and Bonaventure. Thomas may have known of it through his teacher Albert the Great.

For later authors the distinction between the cardinal virtues was primarily a distinction between distinct habits, although the other usage, which is as indicating features of every virtuous act, sometimes remained. The new complete translation of Aristotle's *Nicomachean Ethics* influenced this shift to thinking of the cardinal virtues primarily as distinct habits because of its lengthy account of each of these virtues and of its account of the connection between the virtues through prudence. But Thomas is writing in a transitional period. When reading Thomas's contemporaries on the cardinal virtues, it is important to consider whether they are speaking of these virtues as present in every virtuous act or whether they are speaking of them as specifically distinct habits. Thomas explicitly recognizes both uses, although he prefers to discuss them as distinct habits.

These two ways of using the term "cardinal virtue" influence Thomas's explanation of why the cardinal virtues are principal. In his later writings

---

[75] Philip, *Summa de Bono*, 1071. Lottin, *PM*, 3.1, 220–222.
[76] Lottin, *PM*, 3.1, 222–225; Bonaventure, *In Sent.*, lib. 3, d. 36, art. un., q. 3 (vol. 3, 796–799); Albert, *In Sent.*, lib. 3, d. 36, q. un., art. 1, ad s.c. (Col. ed., vol. 28, 666–667).

he states that they are in a way more principal on account of some special difficulty in the matter and also on account of the way in which they can as general conditions be understood to be present in every virtuous act. But in the *Commentary on the Sentences*, when explicitly discussing the cardinal virtues, he denies that each of the cardinal virtues as a cardinal virtue is a general condition.[77] Thomas mentions that they are general virtues only to the extent that they can move other virtues. For instance, prudence is the most general cardinal virtue because it commands acts that belong to the other virtues. Although he recognizes a general justice, he states that only particular justice is a cardinal virtue. Moreover, temperance and courage are general only with respect to the specific moral virtues that are joined to them and not with respect to every virtuous act.

Only later in the *Commentary on the Sentences* does Thomas mention that these four virtues can be understood as general conditions. He introduces this usage in the same setting that his predecessors did, namely in the question of whether the virtues are connected.[78] If it were important for Thomas's own early discussion of the cardinal virtues, one might expect it to be present in the earlier discussions and not only in this context.

In his more mature works, Thomas makes the distinction between virtues as general conditions and virtues as having distinct matter, which corresponds to the less developed distinction of Philip. Although Thomas clearly defines virtue as a habit, it is interesting that he continues to discuss them also as general conditions.[79] Nevertheless, he clearly states that the two uses signify different things. When the cardinal virtues are general conditions, these virtues differ from each other only conceptually and are not distinct habits. Consequently, the definition of virtue would not apply to them. However, these general conditions can share names with the cardinal virtues because of the way in which the formal natures of the distinct virtues are connected with these general conditions.[80] The formal nature of any cardinal virtue is what distinguishes it from other virtues, including the other cardinal virtues. This formal nature can also be considered as a general condition of any virtuous act. This resemblance between the four conditions of virtuous acts and the four good operative

---

[77] Thomas, *In Sent.*, lib. 3, d. 33, q. 2, art. 1, sol. 1 and sol. 3, ad 2 (Mandonnet-Moos, 3, 1045, 1048). Thomas does however seem to think of legal justice as a cardinal virtue in *In Sent.*, lib. 3, d. 33, q. 3, art. 4, sol. 5, ad 5 (Mandonnet-Moos, 3, 1102).

[78] Thomas, *In Sent.*, lib. 3, d. 36, q un. art. 1, resp. (Mandonnet-Moos, 3, 1216–1217).

[79] Thomas, *S. T.*, I-II, q. 61, art. 3, resp.

[80] Thomas, *DVCard.*, art. 1, resp. and ad 1 (Marietti, 814–815); *S. T.*, I-II, q. 61, art. 2–3, resp. See also Thomas, *DVC*, art. 12, ad 23 (Marietti, 746).

habits explains why such different kinds of things as conditions and operative habits can both be called "cardinal virtues." The term "cardinal virtue" can signify either a condition of a virtuous act or a virtue properly speaking, and a name of any of the cardinal virtues can signify either a general condition of any virtuous act or what is strictly a speaking virtue, namely the particular good operative habit.

Thomas's account of the cardinal virtues as general conditions shows how any one virtuous act can be considered as in some way instantiating each of the different cardinal virtues. Any act of virtue is prudent insofar as it is directed by reason. Moreover, insofar as it produces an operation that is right, it is just. Similarly, every virtuous act is temperate insofar as it resists impulses to other goods and courageous insofar as it resists those passions that draw away from the act. The second and more propter way of considering the cardinal virtues is as having distinct matter, as Aristotle did. For instance, the principal act of prudence is command, and the principal act of temperance is about bodily pleasure. Thomas here more or less repeats Aristotle's claim that courage is concerned with death in battle and justice is about another's due. According to Thomas, the Stoic understanding of the unity of the virtues is based on thinking about the cardinal virtues as general conditions of virtue and not as distinct habits.

In the *De Virtutibus Cardinalibus* Thomas follows tradition in noting that the word "cardinal" (*cardinalis*) comes from the word "hinge" (*cardo*).[81] The virtues are described as cardinal on account of the way in which one enters human life as through a door that has these virtues as hinges. Thomas distinguishes between three kinds of life, namely the bestial life that is based on sensitive pleasure, the active life that depends on moral virtue, and the superhuman life of contemplation. Since the cardinal virtues are hinges by which one leads a properly human life, the cardinal virtues are moral virtues or that intellectual virtue which moral virtue requires, namely prudence. Although Thomas connects the cardinal virtues with the active life, he does not hold that moral virtue is incompatible with contemplation in the way that the subhuman life of the senses is. The activity of moral virtue itself can lead to contemplation.[82] But the cardinal virtues are concerned with ordinary human affairs. In the *Summa Theologiae*, Thomas introduces the cardinal virtues in the context of "human virtue" (*virtus humana*), which similarly seems to connect moral virtue with the human life of moral virtue, since human

---

[81] Thomas, *DVCard.*, art. 1, resp. (Marietti, 814).
[82] Thomas, *DVCard.*, art. 1, ad 4 (Marietti, 816).

virtue is described as the kind of virtue that guarantees correct use and consequently requires a right appetite.[83] The cardinal virtues are virtues that moderate and direct the appetite or require such a rectified appetite. Human life requires not only moral virtue but the intellectual virtue of prudence that they each presuppose.

Thomas does not seem to think that the distinction between formal reasons is only a distinction between general conditions. There is a way in which the formal reasons are connected not only to the general conditions but also to the different matter of specifically distinct virtues and habits. In the *De Virtutibus Cardinalibus* and in the *Summa Theologiae*, Thomas provides slightly different accounts of the way in which the cardinal virtues are distinguished from each other. Both texts give a similar account of the different subjects of the moral virtues. They both differ from the earlier *Commentary on the Sentences*, in which Thomas mentions the difference in subjects only after having used the matter to distinguish between the virtues.[84] In the later texts the distinction in subjects is at least one way of distinguishing the cardinal virtues.[85] This approach is ultimately rooted in Plato, although Thomas connects it to his own account of the essentially rational part of the soul and the three appetitive parts that participate in reason, namely the rational appetite, the irascible appetite, and the sensitive appetite. Consequently, there are four parts of the soul that are concerned with the moral life and they are either essentially rational or rational by participation. Each of these four parts can be the subject of a distinct cardinal virtue. Prudence perfects reason itself insofar as it is concerned with human action. Justice belongs to the will because it is about operations and not about the passions. We have already seen how temperance perfects the concupiscible appetite and courage perfects the irascible.

In the *De Virtutibus Cardinalibus*, art. 1, Thomas gives three ways of distinguishing between the cardinal virtues, namely by quasi-formal reasons, by the matter and the act, and by subject.[86] The contrast between the cardinal virtues considered as condition and considered as specifically distinct habits is present but less clearly marked. When Thomas first mentions the quasi-formal natures and the matter of the cardinal virtues, he

---

[83] Thomas, *S. T.*, I-II, q. 61, art. 1, resp. See also Thomas, *In Sent.*, lib. 3, d. 33, q. 2, art. 1, sol. 2; q. 2, art. 4, sol. 2 (Mandonnet-Moos, 3, 1047, 1063); *DVC*, art. 12, ad 24 (Marietti, 746).

[84] Thomas, *In Sent.*, lib. 3, d. 33, q 2, art. 4 (1059–1067).

[85] Thomas, *DVCard.*, art. 1, resp. (Marietti, 815); *S. T.*, I-II, q. 61, art. 2, resp. See also Thomas, *DVC*, art. 12, ad 25 (Marietti, 746–747).

[86] Thomas, *DVCard.*, art. 1, resp. (Marietti, 815).

does not explicitly distinguish between these two ways of speaking about the virtues, namely as conditions of a virtuous act and as habits strictly speaking. The thesis that the cardinal virtues can be considered as conditions of any virtuous act appears only in his replies to the objections when he wishes to account for authorities who speak of the virtues as inseparable.[87] It plays little role in the overall discussion.

In the *Summa Theologiae*, I-II, q. 61, Thomas notes that the cardinal virtues are principal because they make the act and agent good. Virtues that make the agent good must in some way involve the appetite. Consequently, a cardinal virtue will be a moral virtue that perfects the appetite or an intellectual virtue that is about the good, which is the object of an appetite. Unlike in the *De Virtutibus Cardinalibus*, Thomas does not first introduce the distinction in matter to differentiate between the cardinal virtues. In art.2, he uses the four formal principles and the four subjects to argue that there are four cardinal virtues. He indicates the difference according to matter only in art. 3, when he argues that the cardinal virtues are more principal than other virtues on account of their matter. The full importance of the difference in matter appears only in art. 4, in which Thomas discusses the ways in which these cardinal virtues differ from each other. He then states that the cardinal virtues are better understood as distinct according to matter than as differing according to the way in which they are general conditions. Only in this art. 4 does he more fully explain how the formal characteristics of the different cardinal virtues are related to the general conditions of each virtuous act.

In this text, Thomas argues that understanding these virtues as general conditions entails only a twofold division between the virtues, namely between prudence and the other moral virtues considered together.[88] Taken as a general condition, prudence is distinct from the other three virtues insofar as it is essentially rational, but the other three cardinal virtues are not really distinct because they all direct the appetite to the good of reason Thomas connects these three conditions to the very nature of moral virtue. By the fact that such virtue is a habit, it is firm and therefore can be called courage. By the fact that it is a virtue, it is ordered to a good and consequently able to be described as just. By the fact that it is moral, it can be described as following an order and therefore temperate.

Thomas uses these two different ways of speaking about the cardinal virtues in order to resolve apparent disagreements among his authorities.

---

[87] Thomas, *DVCard.*, art. 1, ad 1, 4 (Marietti, 815, 816).
[88] Thomas, *S.T.*, I-II, q. 61, art. 4, resp.

In his *Commentary on the Nicomachean Ethics*, he attributes the concep-
tion of the cardinal virtues as general conditions to Cicero, Seneca, and
other philosophers.[89] He contrasts this understanding of the cardinal virtues with that of Aristotle, who considers them only as specifically distinct
habits. He notes that the former distinction is less appropriate than that of
Aristotle precisely because their division does not refer to distinct species
and it is not based on the objects of the virtues.

It is unclear whether Thomas thinks that this doctrine of the cardinal
virtues as general conditions can in some oblique way be attributed to
Aristotle. In the *Summa Theologiae* and in the *De Virtutibus Cardinalibus*,
he argues that this understanding in some way seems to be implied by
Aristotle's texts.[90] In both works, Thomas recalls Aristotle's statement in
Book II of the *Ethics* that "First, a human should have knowledge; sec-
ondly, he must choose the acts and choose them for this end; and thirdly,
he must act in a firm and steadfast manner."[91] He gives slightly different
accounts of how this text points to the cardinal virtues. In the *Summa
Theologiae*, the first characteristic indicates that every act must be prudent, whereas the second indicates temperance insofar as the action is
from choice and not passion and justice insofar as the choice is for a due
end. The third element indicates a kind of fortitude. In the *De Virtutibus
Cardinalibus*, Aristotle's text points to only three of the four virtues, since
temperance is not clearly connected with any of these three characteristics.
Consequently, there is at least a difference of emphasis between Thomas's
different discussions.

Despite the differences between them, in these two texts Thomas
seems to connect the conditions that are mentioned by Aristotle with
the doctrine of the cardinal virtues. However, in the *Commentary on the
Nicomachean Ethics*, he discusses these same conditions without making
any reference to the cardinal virtues. Perhaps his silence is due to a belief
that Aristotle himself did not recognize the connection. Moreover, in the
De Virtutibus Cardinalibus, Thomas explicitly states that Aristotle's way
of speaking of the virtues as specifically distinct is not that of the other

---

[89] Thomas, *SLE*, lib. 2, lect. 8 (Leonine, 47.1, 102–103).
[90] Thomas, *S.T.*, I-II, q. 61, art. 4, ad 3; *DVCard.*, art. 1, resp. Thomas also touches on the issue in
DVC, art. 12, ad 23 (Marietti, 746).
[91] "primum quidem, si sciens; deinde, si eligens, et eligens propter hoc; tertium autem, si firme et
immobiliter habeat et operetur." Aristotle, *EN*, 2.4.1105a31–34, cited in Thomas, *S.T.*, I-II, q. 61,
art. 4, obj. 3. Aristotle's text is so compressed as to be awkward, so I have used the somewhat free
translation in Thomas Aquinas, *Treatise on the Virtues*, trans. John A. Oesterle (Notre Dame, IN:
University of Notre Dame Press, 1984), 113.

way of speaking of the virtues as general conditions.[92] Whatever Thomas's view on Aristotle's own understanding, the fact that the connection is not mentioned by Aristotle is not conclusive evidence against the truth of Thomas's other statements that there is such a connection between the properties of the virtuous human and the cardinal virtues, even though it makes the connection appear somewhat tenuous.

In the *Summa Theologiae*, Thomas argues that the cardinal virtues are principal primarily insofar as they are specifically distinct habits with distinct matter. He states:

> But others, and better, take these four virtues as they are determined to special matters, each one of them to the matter in which is principally praised that general condition by which the name of virtues is taken... And according to this, it is clear that the aforesaid virtues are diverse habits, according to the diversity of distinct objects.[93]

In this passage Thomas notes that the formal natures by which the cardinal virtues are general conditions are also principally in the distinct matter or objects that diversify the cardinal virtues insofar as they are distinct habits. In each case the matter indicates a special difficulty. For instance, the proper act of prudence is command, which is more difficult than the acts of deliberation or judgment, which are perfected by *eubulia*, *synesis*, and *gnome*. Similarly, temperance is about the most difficult pleasures to moderate, which is bodily pleasure. Courage insofar as it is a specifically distinct virtue is concerned with the greatest object of fear, which is of bodily death. Last, justice is about what is most strictly owed to another.

In the *De Virtutibus in Communi* Thomas similarly states that the use of the same word for both conditions and habits is a kind of "appropriation" by which the specifically distinct virtues take their names from the general conditions.[94] With respect to naming, the general conditions are prior. But, as we have seen in both the *Summa Theologiae* and the *Commentary on the Nicomachean Ethics*, even though in naming the general conditions are prior, Thomas prefers the usage according to which they are distinct virtues with distinct matter. This emphasis on the matter of the cardinal virtues reflects Thomas's much earlier account in his *Commentary on the*

---

[92] Thomas, *DVCard.*, art. 1, ad 1 (Marietti, 815).

[93] "Alii vero, et melius, accipiunt has quatuor virtutes secundum quod determinantur ad materias speciales; unaquaeque quidem illarum ad unam materiam, in qua principaliter laudatur illa generalis conditio a qua nomen virtutis accipitur ... Et secundum hoc, manifestum est quod praedictae virtutes sunt diversi habitus, secundum diversitatem obiectorum distincti." Thomas, *S.T.*, I-II, q. 61, art. 4, resp. See also Thomas, *DVC*, art. 12, ad 26 (Marietti, 747).

[94] Thomas, *DVC*, art.12, ad 23 (Marietti, 746).

Sentences, in which Thomas discusses the matter at length and passes over the account of the virtues as general conditions.[95]

Thomas allows for some flexibility in these two uses even among his authorities. He usually attributes an understanding of the virtues as general conditions to those who defend the unity of the virtues, such as Cicero and Church Fathers who are influenced by the Stoics. Nevertheless, he provides for another interpretation when he discusses the way in which cardinal virtues have distinct matters.[96] He notes that they could also be describing an overflowing of one virtue into another. For instance, the temperate person is able to restrain lesser desires precisely because she is able to restrain the desire for bodily pleasure, and the courageous person is able to face lesser dangers because of his firmness in face of death. In this way the cardinal virtues can be seen as connected not only as general conditions of virtue but also as overflowing into lesser virtues. Consequently, these authorities can to some extent be read either as holding that these virtues are general conditions or as holding that they are distinct habits. The sources themselves are ambiguous.

When considered primarily as distinct habits, the division between the cardinal virtues provides Thomas with a way of organizing the other moral virtues. He gives slightly different accounts of the ways in which other virtues are joined to the cardinal virtues. In the *Commentary on the Sentences*, he states that the difference between a cardinal virtue and a part of the virtue is not only in the fact that the cardinal virtue's matter is in some way more principal but also in that the associated virtue depends on the cardinal virtue, whereas the cardinal virtue does not depend on the virtue that is joined to it.[97] For instance, the virtue of magnanimity requires cardinal virtue for its exercise, but cardinal virtue does not depend on magnanimity. Similarly, the virtue of liberality presupposes the virtue of justice, because one must rightfully own money in order to give it freely. However, the cardinal virtue of justice does not similarly depend on liberality. In the later discussions Thomas does not emphasize such dependence. Throughout the *Secunda Secundae* of the *Summa Theologiae*, he focuses on the way in which other virtues are reduced to the cardinal virtues as either subjective or potential parts.

Although the schema of the cardinal virtues and their parts is dominant in the *Secunda Secundae* as an organizational principle, it is also present in

---

[95] Thomas, *In Sent.*, lib. 3, d. 33, q. 2, art. 1, sol. 1 (Mandonnet-Moos, 3, 1045).
[96] Thomas, *S.T.*, I-II, q. 61, art. 4, ad 1. Thomas also seems slightly hesitant about attributing the Stoic understanding to Augustine and Gregory (*ita videtur uti*) in the *DVCard.*, art. 1, ad 1 (Marietti, 815).
[97] Thomas, *In Sent.*, lib. 3, d. 33, q. 2, art. 1, qcla 4, ad 2–5 (Mandonnet-Moos, 3, 1050–1051).

Thomas's other works. For instance, in the *De Virtutibus in Communi*, he focuses on the way in which other moral virtues are potential parts of the cardinal virtues. He writes:

> The other associated or secondary virtues are held to be parts of the cardinal virtues, not as integral or subjective [parts], since they have determinate matter and their proper act; but as if they are potential parts, insofar as they in a particular and deficient way participate in the mean which is principally and more perfectly suited to the cardinal virtue.[98]

For instance, playfulness (*eutrapelia*) is joined to temperance insofar as it is a moderation of pleasure, even though it is not primarily about bodily pleasure. Similarly, gentleness and humility are joined to courage, since they involve passions of the irascible power. Here he emphasizes the matter of the specifically distinct cardinal virtues.

Thomas gives a more comprehensive account of the parts of the cardinal virtues in the *De Virtutibus Cardinalibus*, according to which the other moral virtues are joined to the cardinal virtues in different ways, depending on whether the cardinal virtues are considered as general conditions or specifically distinct parts.[99] The account of how the other moral virtues are reduced to distinct cardinal virtues as potential parts is unproblematic and seems consistent with the teaching of the *Summa Theologiae*. On the other hand, the account of these virtues as subjective parts seems to conflict with that of the *Secunda Secundae* of the *Summa Theologiae*. As has been mentioned, subjective parts are usually parts of a whole in the sense that they retain all of what it means to be in the whole. For instance, humans, dogs, and dolphins are all subjective parts of the whole that is "animal." Each is fully animal. In the *De Virtutibus Cardinalibus*, Thomas indicates that those virtues that are subjective parts of a cardinal virtue are reduced to the cardinal virtue if we consider the cardinal virtue as a general condition. A cardinal virtue would then be a whole that could be applied equally to the different virtues that are subjective pars.

This account at least seems inconsistent with that of the *Summa Theologiae*, according to which the subjective parts of a cardinal virtue are simply virtues with more distinct matter. In the *Secunda Secundae*, Thomas assigns every moral virtue to a cardinal virtue as integral,

---

[98] "aliae virtutes adiunctae vel secundariae ponuntur partes cardinalium, non integrales vel subiectivae, cum habeant materiam determinatam et actum proprium; sed quasi partes potentiales, in quantum particulariter participant, et deficienter medium quod principaliter et perfectius convenit virtuti cardinali." Thomas, *DVC*, art. 12, ad 27 (Marietti, 747).

[99] Thomas, *DVCard.*, art. 1, ad 5 (Marietti, 816).

subjective, or potential part.[100] In this latter work, the subjective parts of a virtue seem to be in no way species of a virtue that is a general condition. For instance, military prudence and ruling prudence are both species of prudence, but it is not clear that they should be considered subjective parts of prudence considered merely as a general condition.[101] They differ from the genus of prudence on account of the more limited matter. Prudence as a genus is concerned with right reason in action. These subjective parts are concerned more particularly with right reason about preserving the internal order of the political community or protecting it from extrinsic threats. Similarly, in the *Summa Theologiae*, the cardinal virtue of temperance is concerned with bodily pleasure, and it can be divided into four different subjective parts according to the kinds of bodily pleasure, namely food, drink, sexual pleasure, and the pleasure surrounding the sexual act.[102] These subjective parts are not associated with temperance as to a general condition of every virtue, but with temperance as a genus that is concerned with bodily pleasure. It seems difficult to reconcile the text of the *De Virtutibus Cardinalibus* with the parallel discussions in the *Summa Theologiae*.

Even though the cardinal virtues are in some way more principal than the other virtues, they are not simply speaking the most important moral virtues. This point is clearly seen in the discussion of humility and religion in the *Secunda Secundae*.[103] Religion is a potential part of justice.[104] It is a distinct virtue about the worship of God. It falls short of justice because there is no equality between the agent and God. Nevertheless, it is more important than the other moral virtues because its end is God and not a created good. Humility is similarly more important than the virtue to which it is joined.[105] According to Thomas, humility is a potential part of temperance, since it is primarily about restraint. It differs from temperance insofar as it moderates desires for great things and not simply the desire for bodily pleasure. Since humility orders the agent with respect to all goods, as a moral virtue it is inferior only to legal justice, which is the principal ordering virtue. Neither humility nor religion is a cardinal virtue, and in the organization of the *Summa Theologiae* they are subordinated

---

[100] For Thomas's taxonomy of the virtues, see Thomas M. Osborne Jr., *Aquinas's Ethics* (Cambridge: Cambridge University Press, 2020), 28–39.
[101] Thomas, *S.T.*, II-II, q. 48, art. un.
[102] Thomas, *S.T.*, II-II, q. 143, art. un.
[103] John of St. Thomas, *In I-II*, disp. 16, art. 6, n 1022 (Québec, 315).
[104] Thomas, *S.T.*, II-II, q. 81, art. 2, 4, 6.
[105] Thomas, *S.T.*, II-II, q. 161, art. 4–5.

to temperance and justice respectively. Nevertheless, in a significant way each is more important than the cardinal virtue to which it is joined. For Thomas, the schema of the cardinal virtues helps to organize the moral life, but it does not pick out the most significant moral virtues.

Assimilating Neoplatonic Divisions of Virtue

The division between the cardinal virtues is central for Thomas's taxonomy of human virtue. Nevertheless, he also thinks that the cardinal virtues can exist in ways that exceed ordinary human life and virtue. In the *Summa Theologiae*, he applies to his account of the cardinal virtues a fourfold Neoplatonic distinction between political virtue, purgative virtue, purged virtue, and exemplary virtue. This division comes from the Latin writer Macrobius, who himself is recounting Porphyry's systematization of Plotinus's account of virtue as a preparation for contemplation and in some way even as superhuman.[106] Although in the *Summa Theologiae* Thomas devotes only one article of the question on the cardinal virtues (q. 61) to this fourfold schema, it is important insofar as it reflects the culmination of his own reception of it and also as a way of taking into account a traditional Neoplatonic division of virtue. Thomas in general adopts Aristotle's claim that the human virtues are appropriate to the life proper to humans and that contemplation is in some way superior. He indicates that moral virtue can prepare for contemplation. But he consistently rejects the Neoplatonic thesis that moral virtue is valuable only as a means for contemplation.

The first member of the fourfold division, namely political virtue, is significant not only in this context but also on account of the way in which terminology about the virtues developed in the late twelfth and early thirteenth centuries. Simon of Tournai (d. 1201) and Alan of Lille (d. 1202/1203)

---

[106] Macrobius, *Commentarium in Somnium Scipionis*, 1.8–10, in *Ambrosii Theodosii Macrobii Commentarii in Somnium Scipionis*, ed. James Willis, Bibliotheca scriptorum Graecorum et Romanorum Teubneriana (Leipzig: Teubner, 1963), 36–45. For the history of this distinction and Thomas's appropriation of it, see H. van Lieshout, *La théorie Plotinienne de la vertu: Essai sur la genèse d'un article de la Somme théologique de saint Thomas* (Freiburg: Studia Friburgensia, 1926). For Thomas's account, see also Mary M. Keys, *Aquinas, Aristotle, and the Promise of the Common Good* (Cambridge: Cambridge University Press, 2006), 130–140; Benjamin DeSpain, "*Quaestio Disputata*: Aquinas's Virtuous Vision of the Divine Ideas," *Theological Studies* (8) 2020: 453–466; Paul De Hart, "*Quaestio Disputata*: Divine Virtues and Divine Ideas of Virtues," *Theological Studies* (8) 2020: 467–477. For the reception by Thomas and Bonaventure, see Joshua Hochschild, "Porphyry, Bonaventure, and Thomas Aquinas: A Neoplatonic Hierarchy of Virtues and Two Christian Appropriations," in *Medieval Philosophy and the Classical Tradition: In Islam, Judaism, and Christianity*, ed. John Inglis (London: Curzon, 2002), 245–258.

were among the first to use the term "political virtue" in order to distinguish between the virtues that pagans recognized and the "Catholic" virtues of faith, hope, and charity.[107] Although the terminology was widely adopted, its usage varied. Philip the Chancellor, for instance, used the term "political" to indicate the kind of virtue that was studied by ethics and not that virtue which is given by God.[108] It seems that on Philip's account there can be a distinction between the political and other virtues even among the individual cardinal virtues. For instance, Philip seems to think that a virtue such as prudence can either be considered as a political virtue or as a virtue given through grace. Bonaventure more clearly states that names of each of the cardinal virtues can refer either to a virtue that is acquired by ordinary human efforts or to a corresponding virtue that is given by God.[109]

In Thomas's historical period the term "political virtue" is not used primarily in the context of Macrobius's schema, but in some way it refers to the virtues acquired through ordinary human efforts. In his *De Virtutibus Cardinalibus*, Thomas seems to me to identify Macrobius's political virtue with the political virtue that is acquired moral virtue, which we will discuss more completely in Chapter 4.[110] However, many Thomists have plausibly argued that in the *Prima Secundae*, the distinction between the first three members of Macrobius's division is not between different kinds of virtue but between degrees or states within the same kind of virtue.[111] According to their reading of this text, Macrobius's political virtue is not specifically distinct from purged or purgative virtue but indicates the virtue insofar as it is exercised in political matters. One consideration is that, as will be shown in Chapter 5, Thomas in the *Summa Theologiae* seems to argue that the saints in heaven possess and use acquired moral virtues. Such virtues would be acquired moral virtues but not political in Macrobius's sense. Our focus here is on Thomas's development of Macrobius's description of political virtue as the lowest state of virtue. In the *Prima Secundae*, he introduces Macrobius's "political virtue" before he fully introduces the distinction between moral and theological virtue or the distinction between acquired and infused moral virtue.

[107] Lottin, *PM*, 3.1, 105–115; Istvan Bejcvy, "The Problem of Natural Virtue," in *Virtue and Ethics in the Twelfth Century*, ed. Istvan Bejcvy and Richard Newhauser (Leiden: Brill, 2005), 146–149.
[108] Philip, *Summa de Bono*, vol. 2, 596–597. William of Auxerre distinguishes primarily between political and theological virtues in his *Summa Aurea*, lib. 3, tract. 11, cap. 1 (vol. 3.1, 172); cf. lib. 2, tract. 13, cap. 1 (vol. 2.2, 474). See Lottin, *PM*, 3.1, 142–146.
[109] Bonaventure, *In Sent.*, lib. 3, d. 33, art. un. q. 5, resp. (vol. 3, 722–723).
[110] Thomas, *DVCard.*, art. 4, ad 7 (Marietti, 827).
[111] Cajetan, *In I-II*, q. 61, art. 5, n. 1 (Leonine, 6, 399); John of St. Thomas, *In I-II*, disp. 16, art. 6, nn. 1114–1148 (Québec, 342–350).

Why should the lowest state of virtue be described as "political"? The Neoplatonic division of virtue originally was used in conjunction with the thesis that the exercise of moral virtue in the active life is valuable primarily or perhaps even only as a means to the life of philosophy. Unlike Aristotle, these Neoplatonists seem to completely subordinate the political life to the life of contemplation. In his more significant references to Macrobius's division, Thomas primarily focuses on the way in which the virtues of the political life are contrasted with those that belong to the contemplative.[112] Thomas's earlier major discussions of this division are in his *Commentary on the Sentences*, in the context of the persistence of virtue in the next life, and in the *De Veritate*, in the context of the relationship between the virtues and the passions. He does briefly address this fourfold distinction in an inaugural sermon from the 1250s, but it is mostly in order to differentiate between the three "wisdom" books of the Bible.[113] Perhaps following a tradition that Bonaventure later attributes to Origen, Thomas states that *Proverbs* concerns the political virtues, *Ecclesiastes* is about the purgative virtues, and the *Song of Songs* is concerned with the purged virtues.[114]

In the *Commentary on the Sentences*, Thomas gives his first sustained treatment of the fourfold division in his defense of the position that only the infused moral virtues exist after death. He replies to an objection that the moral virtues, including both the acquired and infused, cannot persist in the next life because there will be no active life there but only contemplation.[115] Thomas argues that the virtues that perfect the active life do not disappear but rather are changed in the contemplative life. The persistence of the virtues is explained by the way in which the active life has the contemplative life as its further end. Thomas accounts for Macrobius's three states of virtue in the context of this relationship between the two lives. Political virtue is concerned with the active life of the city. The citizen uses purged virtue to attain contemplation. Purged virtue is exercised only in this life, and only by those who set aside civil life and devote themselves to contemplation or by the just in heaven. Without the cares of civil life, there is no need for temperance to restrain the desire for bodily pleasure

---

[112] For partial references to this distinction, see Thomas, *DV*, q. 26, art. 7, ad 6 (Leonine, 22.3, 774); *S.T.*, III, q. 7, art. 2, ad 2; q. 41, art. 2, ad 1. See DeSpain, "Divine Virtues and Divine Ideas," 470.

[113] Thomas, *Principium Fratris Thomae de Commendatione et Partitione Sacrae Scripturae*, n. 1207, in *Opuscula Theologica*, vol. 1 (Marietti, 438).

[114] Bonaventure, *Collationes in Hexaëmeron*, 6.25 (vol. 5, 363–364). For Bonaventure, see Hochschild, "Porphyry, Bonaventure, and Aquinas," 249–250.

[115] Thomas, *In Sent.*, lib. 3, d. 33, q. 1, art. 4, ad 2, 5 (Mandonnet-Moos, 3, 1041).

or for courage to overcome fear. Courage and temperance persist but no longer perform the same function. In contrast, the angels and God alone have exemplary virtue.

In his later discussion of the gifts of the Holy Ghost in the same work, Thomas holds the view that these gifts are reduced to the exemplary virtues that are in God and consequently are above and specifically distinct from the political virtues.[116] Although this early work is not entirely clear about the exact nature of the difference between the first three members of Macrobius' division, the implication seems to be that they are all in some way human, whereas the fourth member is above human nature.

In the *De Veritate*, Thomas connects these first three states of virtue to the dispute between the Stoics and the Peripatetics over whether the virtuous person experiences passion.[117] According to Thomas, Macrobius' account of purged virtue as being free of passion can be interpreted in two ways. First, it can be understood in light of the Stoic belief that although the virtuous person might have sudden passion, she does not experience passions that distort reason or disturb the soul. According to this interpretation, purged virtue seems to be the same as Thomas's ordinary description of moral virtue. Second, Thomas states that purged virtue is better understood as the virtue of someone who has separated himself from political life and its attendant goods of money and honor. Such a person will have passions concerning only natural goods such as food, drink, and bodily health and their contrary evils. According to this second interpretation, the difference seems to be not so much in the virtue itself but in the life to which the possessor of the virtue belongs. Although this text differs from that of the *Commentary on the Sentences* by focusing on the passions, it retains the tight connection between Macrobius' distinction between the virtues and the division between the active and contemplative lives.

In this text of the *Summa Theologiae*, Thomas seems to use Macrobius' account of these virtues as part of a transition from a question about the cardinal virtues (q. 61) to a question about the theological virtues (q. 62). He addresses the division in the last article on cardinal virtue.[118] In this work he attributes exemplary virtue only to God and not to the angels. He departs from his earlier accounts by distinguishing between the other three kinds of virtue according to the way in which their possessors are assimilated to God. The focus is no longer on the contrast between the

---

[116] Thomas, *In Sent.*, lib. 3, d. 34, q. 1, art. 1, ad 6 (Mandonnet-Moos, 3, 1115).
[117] Thomas, *DV*, q. 26, art. 8, ad 2 (Leonine, 22.3, 777).
[118] Thomas, *S.T.*, I-II, q. 61, art. 5.

active and contemplative lives. The two extremes, namely exemplary and political virtue, contrast God and human affairs. The former virtues in God preexist as exemplars in which the other virtues participate. The latter virtues are political insofar as they are about human deeds. Thomas introduced the cardinal virtues in the context of human affairs, and he states in this discussion of political virtue that "According to this way we have been speaking of the virtues up to this point."[119] This statement indicates a shift from considering moral virtues as perfecting human life to considering them as involving divine assimilation.

The distinction between purgative and purged virtue corresponds to the higher levels of assimilation to the divine. First, purgative virtues perfect those who are on their way to divine assimilation. They remove obstacles to contemplation. Thomas writes of such virtue:

> In such a way it is clear that prudence despises all worldly things in the contemplation of divine things, and directs every thought of the soul into the divine alone; and temperance leaves behind what the use of the body requires, insofar as nature allows; it belongs to courage not to be terrified of withdrawing from things of the body, and ascending to things above; and justice is such that the whole soul consents to this proposed life.[120]

The distinction between political and purged virtue corresponds to the distinction between actions that belong to ordinary human life and actions that set aside such life in favor of God. In contrast to those who practice purgative virtue, the possessors of purged virtue are already in heaven or at least have become perfect already in this life. These virtues are distinguished from the purgative because their possessors have already set aside human affairs in their assimilation to God.

These three kinds of virtues that humans can possess indicate different ways in which virtues are related to the passions. In the Neoplatonic sense of the term, "political virtue" regulates the passions. Thomas's discussion of the moral virtues and the passions up to this point has primarily been on this kind of virtue. But he also recognizes that purgative virtues take away passions. His praise for such virtue brings to mind the Stoic thesis that the passions are incompatible with virtue. In contrast, the purged virtues of

---

[119] "Secundum quem modum hactenus de his virtutibus locuti sumus." Thomas, *S.T.*, I-II, q. 61, art. 5, resp.

[120] "Ita scilicet quod prudentia omnia mundana divinorum contemplatione despiciat, omnemque animae cogitationem in divina sola dirigat; temperantia vero relinquat, inquantum natura patitur, quae corporis usus requirit; fortitudinis autem est ut anima non terreatur propter excessum a corpore, et accessum ad superna; iustitia vero est ut tota anima consentiat ad huius propositi viam." Thomas, *S.T.*, I-II, q. 61, art. 5, resp.

the perfect and the blessed in heaven do not have passions to moderate or remove. Thomas explains, "human virtues are about the passions, namely the virtues of humans in this world of social intercourse; but the virtues of those who have attained full happiness are without passions."[121]

Thomas's use of Macrobius' division in the *Summa Theologiae* signals a shift in the text from a discussion of virtue as perfecting human affairs to a discussion of virtue as involving God. The distinction itself has greater significance than it held in early texts in which it was connected to the distinction between the active and contemplative lives. However, the nature of the distinction as applied to the first three stages is never fully explained in later parts of the *Summa Theologiae*.[122] For instance, do these three kinds of virtue have distinct formal objects or are they distinct merely on account of the way in which they are possessed? At this point Thomas has not yet in any clear way introduced the relevant distinctions that would help us to address such a question, such as whether this three-fold division applies equally to acquired and infused virtue or whether the formal object of the virtue follows a rule that exceeds human nature. In his later discussions he does not return to this topic. It seems that Thomas is using Macrobius's division here only as a way of making a transition from human affairs to the divine.

---

[121] "virtutes humanae sunt circa passiones, scilicet virtutes hominum in hoc mundo conversantium. Sed virtutes eorum qui plenam beatitudinem assequuntur, sunt absque passionibus." Thomas, *S.T.*, I-II, q. 61, art. 5, ad 2.

[122] For a convincing argument that the difference is not in kind, see John of St. Thomas, *In I-II*, disp. 16, art. 6, nn. 339–356 (Québec, 118–122).

CHAPTER 4

Natural and Supernatural Virtue

Thomas's account of the distinction between intellectual, moral, and cardinal virtues prepares for what is in some way a more profound distinction between natural and supernatural virtues. This latter distinction rests on the difference between a natural order that can be known by natural reason and a supernatural or gratuitous order that is known only through revelation. Natural virtues perfect the agent insofar as she is a citizen of an earthly or temporal city. Supernatural virtues perfect the agent insofar as she belongs to the heavenly city, or the city of God. As a work of theology, the *Summa Theologiae* is concerned primarily with these latter virtues. However, Thomas's account of the supernatural virtues depends in large part on his previous discussion of natural virtue. Moreover, his account of the relationship between the two kinds of virtue sheds further light on natural virtue.

In the *Prima Secundae*, Thomas describes two kinds of supernatural virtues. First, in q. 62, he introduces three supernatural virtues that were generally called "theological" virtues, namely faith, hope, and charity. These virtues are called theological because they are distinctively Christian or Catholic. They are about God and unknown apart from revelation. Second, in q. 63, Thomas states that there are moral virtues that are caused by God, have a different mean than the humanly acquired moral virtues, and are essentially ordered to a supernatural end. There are consequently supernatural virtues that correspond to the ordinary natural moral virtues. They are supernatural counterparts to the virtues that the non-Christian philosophers discuss. Even the cardinal virtues can be considered either as natural or as supernatural in this way. The natural moral virtues are called "acquired" and the supernatural moral virtues are called "infused." The names for these broad kinds of virtues are taken from their efficient causes, although the efficient cause does not indicate the essential difference between them.

Acquired moral virtues are ordinarily acquired or caused by human acts, and infused moral virtues must be directly infused or caused by God. But more fundamentally these virtues are distinct according to their moral objects. For instance, the acquired virtue of temperance has a different mean from the corresponding infused virtue. The mean of an infused moral virtue is distinct from that of the corresponding acquired virtue because it is concerned with acts that perfect the agent with respect to the supernatural end. Christian temperance requires a stricter fasting and abstinence than acquired temperance does. But acquired and infused moral virtues share the same proper names because they have the same matter. For example, infused temperance and acquired temperance are both called "temperance" because they are about bodily pleasure.

In order to discuss such supernatural moral virtues, it will be helpful to follow Thomas's own order and consider theological virtue first. Thomas's writings on the theological virtues integrate and pass on elements that he has learned from the previous theological tradition. His account of the infused moral virtues seems to be somewhat innovative, although it develops views that were previously defended by Bonaventure and perhaps others. After considering the distinction between the acquired and infused moral virtues, we will look at how they are related. At least the broad outline of this relationship between acquired and infused moral virtue is of central importance for understanding not only Thomas's theology but also what he writes about the connection between the acquired and the moral virtues, which will be addressed in the next chapter.

Infused and Theological Virtue

According to Thomas, humans need theological virtue because they are ordered to an ultimate end that exceeds the requirements and abilities of human nature, namely the beatific vision of God in the next life. He states that this end is attained primarily through the exercise of the theological virtues in this life. These virtues are distinctively Christian virtues and rooted in Scripture. The standard source is St. Paul's First Epistle to the Corinthians (1 Cor 13:15), although there are references to these virtues throughout St. Paul's Epistles and in the Bible as a whole. Thomas's account of these virtues depends on the way in which he understands this ultimate end as compatible with but not the same as the natural end of humans.

Thomas emphasizes not only that humans are unable to achieve the beatific vision through their natural powers but also that apart from grace they lack an ordering to this end.[1] This ordering is not natural, but neither does it violate human nature. The supernatural last end and means are thoroughly compatible with human nature. Thomas describes this ability to be raised to a supernatural order as a kind of passive potency. Human nature is a kind of nature that can be raised to a higher order. In general, a passive potency is a potency that corresponds to some active power. For instance, water has a passive potency to be heated by fire and to be moved in a different way by the heavenly bodies. Similarly, water could be changed not only by such natural agents but also by God, who, for instance, parted the Red Sea. These changes do not contradict what it means to be water but are compatible with it. A natural agent or even God would be unable to make water rational or dry. Similarly, not even God could make humans nonrational or avian. But God can elevate human nature, since humans as rational animals are capable of being raised to a supernatural knowledge and love for God.

Humans by nature have active principles for achieving their natural ends. For instance, humans by nature are able to attain connatural ends through the exercise of natural moral virtues. In the *Summa Theologiae*, Thomas indicates that this inclination has been wounded by original sin with respect to each of the four powers that are subjects of the cardinal virtues.[2] Human reason has been darkened by ignorance, especially in practical affairs, and such ignorance is an obstacle to prudence. The appetitive powers are also affected. The will, which is the subject of justice, is wounded by malice. The irascible power is wounded by weakness and cannot easily acquire courage. Moreover, the concupiscible power is wounded by concupiscence, which is an obstacle to temperance. These wounds result from original sin and belong to human nature not as it was originally created but only insofar as it is transmitted from Adam. Grace is needed to heal these wounds. Such healing grace is needed for our fallen nature to be further elevated by grace, but it does not on its own raise human nature. It allows human nature to act in accordance with human natural inclinations that are themselves good and uncorrupted.

---

[1] Thomas, *DVC*, art. 10, resp. (Marietti, 735–736); *DV*, q. 15, art. 3, ad 9 (Leonine, 22.2, 447–448).

[2] Thomas, *S.T.*, I-II, q. 85, art. 3. In earlier passages Thomas does not so clearly connect the corruption of original sin with the corruption of the subjects of virtue. See Thomas, *In Sent.*, lib. 3, d. 30, q. 1, art. 3 (Mandonnet-Moos, 3, 773–776); *DV*, q. 25, art. 6 (Leonine, 22.3, 740–743); *DM*, q. 4, art. 5 (Leonine, 23, 17–118). For a discussion of the *S.T.* passage, see Thomas Hibbs, "The Fearful Thoughts of Mortals: Aquinas on Conflict, Self-Knowledge, and the Virtue of Practical Reasoning," in *Intractable Disputes about the Natural Law: Alasdair MacIntyre and Critics*, ed. Lawrence Cunningham (Notre Dame, IN: University of Notre Dame Press, 2009), 289.

More importantly, sanctifying grace elevates humans so that they are ordered to a supernatural end.[3] But human nature lacks the principles for achieving such an end, even though it is capable of being assisted by God to the achievement of such an end. In the *De Virtutibus in Communi*, Thomas describes such a potency for supernatural life as an "obediential potency," since it is an ability of human nature to obey God's activity. Such an obediential potency is a kind of passive potency.[4] This obediential potency to the supernatural end in some way results from human nature even though the elevation itself does not belong to human nature. It is God's free gift. Nevertheless, humans, unlike other material creatures, are capable of receiving such a gift. It would be impossible for water to be the subject of any supernatural knowing or loving. Consequently, water does not have an obediential potency to be so elevated. But since humans are rational, God can raise humans to such a life. It is important to recognize that this elevation is a result of God's free choice and in no way required by nature. God does not need to order humans to such an end, but he can and has done so.

Even though God offers all adult humans the possibility of an order to the supernatural ultimate end through grace, we can still distinguish between the supernatural happiness of heaven, its anticipation in this life, and a natural happiness that is proportionate to human nature. In Chapter 5, when discussing the connection of the virtues, we will briefly give reasons for thinking that in our present state there is no natural happiness that can be achieved apart from or in opposition to supernatural happiness. When first looking at the theological virtues, it is primarily important to grasp that humans are directed to a happiness that exceeds

---

[3] This issue was subject to many and perhaps not particularly illuminating disputes in the twentieth century, starting primarily with Henri de Lubac, *Surnaturel: Études Historiques* (Paris: Aubier, 1946). For some recent criticisms of de Lubac, see Bernard Mulcahy, *Aquinas's Notion of Pure Nature and the Christian Integralism of Henri de Lubac* (New York: Peter Lang, 2011); Steven A. Long, *Natura Pura: On the Recovery of Nature in the Doctrine of Grace* (New York: Fordham University Press, 2010). For a review essay that contains some references to the voluminous literature, see Thomas M. Osborne Jr., "Natura Pura: Two Recent Works," *Nova et Vetera, English Edition* 11 (2013): 265–279. It seems to me that the best guides to the issues under discussion remain T.-H. Deman, Review of *Surnaturel: Études historiques*, by Henri de Lubac, *Bulletin Thomiste* 7 (1943–46, pub. 1950): 422–446; J.-H. Nicolas, *Les profondeurs de la grace* (Paris: Beauchesne, 1969), 331–397.

[4] Thomas, *DVC*, art. 10, ad 2, 13 (Marietti, 737). For the history of the medieval use of the term "obediential potency," see L.-B. Gillon, "Aux origines de la 'Puissance Obédientielle,'" *Revue Thomiste* 48 (1947): 304–310. For a similar use of the term *potentia oboedientiae* in Albert the Great, see his *Super Dionysium de Divinis Nominibus*, cap. 1 (Col., 37.1, 13). For Thomas's account of obediential potency in light of recent scholarly disputes, see Mark Johnson, "St. Thomas, Obediential Potency, and the Infused Virtues: *De virtutibus in communi*, a. 10, ad 13," *Recherches de Théologie ancienne et médiévale*, suppl. 1: *Thomistica* (1995): 27–34; Steven A. Long, "Creation *ad imaginem Dei*: The Obediential Potency of the Human Person to Grace and Glory," *Nova et Vetera* 14 (2016): 1175–1192.

the capabilities and inclinations of a human nature that has not been elevated by grace to a higher order. These considerations should not lead us
to think that a separate purely natural happiness is possible for us.

In the *Summa Theologiae* and throughout his writings, Thomas emphasizes that the theological virtues are themselves supernatural precisely
because of the way in which they are directed to an end for which there
is no natural inclination. Humans can be made participants in God's life
through a kind of knowledge and love that entirely exceed human nature
and the natural ordering to God.[5] In the first five questions of the *Prima
Secundae*, Thomas had distinguished between the imperfect happiness
that is achieved through the exercise of virtues in this life and the perfect
happiness that the blessed enjoy in heaven. He uses this twofold happiness
in order to distinguish between natural virtue and infused virtue and in
particular to introduce the theological virtues. The distinction between
the happiness of natural virtue and that of supernatural virtue should
not be identified with a distinction between an ultimate end that is not
God and God as the ultimate end. Thomas clearly states that humans are
directed to God naturally. The difference is in the way in which God is
the ultimate end of human action.

Thomas emphasizes that this ordering to the supernatural vision of God
is first made possible through grace, which gives a kind of spiritual being
(*esse*) to the creature.[6] In general, the word "grace" refers to any freely given
gift. "Grace" or something gratuitous is therefore understood in opposition to something that is due. According to Thomas, something can be
due to someone in two ways.[7] First, someone might deserve a reward on
account of a good deed. Second, it is in some way due to a human that she
has a hand and the power of reason. In a theological context, grace can
refer to the Holy Ghost or to a created gift that God gives apart from any
such merit or naturally due property. Such created grace can be either for
the benefit of the recipient or for that of others.[8] For instance, a prophet
might receive the gift of prophecy entirely for the benefit of other hearers
and not of the prophet. Grace is sometimes a motion according to which
God helps the exterior act or interiorly moves the will.[9] In the context of
virtue, we are most concerned with the grace that makes the possessor
in some way pleasing to God (*gratia gratum faciens*), and more narrowly

---

[5] Thomas, *S. T.*, I-II, q. 109, art. 3, resp. et ad 2; art. 4.
[6] Thomas, *DVC*, art. 10, resp. (Marietti, 735–736).
[7] Thomas, *S. T.*, I-II, q. 111, art. 1, ad 2.
[8] Thomas, *S. T.*, I-II, q. 111, art. 1, resp.
[9] Thomas, *S. T.*, I-II, q. 111, art. 2, 4.

within this wider category the grace by which someone in this life is justified. It is a quality of the soul that raises its possessor to a new kind of being. The Christian ordinarily receives such grace with baptism, loses it through mortal sin, and regains it through a perfect contrition or confessing one's sin with a kind of imperfect contrition or attrition. Such grace is generally called "sanctifying grace" by later writers.

Sanctifying grace is prior to the virtues since it exists in the essence of the soul and makes its recipient a sharer in God's own life. Thomas writes, "the gift of grace exceeds every faculty of created nature, since it is nothing other than a certain participation in the divine nature, which exceeds every other nature."[10] This grace is distinct from virtue since it not an operative habit but a quality that inheres in the soul's essence.[11] The order that such habitual grace establishes, namely the order to God as a supernatural end, is achieved through three operative habits, namely the theological virtues of faith, hope, and charity.

Sanctifying grace is a habit, but it is not an operative habit. It is a distinct kind of habit from the theological virtues.[12] Grace makes someone participate in God insofar as she resembles God by being a new creation or generation. The theological virtues belong to someone insofar as she participates in this divine nature. The first manifestation of the sanctifying grace by which someone participates in God is an act of faith that is made through charity. Whereas grace exists in the soul's essence, the theological virtues are operative powers that are in the soul's powers. Consequently, the theological virtues flow from grace in the way that the soul's powers flow from its essence. Theological virtue makes some participate in God through acts such as loving God through charity and knowing him through faith.

These theological virtues, and, as we will see, the infused virtues more widely, share many of the same functions that are performed by the acquired moral virtues. For example, whereas acquired moral virtue makes the agent and the act good with respect to human nature, theological virtue makes them good in the order of grace. The infused virtues are related to grace in the way that the acquired virtues are related to the natural light of reason.

The theological virtues play a larger role in the supernatural order than the acquired moral virtue plays in the natural order.[13] Moral virtues do

---

[10] "Donum autem gratiae excedit omnem facultatem naturae creatae, cum nihil aliud sit quam quaedam participatio divinae naturae, quae excedit omnem aliam naturam." Thomas, *S.T.*, I-II, q. 112, art. 1, resp.
[11] Thomas, *S.T.*, I-II, q. 110, art. 4.
[12] Thomas, *S.T.*, I-II, q. 62, art. 1, ad 1; q. 110 art. 3.
[13] Thomas, *S.T.*, I-II, q. 62, art. 3.

not supply but depend upon the intellect's natural grasp of an end and a natural inclination to the end. But there is no such natural knowledge or natural inclination to the supernatural end. Whereas the first principles of understanding are known through the habit of understanding, the first principles of the supernatural life are known only through faith. Similarly, the will's nature on its own has a natural inclination that is sufficient both for intending the end that is proportionate to nature and for conforming to it. But in the supernatural order the virtues of hope and charity themselves supply the corresponding supernatural inclination. Hope moves to the supernatural end insofar as it is possible, and charity unites the agent to the end. Charity in a way transforms the agent into God. This transformation exceeds anything natural. Just as the will on its own naturally tends to the good for reason, so the Christian tends to the beatific vision. Unlike the moral virtues, the theological virtues supply the knowledge of and inclination towards their end.

Like sanctifying grace, the theological virtues are essentially supernatural. In both the *Summa Theologiae* and the *Commentary on the Sentences*, Thomas states that the theological virtues exceed nature with respect to their divine object and cause.[14] Moreover, he states that we know about them only through revelation. It is important that, for Thomas, grace is not simply an aid to action or a mere decision by God to accept someone as just. According to him, the life of grace is a participation in God's own life that exceeds the natural life in its acts, abilities, and formal end. In his *Commentary on the Sentences*, he more clearly explains this threefold need for special virtues in this supernatural order. First, there must be virtues that have a supernatural object. Since by grace humans have an inclination to God himself, there needs to be supernatural virtues that are about actions concerning God himself. Second, there must be virtues that have only God as a cause. Natural virtues can be caused by human acts, since humans naturally can act in accordance with their nature, which is sufficient for the achievement of a natural end. But since through grace humans are ordered to God in a way that exceeds human nature and the natural order, God must be the cause of some virtue in a way similar to how he is the cause of the supernatural ordering. Third, since human reason is sufficient for knowing about the natural inclination to this end, it also suffices for knowing

---

[14] Thomas, *In Sent.*, lib. 3, d. 23, q. 1, art. 4, sol. et ad 1, 3 (Mandonnet-Moos, 3, 714–715); *S. T.*, I-II, q. 62, art. 1, resp. For a translation of and introduction to the article of the *S. T.*, see J. Budziszewski, *A Commentary on Thomas Aquinas's Virtue Ethics* (Cambridge: Cambridge University Press, 2017), 64–79.

the virtues that correspond to the natural end.[15] But the supernatural virtues are ordered to an end that exceeds such an inclination and can consequently only be known through revelation. The fact that they are known only through revelation is one of the reasons why they are called "theological." Philosophers such as Aristotle lacked revelation and only knew about the virtues that belong to the natural order.

In the *De Virtutibus in Communi*, art. 10, Thomas discusses the distinction between infused virtues, which include theological and infused moral virtues, and acquired moral virtues in light of Aristotle's distinction between virtue that makes a human good and those that make a citizen good.[16] This text is important for several reasons. First, it indicates how he appropriates arguments and distinctions from Aristotle in a theological context. Second, it explains in relatively expansive detail how his understanding of the distinction between the natural and the supernatural is connected to the distinction between the political community and the community of Christians.

It is puzzling why Aristotle would distinguish between human goodness and a goodness that is relative to the regime under which the citizen lives. In his *Commentary on Aristotle's Politics*, Thomas understands Aristotle to give three distinct arguments for the existence of this difference between goodness as a human and goodness relative to a regime. In this text "virtue" does not seem to narrowly mean moral or even intellectual virtue. It seems to include even what would make the ruler or perhaps the ruled good in only a qualified way. Some remarks seem to include even that "virtue" which assists in the preservation of a corrupt regime. Paradoxically, such "virtue" would make someone good in relation to a regime that is bad, since it is directed towards only the good of the rulers. Tyranny, oligarchy, and even mob rule are examples of such bad regimes. The regime-relevant excellence or virtue is understood in the context of the role of a ruler or perhaps a citizen.

In the first argument for the distinction between the two kinds of virtue, Aristotle compares the community to a ship. Different members of a ship each have virtues or excellences that are relative to their role, even though they share the same goal of safe navigation.[17] For instance, someone who steers must have different virtues or excellences from someone who rows. Similarly, different members of the political community, such

---

[15] See also Thomas, *DVC*, art. 12, ad 6 (Marietti, 745).
[16] Aristotle, *Pol.*, 3.4.
[17] Thomas, *SLP*, lib. 3, cap. 3 (ed. Leonina, vol. 48A, 193–194).

as rulers and the ruled, will have excellences or virtues that are appropriate to their role even though they are all concerned with the conservation of the community. This distinction between virtue as such and a kind of regime-relative virtue is important because of the way in which regimes are ordered to self-preservation.

According to Thomas, this first argument considers virtues or excellences as preserving both good and bad regimes. The virtue that makes someone a good human being will be the same as political virtue only in the best regime. This argument might in some way shed light on Thomas's use of the distinction in the *De Virtutibus* in the context of the division between the natural and the supernatural. But it also indicates a possible conflict between political goodness and human goodness that cannot exist between the natural and supernatural orders. The good citizen may lack political virtue, and we can even imagine that the virtuous individual in a bad regime might be a "bad" citizen, in that her activities fail to further the ends of the regime. Perhaps this conflict appears because "virtue" is used more widely here as any kind of excellence, as when we might describe the virtue or excellence of someone who is good at stealing.[18]

Aristotle's second argument shows that even in the best political community the virtue of the good citizen differs from the good human.[19] This argument rests on the fact that in the best regime the ruler will be good and the citizens will at least be good citizens. But it is impossible for every citizen to be a good human being.[20] Consequently, in the best city there must be good citizens who are not good human beings. Such citizens will only have that virtue that makes them good citizens and lack the virtue that makes them good human beings. At first this distinction might seem irrelevant to the distinction between acquired virtue and infused virtue, because acquired virtue makes the agent good in a way proportionate to nature. But although the two distinctions are not the same, the second argument might be relevant to the distinction between infused and acquired virtue because it indicates how different kinds of virtue or excellence have distinct criteria. Just as the virtue of the good human being has narrower criteria than that of the good citizen, so might infused virtue have narrower criteria than that of acquired virtue.

Aristotle's third argument is based on the way in which a virtue or excellence of a part should be considered in relation to the whole. Thomas

---

[18] Thomas, *S.T.*, I, q. 55, art. 4, ad 1.
[19] Thomas, *SLP*, lib. 3, cap. 3 (ed. Leonina, vol. 48A, 194–195).
[20] See also Thomas, *S.T.*, I-II, q. 92, art. 1, ad 3.

shows that he understands Aristotle to be taking virtue in a wide sense, namely as a quality that makes a person good in any way, not just good as a human being or even citizen.[21] This argument depends on how parts have different excellences or virtues with respect to different wholes. For instance, in a household there are different excellences for slaves and masters, as well as for men and women. What counts as courage for a woman would be cowardice for a man. Similarly, the choir leader has a different excellence from the person who merely sings in the choir. According to Thomas, the same differences exist in the political community. Citizens have different virtues according to the different roles that they possess in a city. The virtue that makes someone good is one and the same for everyone. But rulers have a distinct virtue by which they direct the others. The citizen who rules and is ruled will have both virtues.

Aristotle thinks that the distinction between the good citizen and the good human being depends on the nature of the regime and the role that the citizen plays in it. The virtue of the good citizen here seems to be that of the citizen who also participates in ruling, such as in a polity. In such a political community the citizen is a perfect or complete citizen, since he more fully participates in politics. Thomas sums up Aristotle's account by stating:

> [I]n some city, namely the aristocratic, the good man and the good citizen are the same, because evidently rule is given according to the virtue which belongs to the good man. But in some cities the good man is other than the good citizen, namely in corrupt political communities in which rule is not given according to virtue. And that citizen who is the same as the good man, is not just any citizen, but he who is political (*civilis*), that is the ruler of the city and the lord or able to be the lord, either alone or with others, of those things which pertain to the care of the community. For it is said above that the virtue of the ruler is the same as that of the good man; but therefore if the citizen is taken to be the ruler or the one who can be the ruler, his virtue and that of the good man is the same. However, if the citizen is taken to be an imperfect one who is not able to be a ruler, the virtue of the good citizen and of the good man will not be the same, as is clear from what has been said.[22]

---

[21] Thomas, *SLP*, lib. 3, cap. 3 (ed. Leonina, vol. 48A, 195–196).

[22] "in aliqua ciuitate, scilicet aristocratica, idem est bonus uir et bonus ciuis, quia scilicet principatus dantur secundum uirtutem quae est boni uiri; in aliquibus autem alius est bonus uir et alius bonus ciuis, scilicet in corruptis politiis in quibus principatus dantur non secundum uirtutem. Et ille ciuis qui est idem cum bono uiro non est quicumque ciuis set ille qui est ciuilis, id est rector ciuitatis et dominus uel potens esse dominus eorum quae pertinent ad curam communitatis, uel solus uel etiam cum aliis. Dictum est enim supra quod eadem est uirtus principis et boni uiri; unde si ciuis accipiatur qui est princeps uel qui potest esse, eadem est uirtus eius et boni uiri; si autem accipiatur ciuis imperfectus qui non potest esse princeps, non erit eadem uirtus boni ciuis et boni uiri, ut ex predictis patet." Thomas, *SLP*, lib. 3, cap. 3 (Leonine, 48A, 199).

The discrepancy between the good citizen and the good man in some political communities has two causes. First, the regime might not be good. Second, even in some good regimes the virtuous man might not be fully a citizen. He will be ruled but unable to rule. In such a case, both the man and the political community might be good. But such a good citizen will not be fully a citizen or have the regime-relevant virtue that the rulers will have. This last possibility results from the variety of ways in which individuals can be part of regimes. In Thomas's account of Aristotle's first argument, the discrepancy between a good human being and a good citizen in a corrupt community results from the fact that in corrupt political communities the virtuous do not rule. In the third argument and more completely in the above summary, he notes that even in some good regimes, some virtuous persons will not be full citizens, taking part in ruling and being ruled.

Thomas uses this distinction between the good citizen and the good human being to explain how there is a difference in kind between the virtue that makes someone a good member of the political community and that which makes him a good member of the city of God. In the former case, "virtue" is used in a wide sense and can even apply to habits by which someone is a "good" citizen by fulfilling well his bad role in a bad political community. The goodness of such a citizen is like the goodness of a thief who is good at stealing. A citizen with such "virtue" could not be a good human.

The existence of bad regimes makes possible the incompatibility between the virtue of the good citizen and that of the good human being. The citizen's virtue is not merely different from that of the good human being, but in such regimes it makes the good citizen a bad person. But there is no parallel conflict between being a good human on the natural level and being good on the supernatural level. Grace elevates but does not do violence to human nature. Natural virtue makes someone good as a human being according to the happiness that is proportionate to his nature. Theological virtue makes someone good as a Christian who is ordered to the beatific vision. Theological virtue does not depend on natural virtue directly, but it is incompatible with mortal sin, and consequently the proper acts of the more prominent vices.

The theological virtues are essentially supernatural and consequently both are about God and come from God.[23] Many later scholastic theologians, such as John Duns Scotus and William of Ockham (d. 1347), think

---

[23] Thomas, *S.T.*, I-II, q. 62, art. 2.

that there are both acquired and infused versions of faith, hope, and charity.[24] On their accounts, the acquired theological virtues do or at least can share the same object as the infused. Each of the supernaturally produced theological virtues would have a natural counterpart that is about God in the same way. For instance, someone might love God more than self on account of a natural habit or on account of the charity that is infused by God. Similarly, one might believe in revelation on the basis of natural reason instead of or in addition to the faith that is given by God. In contrast, Thomas holds that the theological virtues are essentially supernatural. They lack any natural counterparts.

Thomas emphasizes the difference between the natural happiness that is known by philosophers such as Aristotle and the Christian understanding of happiness as the beatific vision. Virtues are defined by their formal objects. The theological virtues have as their formal objects God "insofar as he exceeds the knowledge of our reason."[25] Many other virtues in some other way involve God or are about God. For instance, the intellectual virtue of wisdom, which is discussed by Aristotle, is concerned with knowing God.[26] But through this intellectual virtue we know God in a different way, namely through natural reason. Both wisdom and the theological virtues consider God, but the difference is in the way in which God is considered. In contrast to these virtues, the moral virtue of religion involves God although it is not about God in the way that wisdom or the theological virtues are.[27] Religion has God as its end but the worship as its proper object. The distinction between the theological virtues and the other virtues consequently is not a distinction between virtues that recognize God and those that do not, but instead it involves the order that a Christian has to God as directly known, relied on, and loved in a way that exceeds nature.

The three theological virtues have distinct formal objects even though they have God at least as their primary material object.[28] It is not unusual for distinct habits or powers to have the same material object. For instance,

---

[24] See, for instance, John Duns Scotus, *Ord.* 3, d. 26, q. un., n. 102, in his *Opera Omnia* (Vatican City: Typis Vaticanis, 1950–), vol. 10, 31–32; William of Ockham, *Quaestiones Variae*, q. 7, art. 2, in his *Opera Theologica*, 10 vols., ed. G. Gál et al. (St. Bonaventure, NY: 1967–1986), vol. 8, 338. For other texts on acquired faith, see Thomas M. Osborne Jr., "Spanish Thomists on the Need for Interior Grace in Acts of Faith," in *Beyond Dordt and De Auxiliis: The Dynamics of Protestant and Catholic Soteriology in the Sixteenth and Seventeenth Centuries*, ed. Jordan Ballor, Matthew Gaetano, and David Sytsma (Brill: Leiden, 2019), 67–70.

[25] "prout nostrae rationis cognitionem excedit." Thomas, *S.T.*, I-II, q. 62, art. 2, resp.

[26] Thomas, *S.T.*, I-II, q. 62, art. 2, ad 2.

[27] Thomas, *DVC*, art. 12, ad 11 (Marietti, 745).

[28] Thomas, *DVC*, art. 12, resp. et ad 10 (Marietti, 744, 745); *DVSpe*, q. 1, art. 1 (Marietti, 804–805).

the same ball can be the object of different senses such as sight and touch. But each of the senses approaches the material object under a different formality, such as color or heat. Similarly, although faith, like the other theological virtues, has God as its material object, the formal object of faith is God as the first truth.[29] Moreover, the material object of faith includes not only truths about God but also secondary truths that are in some way about God. The formal object of faith indicates the mean by which the truths are believed. The believer assents to these truths because they have been revealed by God. Since these truths are unknown to the believer's unaided reason and only enigmatically seen in this life, this assent is not forced by the evidence of the objects but instead is commanded by an act of the will.[30] The believer is moved by grace to see the truths in the light of faith and to assent to them with a certitude that is not based on the believer's own natural knowledge. This faith provides the believer with an inchoate grasp of that which is seen in the beatific vision and which is necessary for its attainment.

Hope is a confidence or trust in God's provision of the means necessary to attain the beatific vision.[31] Like faith, hope necessarily results from sanctifying grace in this life and also can be possessed by those who lack such grace. Thomas sharply distinguishes this virtue of hope from the passion of hope whereby one has confidence in attaining any difficult good or a kind of magnanimity or optimism whereby the naturally virtuous person overcomes difficulties. The theological virtue of hope is essentially supernatural because it is about the beatific vision. Moreover, it depends on another supernatural virtue, namely the theological virtue of faith. Later scholastics often emphasized the way in which hope involved a love of beatitude for one's own sake.[32] But Thomas thinks that hope is primarily about relying on God's help. Someone who trusts in herself and not in God is guilty of the sin against hope that is presumption. Someone who doubts her ability to attain the beatific vision is guilty of the sin of despair,

---

[29] In addition to the texts cited in the previous note, see Thomas, *S.T.*, II-II, q. 1, art. 1; q. 2, art. 2; *In Sent.*, lib. 3, d. 24, art. 1, sol. 1 (Mandonnet-Moos, 3, 762); *DV*, q. 14, art. 8, resp. (Leonine, 22.2, 459–460).

[30] Thomas, *S.T.*, II-II, q. 6, art. 1; *DV*, q. 18, art. 1 (Leonine, 22.2, 435–439).

[31] Thomas, *S.T.*, II-II, q. 17, art. 1; *In Sent.*, lib. 3, d. 26, q. 2, art. 1 (Mandonnet-Moos, 3, 831–833); *DVSpe*, art. 1 (ed. Mandonnet, vol. 2, 803–806). For an introduction to Thomas' teaching on hope, see Romanus Cessario, "The Theological Virtue of Hope (IIa IIae, qq. 17–22)," in *The Ethics of Aquinas*, ed. Stephen J. Pope (Washington, DC: Georgetown University Press, 2002), 232–243.

[32] P. de Letter, "Hope and Charity in St. Thomas," *The Thomist* 13 (1950): 204–324, 325–352; Mary Michael Glenn, "A Comparison of the Thomistic and Scotistic Concepts of Hope," *The Thomist* 20 (1957): 27–74; Thomas M. Osborne, Jr., "Thomas, Scotus, and Ockham on the Object of Hope," *Recherches de Théologie et Philosophie Médiévales* 87 (2020): 1–26.

which is also against hope. The virtue of hope is that by which someone is able to rely on God's help to attain the supernatural end, which is naturally impossible to him.

Charity is the virtue by which God is loved primarily for his own sake as the source of supernatural goods, and one's neighbor is loved for God's sake.[33] One loves one's neighbor's supernatural good because both are called to the same supernatural common good, which is the direct vision of God. One loves one's own salvation through charity in a way that is subordinated to his love for God. Charity differs from faith in that it is concerned with God's supernatural goodness rather than his truth, and consequently its act belongs to the will rather than to the intellect. Charity differs from hope in that it is not about our attainment of God's goodness but instead directly about God's goodness.

Grace and consequently the theological virtues make God present in a special way in their subjects.[34] God is present everywhere insofar as all creatures are under his power, everything is known to him, and he sustains everything in being. But he is present in intellectual creatures as an object of the intellect and will. For instance, he is present through faith to the believer's intellect and he is present through love to the believer's will. This special presence exceeds the natural order and the abilities of the unaided human. It results from the way in which through grace humans are lifted to a higher order of being and are consequently able to act in a higher way.

Since these three theological virtues are essentially supernatural, they must be efficiently caused by God and not by the repetition of merely human acts. In particular, charity is the principal virtue that makes an agent and his acts good in the supernatural order.[35] It directly results from that sanctifying grace by which the agent is made pleasing to God. Thomas, like his other contemporaries, rejects Peter Lombard's opinion that the virtue of charity is really the uncreated Holy Ghost and instead states that it is a created habit that God causes in the soul through grace.[36] He writes in his *Commentary on the Sentences*:

> [T]he whole goodness of the soul itself is from charity ... But it is sure that the soul through charity does not have less of goodness in the being of grace than [it has] through acquired virtue in political being. But political virtue

[33] Thomas, *S.T.*, II-II, q. 25, art. 1, 12; *In Sent.*, lib. 3, d. 27, q. 2, art. 4, sol. 1 (Mandonnet-Moos, 3, 885–886); *DVCarit.*, art. 4 (Marietti, 762–765).
[34] Thomas, *S.T.*, I, q. 8, art. 3; q. 43, art. 3.
[35] Thomas, *S.T.*, I-II, q. 114, art. 4.
[36] Thomas, *S.T.*, II-II, q. 23, art. 2; *In Sent.*, lib. 1, d. 17, q. 1, art. 1 (Mandonnet-Moos, 1, 391–397); *DVCarit.*, art. 1 (Marietti, 753–757).

does two things, since it makes the one having it good, and it renders his work good. More powerfully therefore charity does this. But it would be able to do none of these, if it were not a created habit ... Therefore, just as it cannot be understood that a wall is white without inhering whiteness; so it cannot be understood that a soul is good in gratuitous being without charity and grace informing it.[37]

Being in the supernatural order requires some sort of inherent form in the same way that being in the natural order requires an accidental or substantial form, such as that by which a surface is white through the form of whiteness. The virtue of charity must be both created and supernatural. It is created because of the way in which it enables the agent to perform supernaturally good acts that make him pleasing to God. It is supernatural primarily by its object and derivatively by its efficient cause.

In the *Summa Contra Gentiles*, III.151–153, Thomas provides a detailed and unified account of grace and these virtues. This discussion immediately follows an account of God's help to humans in general and in particular that sanctifying grace (*gratia gratum faciens*) by which the Christian is made pleasing to God. One argument in particular emphasizes the way in which grace is like a new nature that orders humans to a higher end.[38] Thomas notes that sanctifying grace is a created form that inheres in the soul's essence and orders him properly to the ultimate end. The human is moved to God as a supernatural end through this form of grace in a way similar to how a stone is moved downward though the form of gravity. This supernatural motion that comes from sanctifying grace is the love of charity, which is based on the likeness to God that grace causes.

Thomas's other arguments similarly emphasize the way in which grace causes love through creating a new kind of likeness to or union with God.[39] Such grace results from God's special love for a human and consequently leads to the human agent's returning the love of charity back to God. Moreover, through this grace a human is united to God as a supernatural end in the way that humans are united with each other in the common

---

[37] "tota bonitas ipsius animae est ex caritate ... Constat autem quod per caritatem anima non habet minus de bonitate in esse gratiae, quam per virtutem acquisitam in esse politico. Virtus autem politica duo facit: quia facit bonum habentem, et opus ejus bonum reddit. Multo fortius igitur hoc facit caritas. Neutrum autem horum effici poterit, nisi caritas sit habitus creatus ... Sicut igitur non potest intelligi quod paries sit albus sine albedine inhaerente; ita non potest intelligi quod anima sit bona in esse gratuito sine caritate et gratia informante ipsam." Thomas, *In Sent.*, lib. 1, d. 17, q. 1, art. 1 (Moos-Mandonnet, vol. 1, 393).
[38] Thomas, *SCG* 3, cap. 151 (ed. Leonina Manualis, 410).
[39] Thomas, *SCG* 3, cap. 151 (ed. Leonina Manualis, 409–410).

good of the political community. Such union presupposes a conformity of wills that are directed to a shared end. Since such a conformity of wills consists in love, sanctifying grace leads to the conformity of the human will with the divine will in sharing the supernatural end.

Although faith is a necessary condition for sanctifying grace, faith can exist without such grace. Nevertheless, faith on account of its supernatural object requires the assistance of grace in some way. Thomas's view on the need for God's grace for acts of faith follows from his understanding of faith's supernatural object and the limitations of human reason. Since the object of faith is obscure, unaided natural reason cannot assent to the articles of faith with the same certitude as it assents to truths that are known through science and understanding. Nevertheless, the certitude of faith exceeds that of the intellectual virtues. Moreover, faith is infallible in the sense that it never elicits an act that is formally against faith. Natural reason by itself is incapable of such infallibility. Consequently, the act of faith itself is caused by a will that is efficiently moved by God. Such faith is the beginning of justification. Even though such reasoning shows that human powers on their own are insufficient to elicit the acts of the theological virtues, Thomas also holds this position because it is Scriptural and necessary to avoid the heresy that the beginning of faith (*initium fidei*) can come from human beings. Thomas himself describes this heresy as "Pelagian," and later writers sometimes call it Semi-Pelagian.[40] This heresy differs from the Pelagian heresy as normally understood in that it admits that grace is necessary for salvation. But it holds that the beginning of justification lies in the individual's own power and in particular in the individual's choice to accept faith. According to this view, God gives the same grace to someone who accepts or rejects faith, and the decision to make an act of faith and to accept the grace is primarily and ultimately only in the believer's power. Thomas was unusual in his time for his adherence to and knowledge of Augustine's anti-Pelagian writings, and in particular Augustine's account of faith.[41]

When he wishes to argue for the thesis that only God can cause faith, Thomas frequently emphasizes the superiority of the ultimate end to

[40] Thomas, *SCG 3*, cap. 152 (ed. Leonina Manualis, 411). For controversies over the *initium fidei* and the reception of the Second Council of Orange, see Alister McGrath, *Iustitia Dei: A History of the Christian Doctrine of Justification*, 2nd ed. (Cambridge: Cambridge University Press, 1998), 72–78. For the origin of the term, see Irena Backus and Aza Goudriaan, "'Semipelagianism': The Origins of the Term and Its Passage into the History of Heresy," *Journal of Ecclesiastical History* 65 (2014): 25–46.
[41] Henri Bouillard, *Conversion et grâce chez S. Thomas d'Aquin* (Aubier: Montaigne, 1944), 92–122.

the natural order.[42] For instance, in one argument he compares the movement of the human to her ultimate end with the heating of a stick through fire or the teaching of a student. Fire is the efficient cause of a wood's burning. At first the fire is external to the wood. But the heat causes the wood itself to be on fire and to heat. The subject that undergoes the change must have an external cause that possesses the form that the subject begins to possess. Similarly, a teacher causes learning in a student by introducing her to concepts that she does not understand. After learning them the student herself has this knowledge, but it must exist in a prior way in the external cause, which is the teacher. The acquisition of the knowledge is gradual. With respect to faith, the final term of the change is the possession of the beatific vision. Even in this life God must give us some knowledge in order to attain this vision. But such knowledge is inchoate and incomplete. Consequently, in this life we need to have from God the inchoate knowledge of God by faith in order to arrive in the next life at the complete knowledge of God in the beatific vision.

In this same text Thomas argues further that God must cause faith by appealing to the way in which the elevation of human nature requires knowledge that can be gained only through revelation. For instance, humans reach their ends through voluntary action, which requires intellectual knowledge of the end. Consequently, in order for humans to reach the ultimate end, they must know it in some way in this life. But humans without God's special assistance cannot know this end in this life. Therefore, God provides humans the knowledge of faith. Thomas similarly notes that humans have a mode of knowing that is between that of angels, who know immaterial objects, and brute animals, who know only sense objects and sensible intentions. Humans have a mode of knowing that is properly about the natures of material bodies. But the ultimate end of directly knowing God exceeds this properly human mode. Therefore, it must be caused supernaturally.

These arguments for the necessity of revelation might seem to establish only that some revelation is necessary, and not that God must cause a special habit in the Christian, namely the theological virtue of faith. Assuming that the truths are revealed, why does someone need God's special help to accept these truths? In the *Summa Contra Gentiles* Thomas does not as clearly develop his points of the insufficiency of the unaided will to assent to these truths as he does in some other texts, such as the

[42] Thomas, *SCG* 3, cap. 152 (ed. Leonina Manualis, 410).

Summa Theologiae. In the *Secunda Secundae* of this latter work Thomas distinguishes between the supernatural revelation and the supernatural assistance in the assent.[43] With respect to revelation, two individuals might hear the same preaching of supernatural truths and they can also observe the same miracles. But one will believe and another will not, even though they both have sufficient reasons to believe on account of the articles and miracles. The difference is in the will. The one who believes assents to the belief because she has chosen to do so, and her choice is ultimately explained by God's efficient causality. The obscurity of the object explains why the will must be involved. The very nature of faith itself, with its supernatural object, certitude, and inability to err at least formally, indicates why the will needs assistance to make the act. Only God's special help explains the possibility of such an act.

In the *Summa Contra Gentiles,* Thomas's main arguments for the thesis that God causes hope are ultimately based on his account of how through charity and sanctifying grace someone is made a friend of God.[44] In general, friendship involves a mutual goodwill between the friends and consequently a reliance on a friend for necessary help. By charity one loves God for God's own sake while knowing that God has first loved the created lover. Since a person with charity is a friend of God, she expects help from him. A second argument is similarly based on friendship. Thomas notes that generally lovers desire to be united with those whom they love. Although union with God is impossible for humans who are unaided by grace, through faith the believer knows about such union with God. Since she knows that this union is possible, she can desire such union through charity. But this union can be attained only with God's help. The very desire for such union with God presupposes a confidence that the union is possible through God's help. Hope is primarily this confidence in God's help. The friendship with God that is possessed by someone who has charity is unknown to those who lack revelation and unavailable to those who lack grace.

Hope depends on faith and is necessary for charity. Both in the *Summa Contra Gentiles* and in his other writings, Thomas emphasizes that hope in attaining the supernatural end is a necessary condition for striving towards this end. This order follows from a recognition through faith that

---

[43] Thomas, *S.T.,* II-II, q. 6, art. 1; q. 2, art. 9, ad 3. See Thomas M. Osborne Jr., "Natural Reason and Supernatural Faith," in *Aquinas's Summa Theologiae: A Critical Guide,* ed. Jeffrey Hause (Cambridge: Cambridge University Press, 2018), 198–203.
[44] Thomas, *SCG* 3, cap. 153 (ed. Leonina Manualis, 411).

God has directed humans to the beatific vision and also that through his providence God has provided the necessary means by which this end can be attained.

In his other writings, Thomas more clearly explains that the three theological virtues are ordered among themselves in two distinct ways, namely according to their generation and to their perfection.[45] According to generation, faith is prior to hope because hope depends on the prior recognition that heaven is possible. Moreover, faith can exist without hope in someone who despairs. Similarly, hope is prior in generation to charity. The love for God as the source of supernatural goods, which is charity, depends on the belief that these goods can be obtained through his help. Hope that lacks charity requires some love for this end, but this love is specifically distinct from charity.

Even though there is an order of generation among the theological virtues, Thomas states that they are ordinarily received at the same time as habits. This order of generation does not need to be an order of generation in time. Presumably Thomas has in mind baptized infants or adults who place no obstacles to charity when they are baptized. Infants who are baptized receive the three theological virtues along with sanctifying grace even though they cannot exercise the virtues until later. Adults receive these virtues in a similar way unless they have some continued attachment to mortal sin, which blocks charity but not faith.[46] Someone who intends to persist in mortal sin such as adultery or theft can be validly baptized, but charity cannot exist in such a person.[47] She can receive charity once she repents, and she does not need to be baptized again. Consequently, it is possible but not necessary for faith and even hope to be temporally prior to charity.

The theological virtues are related quite differently according to the order of perfection, according to which charity is prior to the other virtues. Thomas repeats the common teaching that charity is "the mother and root of all of the virtues."[48] If charity is posterior in generation to faith and charity, how can it be their root? Thomas explains that charity gives life to the other two theological virtues. Although faith and hope can exist without charity, they are in a way dead, since they do not make

---

[45] The major passages are Thomas, *S.T.*, I-II, q. 62, art. 3; *DVSpe*, art. 3 (Marietti, 807–809); *In Sent.*, lib. 3, d. 23, q. 2, art. 5 (Mandonnet-Moos, 3, 738–740).

[46] Thomas, *S.T.*, II-II, q. 6, art. 2, ad 3.

[47] Thomas, *S.T.*, III, q. 68, art. 4; art. 8, ad 4.

[48] "mater omnium virtutum et radix." Thomas, *S.T.*, I-II, q. 62, art. 4, resp. Thomas in the ad 1 and many other texts cites in this context Eph 3:17: "in caritate radicati et fundati."

the agent good. Without charity they cannot produce meritorious acts that are ordered to eternal life. Consequently, without the virtue of charity they lack the full character of virtue, insofar as virtue makes both the agent and the act good.[49] We might expect the order of perfection to be reverse to the order of generation, so that hope is prior to faith in perfection even though it is posterior to faith in generation. But Thomas does not explicitly address the issue. According to Thomas, the virtue of hope is closer to the ultimate end than faith is, and can help it to last longer, even if it is not clearly more perfect than faith in the way that charity is.[50]

Acquired and Infused Virtue

In the *Nicomachean Ethics*, Aristotle has discussed the causation of moral virtue in Book II. He turns to the causes of virtue immediately after including virtue in the definition of happiness at the end of Book I. In this account he focuses on moral rather than on intellectual virtue. The order of the discussion differs in the *Summa Theologiae*, in which Thomas discusses the causation of habits in general before considering any of the virtues. Nevertheless, in this work he returns to the causation of virtue in q. 63. After introducing the theological virtues, he must revisit how habits can be caused. The theological virtues are not caused in the same way that the previously discussed habits are. The introduction of a class of virtues that must be caused by God allows Thomas to introduce a category of virtue that was not discussed by Aristotle, namely infused virtues, which include not only the theological virtues but also infused moral virtues. Thomas introduces a new distinction within the moral virtues that requires a difference between their possible efficient causes.

In both the *Summa Theologiae* and in the *De Virtutibus in Communi*, Thomas applies the distinction between nature and grace to the causation of the virtues and not only to their objects.[51] He uses philosophy in

---

[49] Thomas, *S. T.*, I-II, q. 65, art. 4; II-II, q. 3, art. 5; q. 23, art. 7, ad 1.
[50] Thomas, *S. T.*, II-II, q. 4, art. 7, ad 2; *In Sent.*, lib. 3, d. 23, q. 2, art. 5, ad 4 (Mandonnet-Moos, 3, 740).
[51] Thomas, *S. T.*, I-II, q. 63, art. 1; *DVC*, art. 8 (Marietti, 725–729). See also Thomas, *In Sent.*, lib. 1, d. 17, q. 1, art. 3 (Mandonnet-Moos, 1, 399–401); 3 Sent, d. 33, q. 1, art. 2, sol. 2–3 (Mandonnet-Moos, 1028–1030). For a translation of and introduction to Thomas, *S. T.*, I-II, q. 53, art. 1–2, see Budziszewski, *Commentary on Aquinas's Virtue Ethics*, 80–111. A defense of the need for infused virtue can be found in Jeffrey Hause, "Aquinas on the Function of Moral Virtue," *American Catholic Philosophical Quarterly* 81 (2007): 1–20. For the radical difference between infused and acquired moral virtues, see Andrew Pinsent, *The Second-Person Perspective in Aquinas's Ethics: Virtues and Gifts* (New York: Routledge, 2012), 12–23.

order to explain the different ways in which forms are brought about in subjects that had lacked them.[52] Thomas argues that the virtues that are recognized by philosophers are caused through human acts. In the ordinary order, God causes them through the operations of the secondary cause, namely the agent. Some virtues are caused directly by God apart from such causality, but they were unknown to the non-Christian philosophers. In the *De Virtutibus in Communi*, Thomas ultimately defends his own view that some moral virtues are acquired through human acts by comparing Aristotle's account of causation to the views of other philosophers. In the *Summa Theologiae*, he merely mentions that according to Aristotle's account of causation, habits such as natural virtues are caused by the agents, whereas other virtues must be infused by God.

In the *De Virtutibus in Communi*, Thomas compares Aristotle's account of causation with the incorrect or incomplete views of Anaxagoras, Plato, and Avicenna.[53] He eventually argues that the virtues are no more innate than the effect of an efficient cause is innate. In order to argue for this point, he first explains why these philosophers failed to see the way in which efficient causes bring about their effects. According to Thomas, Anaxagoras holds the view that the agent merely makes manifest the forms that were previously hidden. For example, on Anaxagoras's account, a carpenter by making a chair would be drawing out the form that existed but was hidden in the wood. Others think that the forms are entirely external, whether in the agent intellect (according to Avicenna) or as separately existing ideas (Plato). According to Thomas, both Plato and Avicenna are reluctant to assign efficient causality to ordinary terrestrial agents.[54] Avicenna attributed such causality in large part to the separate substance that is connected with the moon, which is the agent intellect. He thought that this separate substance agent intellect not only infused intelligible species into human intellects but also that it supplied the forms that were produced in sublunary change. On this account, a chair is a chair because the carpenter prepares the wood and the agent intellect introduces the form. The agent intellect and not the carpenter would be the cause of the form. On Plato's account, the material agent plays even less of a role. Aristotle in contrast is of the view that the agent reduces the potency in

[52] He similarly discusses intellectual virtue in *DV*, q. 11, art. 1 (Leonine, 22.2, 347–354)
[53] Thomas, *DVC*, art. 8, resp. (Marietti, 727).
[54] For Avicenna's own view, see Jon McGinnis, *Avicenna* (Oxford: Oxford University Press, 2010), 187–195; Kara Richardson, "Avicenna and Aquinas on Form and Generation," in *The Arabic, Hebrew and Latin Reception of Avicenna's Metaphysics*, ed. Dag Hasse and Amos Bertolacci (Berlin and Boston: Walter de Gruyter, 2011), 251–274.

the matter to act. For instance, a carpenter might make wood, which is only potentially a chair, actually into a chair.

According to Thomas, the differences between different positions on the causation of virtue reflect these different accounts of efficient causality. Both Platonists and Avicenna think that the agent plays little role in the causation of virtue. The Platonists hold that sciences and moral virtues exist within the agent's soul in such a way that learning and good acts merely remove impediments to them. These impediments are caused by the union of the soul with the body. Similarly, Avicenna holds that the sciences and virtues are caused entirely extrinsically by the agent intellect.

According to Thomas, Aristotle's account of the causation of virtue is superior to the others in the same way that his account of efficient causality in general is. Virtues are potentially in their subjects in the way that forms are potentially in the matter that receives them. On Aristotle's account, the agent who studies or acts well acquires the sciences and virtues through his own action. Virtues are innate and natural but only in an inchoate way.[55] The sciences are inchoate because humans by nature only know certain principles through the understanding. Similarly, the moral virtues are inchoate because humans by having bodies or even particularly bodily characteristics are only disposed in a particular way to act. For instance, by having a certain balance of humors one might be more inclined to study, or to act gently, or to be brave. The sciences and virtues are acquired in their perfection only when such acts lead to the full acquisition of the habit by which the agent can understand a demonstration or act gently or bravely in the right way and for the right reason.

Even though Thomas establishes that the sciences and some virtues preexist in us only in an inchoate way, his argument does not exclude the position that some virtue might be entirely extrinsic in the way that Avicenna suggested. However, he denies that pagan philosophers or Avicenna knew about such virtue. According to Thomas, the theological virtues are the kinds of virtues that must be caused directly by God. The existence of such virtues is known only through revelation and not through unaided human reason.

One distinction between the efficient causes of the virtues corresponds to the distinction based on whether the virtues are regulated by human reason or directly by divine law.[56] All virtues are measured by divine law

---

[55] For Thomas's account of the preexistence of such virtue, see Dominic Farrell, *The Ends of the Moral Virtues and the First Principles of Practical Reason in Thomas Aquinas* (Rome: Gregorian and Biblical Press, 2012), 131–134.

[56] Thomas, *S. T.*, I-II, q. 63, art. 2.

insofar as it is superior to human reason and includes the objects of human reason. Nevertheless, some virtues are ordered to the good that is determined by a rule that is known or knowable by human reason apart from revelation. Such virtues might be miraculously caused by God, but under normal conditions they can proceed from human reason and those intrinsic principles that are ordered by reason.[57] They come from principles that preexist in us.[58] In contrast, virtues that are concerned with the good insofar as it is regulated by the divine law, such as the theological virtues, must be caused directly by God. Human reason and subject human powers are insufficient for the production of the relevant acts and virtues. The difference between these virtues is not simply the fact that one is produced by God apart from secondary causes and the other is produced through secondary causes. The infused virtues cannot be caused through secondary causes because of what they are. The essence of such virtue is due to its rule and end.

The different rules of acquired and infused virtue are ordered in such a way that the lower are included in the higher. As a political animal, humans are guided by a rule in relation to others.[59] This rule itself is subordinate to the general order of reason that measures human actions and passions. But this order of reason itself is subordinated to the divine rule, which governs actions in a way that exceeds reason. Consequently, acts that are against one's neighbor are also against the rule of reason with respect to one's own good and against God. Similarly, acts against one's own good are by the fact directly against God. But sins that are directly against God are not so directly against one's neighbor or against natural reason. Thomas's point is not that sins against God are harmless with respect to the merely political or natural order. The issue is not one of whether they have bad effects but of how they are specified. He argues that sins against God are specifically distinct insofar as they take their species from something higher and more important than the political and even natural order.

All sin violates the rule of reason, even though there is a special way in which sins against one's own self are against reason. The basic precepts of the moral law, namely the natural law, are not isolated from the other precepts. Human law and divine law determine the natural law. For instance,

---

[57] Thomas, *S.T.*, I-II, q. 63, art. 4, ad 3; *DVC*, art. 10, ad 7 (Marietti, 737).
[58] Thomas, *S.T.*, I-II, q. 63, art. 2, ad 3.
[59] Thomas, *S.T.*, I-II, q. 72, art. 4. See also q. 63, art. 2; *In Sent.*, lib. 2, d. 42, art. 2, sol. 2 et ad 1–4 (Mandonnet-Moos, 2, 1074–1075); *DM*, q. 16, art. 2, resp. (Leonine, 23, 289).

it is a precept of the natural law to worship God.[60] But the Mosaic Law contained many determinations of how God was to be worshiped. Those who sinned against the Mosaic Law also violated the natural law by doing so. This revealed and divine law is not contrary to the basic precepts of natural reason, but it determines the way in which the precept of natural reason could be carried out and adds to it.

Thomas's predecessors and contemporaries had disagreed sharply over the way in which God might be necessary for the causation of the cardinal virtues. Although previous thinkers had disagreed to some extent over the proper understanding of the relationship between cardinal, political, and Catholic or theological virtue, until the 1250s there seems to have been no clear discussion of the distinction between infused and acquired moral virtues.[61] Bonaventure was among the first to distinguish between political cardinal virtues that are given by God and the same virtues that arise from human acts.[62] He might be interpreted as holding that this distinction is between different considerations of the same kind of virtue. Nevertheless, Bonaventure's account of their qualities seems to indicate a difference between kinds of virtue. Whereas the political cardinal virtues make an act easier to perform, the infused cardinal virtues elevate the powers and make the acts supernatural. Grace can help with the political virtues, but they ultimately are rooted in nature and perfected through works.

Thomas explains more clearly than Bonaventure does why God must be the efficient cause of not only the theological virtues but also a set of moral virtues that differ from others insofar as they are proportionate to the supernatural end.[63] According to Thomas, these moral virtues are infused by God along with charity; they are distinct from the other moral virtues, which are acquired through acts. Although they are not caused by acts, these infused moral virtues produce acts that are ordered to the supernatural end. They do not have this supernatural end directly as their object. Their order to this end depends on the theological virtues, which are directly about this end.

The infused moral virtues are related to the theological virtues in the way that the moral and intellectual virtues are ordered to the principles

---

[60] Thomas, S. T., I-II, q. 99, art. 3, ad 2. For human law, see Thomas, S. T., I-II, q. 95, art. 2.
[61] Lottin, PM, 459. For difficulties in Bonaventure and Albert, see William Mattison, "Thomas' Categorizations of Virtue: Historical Background and Contemporary Significance," The Thomist 74 (2010), 210–212. For the Dominican context of Thomas's account, see John Inglis, "Aquinas's Replication of the Acquired Moral Virtues," Journal of Religious Ethics 27 (1999): 3–27.
[62] Bonaventure, In Sent., lib. 3, d. 23, art. un., q. 5, resp. (vol. 3, 722–723).
[63] Thomas, S. T., q. 63, art. 3; DVC, art. 10 (Marietti, 733–738).

of natural virtue. In both cases the principles are in a way nobler than the virtues. For instance, the natural understanding of the principles of science can be described as superior to the knowledge of conclusions, and the rectitude of reason to the rectitude of the appetite that participates in reason. In the supernatural order, the theological virtues order us immediately to God in himself, although in an inchoate way. The infused moral virtues perfect us with respect to other acts insofar as they are ordered to God himself. For example, infused fortitude might cause a courageous act by which someone sacrifices life for the Catholic faith, or infused temperance might cause fasting or celibacy for the sake of heaven.

It might seem implausible that everyone with theological virtues possess infused moral virtues. Does a coward become brave after repenting and confessing, or does an intemperate person upon doing so immediately learn to avoid excess in food and drink? Even though Thomas clearly states that the infused moral virtues are caused along with the infusion of sanctifying grace in the soul and the theological virtue, he denies that the vicious person who receives baptism with good dispositions is entirely the same as one who is baptized without these vices or that the vicious sinner who makes a good confession is the same as the virtuous person who has committed mortal sin. So long as the once vicious sinner has sanctifying grace she will not sin mortally. Her vice becomes inactive. Consequently, such qualities are no longer fully habits. Nevertheless, insofar as they remain as dispositions, they can affect the agent's conduct.[64]

In his discussion of the causes of virtue, Thomas distinguishes between virtues that are acquired through human acts and those that must be directly infused by God. This distinction results from the nature of the virtues themselves. The infused virtues are either theological or moral. All theological virtues are infused, and they are entirely about God. They establish an order to God that exceeds mere human abilities. The infused moral virtues are not directly about God. They are distinct from the acquired moral virtues because of the way in which they have a higher rule than the acquired do and the way in which their acts have God as their supernatural end. Nevertheless, they share the same matter that the acquired virtues do. For instance, both infused and acquired temperance are about bodily pleasure.

---

[64] Michael Sherwin, "Infused Virtue and the Effects of Acquired Vice: A Test Case for the Thomistic Theory of the Infused Cardinal Virtues," *The Thomist* 69 (2005): 29–52; Bonnie Kent, "Losable Virtue: Aquinas on Character and Will," in *Aquinas and the Nicomachean Ethics*, ed. Tobias Hoffmann, Jörn Müller, and Matthias Perkams (Cambridge: Cambridge University Press, 2013), 91–109.

The difference between infused and acquired virtue can be seen more clearly when we consider the concrete ways in which they are gained and lost. For instance, infused temperance and acquired temperance are both about bodily pleasure, but they are gained and lost in different ways. Whereas the infused virtues are gained immediately alongside charity, the acquired virtues are gained through repeated actions.[65] Consequently, once charity has been infused, the formerly intemperate person will possess the infused virtue of temperance until she sins mortally. Similarly, the formerly cowardly person will possess infused courage. They also lack the relevant vices, since vices, like virtues, are operative habits. If their vices continued to cause gravely vicious operations, then the agent would lose charity. Serious acts of intemperance or cowardice are mortally sinful.

Nevertheless, although such agents lack the vices, they do not immediately possess the acquired virtues. Under normal conditions it will be more difficult for a repentant fornicator to be temperate or for a repentant coward to be brave. The disposition to vicious acts remains in someone who had the vices. It is a disposition and not fully the habit because the agent does not commit mortal sins. Consequently, infused virtues such as infused temperance or infused fortitude cannot exist alongside their vicious counterparts, although they can and often do exist alongside the corresponding dispositions to evil acts. The penitent intemperate person is more likely to sin concerning bodily pleasure than someone who lacks the disposition to intemperance, just as the penitent coward is more likely to sin concerning dangers to his bodily life. But so long as such agents possess charity they are able to avoid them and do so.

Infused and acquired virtues differ not only with respect to their causation but also with respect to their diminution and loss. Sanctifying grace, the principle of the supernatural life, and the theological virtue of charity are lost through one mortal sin by which the agent directs himself away from God as a supernatural end. Such mortal sin corrupts the supernatural and even natural love of God over self. Since the infused moral virtues come from grace and charity, they too are lost through one mortal sin. Someone who sins mortally against faith or charity loses the infused moral virtues, including such virtues as temperance and fortitude. For instance, someone who denies an article of faith thereby loses his ability to risk his life through infused fortitude or to fast through infused temperance.

In contrast to the infused virtues, acquired virtues are corrupted only through repeated acts that are contrary to them. For example, the acquired

---

[65] Thomas, *S.T.*, I-II, q. 63, art. 2, ad 2; *DVC*, art. 10, ad 16 (Marietti, 737).

virtues of fortitude and temperance are lost only through repeated acts of cowardice and intemperance respectively. A temperate person who overeats once does not thereby entirely lose the virtue of temperance. We should not conclude from this fact that the acquired virtues are unaffected by the loss of charity and grace or that an acquired virtue is completely unaffected by the practice of repeated acts against another acquired virtue. The connection between the virtues will be discussed in the next chapter. The point here is simply that infused virtues are caused along with grace and charity and consequently are corrupted by their loss, whereas the acquired virtues are corrupted by acts that are contrary to the particular acquired virtue.

The Augustinian definition of virtue found in Peter Lombard includes the phrase "which God operates in us without us."[66] Since the efficient cause is part of this definition, Thomas uses it to argue that there is a specific difference between infused and acquired virtues. But the difference in efficient causes by itself is insufficient to establish the distinction, since God can directly cause both acquired and infused virtue in the same way that God can cause other natural effects.[67] For instance, if God miraculously restores someone to health, this health is specifically the same as the health that is naturally restored. Similarly, God can cause in someone an acquired virtue of temperance that is the same as the temperance that another achieves only through repeated temperate actions. Infused virtues are distinct from the acquired ones because they not only can but must be caused by God and not by their possessors. Although such miracles are unusual, acquired virtues can be miraculously infused.

The specific difference between the two virtues rests more on the divergence between their objects, which are determined by different rules and their ends.[68] The difference between the formal natures (*rationes*) and objects of acquired and infused virtues is based on the fact that the virtues follow different rules. For instance, acquired temperance follows the rule that preserves human health and reason, whereas by infused temperance the Christian "castigates his body and reduces it to servitude."[69] The matter is the same in that both virtues are concerned about bodily pleasure. But infused temperance regulates this pleasure according to revelation.

---

[66] Thomas, *S.T.*, q. 63, art. 4, sc.
[67] Thomas, *S.T.*, I-II, q. 63, art. 4, ad 3; *DVC*, art. 10, ad 7.
[68] See also Thomas, *In Sent.*, lib. 3, d. 33, q. 1, art. 2, sol. 4 (Mandonnet-Moos, 3, 1031); *DVCard.*, art. 4, resp. (Marietti, 826–827).
[69] "castiget corpus suum et in servitutem redigat." 1 Cor 9:27, cited in Thomas, *S.T.*, I-II, q. 63, art. 4, resp.

This distinction between the formal rules of acquired and moral virtues helps to explain the different ways in which these virtues regulate the passions.[70] By the very acquisition and possession of the virtue, a person with acquired virtue has more moderate passions than someone who lacks the virtue. The passions themselves become more reasonable. In contrast, infused virtue is to some extent compatible with unruly passions. For example, infused temperance subjugates and castigates even unruly passion to a higher rule than that which is known through natural reason. A person who receives the infused virtue of temperance without the acquired will be able to subdue her unruly passions, but she will still feel them. The infused virtues are an ability to act in accordance with this higher rule, but they do not cause a miraculous transformation in the emotions of those who possess them. Their acts need not be accompanied by some sort of sensibly perceived pleasure.

Acquired and infused virtues also differ with respect to their ends. Most obviously they differ insofar as acquired virtues order the agent with respect to human affairs, whereas the infused virtues order the agent to the city of God. This difference in the end does not specify the acts of the different virtues, but it does account for the differences in the objects that do specify them.[71] For instance, a person with acquired temperance follows the rule of human reason and consequently castigates and subjugates his body less than someone with infused temperance does, since the latter is concerned with ordering bodily pleasure to beatitude. The supernatural end in some cases requires a temperance with a distinct rule and object. Thomas connects this difference between acquired and infused virtue to the distinction between being a citizen of an earthly city and St. Paul's description of Christians as "citizens of the saints and members of the household of God."[72] Thomas had previously used the example of miraculously caused health and naturally caused health to indicate how different natural effects are not distinguished by their causes. In this context he uses the example of health to show that specific differences can result from ends. For instance, human health and equine health are distinct species of health because they are ordered to different ends, namely human nature and equine nature. Similarly, acquired virtue and infused virtue are distinct species of virtues because they are ordered to distinct ends, namely human affairs and the heavenly city.

---

[70] Thomas, *S.T.*, III, q. 69, art. 5, ad 3; *DVC*, art. 10, ad 14–15 (Marietti, 737).
[71] Thomas, *DVC*, art. 10, ad 8, 10 (Marietti, 737–737).
[72] "cives sanctorum et domestici Dei." Eph 2:19, cited in Thomas, *S.T.*, I-II, q. 63, art. 4, resp. See also Thomas, *DVC*, art. 9, resp. (Marietti, 731); *DVCarit.*, art. 2, resp. (Marietti, 758).

Although the distinct end requires that there be a distinct rule and formal object, and even that there be distinct species of acts, Thomas is unclear about whether these different virtues might be engaged in an act that is materially the same. For instance, it might be possible for someone to resist a fourth beer on account of a rule that belongs to acquired temperance and another distinct rule that belongs to infused temperance. There might be two distinct formal acts.[73] It seems to me that more likely the acquired act is in some way virtually contained or ordered by the infused.[74] Thomas himself never addresses the issue at length.

Some scholars have suggested that since acquired virtues and infused virtues are specifically different, they cannot be present in the same agent.[75] On such a reading, acts of acquired virtue could not be referred by charity to the ultimate end. However, in many texts, Thomas states that acts of the acquired virtues can be directed to the ultimate end by charity.[76] Moreover, in two places Thomas explicitly states that the two kinds of virtue coexist.[77] First, in the *De Virtutibus in Communi*, art. 10, he states:

> [S]ince no merit is without charity, an act of acquired virtue cannot be meritorious without charity. However, the other virtues are infused along with charity: whence the act of acquired virtue can only be meritorious by

---

[73] Renée Mirkes, "Aquinas's Doctrine of Moral Virtue and Its Significance for Theories of Facility," *The Thomist* 61 (1997): 189–218.

[74] For various accounts of how they might be involved, see especially Robert Florent Coerver, *The Quality of Facility in the Moral Virtues* (Washington, DC: The Catholic University of America Press, 1946); John Harvey, "The Nature of the Infused Moral Virtues," *Catholic Theological Society of America Proceedings* 10 (1955): 193–212; Gabriel Bullet, *Vertus morales infuses et vertus morales acquises selon Saint Thomas d'Aquin* (Fribourg: Éditions Universitaires, 1958), 122–163; Renée Mirkes, "Aquinas on the Unity of Perfect Moral Virtue," *American Catholic Philosophical Quarterly* 71 (1998): 589–605; Inglis, "Aquinas's Replication of the Acquired Moral Virtues", 18–22; W. Scott Cleveland and Brandon Dahm, "The Virtual Presence of Acquired Virtues in the Christian," *American Catholic Philosophical Quarterly* 93 (2019): 75–100.

[75] William Mattison, "Can Christians Possess the Acquired Cardinal Virtues?," *Theological Studies* 72 (2011), 558–585; Angela McKay Knobel, "Two Theories of Christian Virtue," *American Catholic Philosophical Quarterly* 84 (2010): 599–618; "Can the Infused and Acquired Virtues Coexist in the Christian Life?," *Studies in Christian Ethics* 23/4 (2010): 381–396; Nicholas Austin, *Aquinas on Virtue: A Causal Reading* (Washington, DC: Georgetown University Press, 2017), 168–189. For an overview of some issues, see Thomas M. Osborne Jr., "What Is at Stake in the Question of whether Someone Can Possess the Natural Moral Virtues without Charity?," in *The Virtuous Life: Thomas Aquinas on the Theological Nature of Moral Virtues*, ed. Harm Goris and Henk Schoot (Leuven, Paris, and Bristol, CT: Peeters, 2017), 117–130.

[76] For Thomas's understanding of referral, see especially Thomas M. Osborne Jr., "Thomas Aquinas and John Duns Scotus on Individual Acts and the Ultimate End," in *Philosophy and Theology in the Long Middle Ages, A Tribute to Stephen F. Brown*, ed. Kent Emery Jr., Russell L. Friedman, and Andreas Speer (Leiden: Brill, 2011), 351–374; "The Threefold Referral of Acts to the Ultimate End in Thomas Aquinas and His Commentators," *Angelicum* 85 (2008), 715–736.

[77] These texts and their interpretation are discussed in Jacques Maritain, *Science et sagesse: Suivi d'eclaircissements sur la philosophie morale* (Paris: Labergerie, 1935), 346–358.

the mediation of infused virtue. For a virtue ordered to an inferior end does not make an act ordered to a superior end except by mediation of a superior virtue; just as that courage which is the virtue of a human insofar as he is a human, does not order its act to the political good, except by mediation of the fortitude which is the virtue of a human insofar as he is a citizen.[78]

This text is subject to different interpretations perhaps in part because it is unclear how Thomas understands the distinction between courage that perfects the individual and courage that perfects the citizen. The virtue that makes a citizen good does not seem to be simply "political virtue" insofar as such virtue is acquired moral virtue, nor is it a kind of purificatory virtue that prepares the soul for contemplation.

Thomas's remarks in the body of the article show that in this context he is using "political virtue" to indicate the virtue that is relative to a political regime. In this sense the temperance or fortitude of the ruler is specifically distinct from that of the good human being who is merely ruled.[79] Thomas writes:

> Virtue, as the Philosopher says, is what makes the one having it good, and renders his work good. Therefore, according to that good which is diversified in the human, it is even necessary that also virtue be diversified; just as it is plain that the good of the human insofar as he is a human is other than the [good of man] insofar as he is a citizen. And it is manifest that some operations can be fitting to a human insofar as he is a human, which are not fitting to him insofar as he is a citizen. And on account of this the Philosopher says in Book III of the *Politics*, that the virtue which makes a human good is other than the virtue that makes a good citizen.[80]

---

[78] "cum nullum meritum sit sine caritate, actus virtutis acquisitae, non potest esse meritorius sine caritate. Cum caritate autem simul infunduntur aliae virtutes; unde actus virtutis acquisitae non potest esse meritorius nisi mediante virtute infusa. Nam virtus ordinata in finem inferiorem non facit actus ordinatum ad finem superiorem, nisi mediante virtute superiori; sicut fortitudo, quae est virtus hominis qua homo, non ordinat actum suum ad bonum politicum, nisi mediante fortitudine quae est virtus hominis in quantum est civis." Thomas, *DVCard.*, art. 10, ad 4. For various readings, see Angela Knobel, "A Confusing Comparison: Interpreting *DVC* A. 10 AD 4," in *The Virtuous Life*, 97–115; David Decosimo, "More to Love: Ends, Ordering, and the Compatibility of Acquired and Infused Virtues," in *The Virtuous Life*, 47–72.

[79] Knobel, "Interpreting *DVC*," 106–111, seems to be at least partially correct in her assertion that the distinction between the fortitude of the good man and the good citizen is similar to the distinction between individual prudence and ruling prudence.

[80] "virtus, ut dicit philosophus, est quae bonum facit habentem, et opus eius bonum reddit. Secundum igitur quod bonum diversificatur in homine, oportet etiam quod et virtus diversificetur; sicut patet quod aliud est bonum hominis in quantum et homo, et aliud in quantum civis. Et manifestum est quod aliquae operationes possent esse convenientes homini in quantum est homo, quae non essent convenientes ei secundum quod est civis. Et propter hoc philosophus dicit in III Politic., quod alia est virtus quae facit hominem bonum, et alia quae facit civem bonum." Thomas, *DVC*, art. 10, resp. (Marietti, 735).

This use of the term "political virtue" to seemingly indicate regime-relative virtue suggests that in the *ad 4* of the same article, Thomas is comparing the way that acquired moral virtue orders acts of regime-relative virtue to the political good to the way in which charity orders the acts of acquired moral virtue to the supernatural end.

To the extent that infused virtue somehow directs acquired virtue to a higher end, the relationship between the infused virtue and the acquired is parallel to the relationship between the courage of the good human and that of the good citizen or ruler. As David Decosimo notes, Thomas in other texts uses the very same phrase used in the *De Virtutibus in Communi*, "by the mediation" (*mediante*), in order to describe the way in which a higher virtue, such as a theological virtue, orders a lower one.[81] Thomas never suggests that the acts of acquired virtues would conflict with the infused. But they certainly lack any sort of supernatural goodness or merit on their own. The point of Thomas's example of the kinds of courage should be clear enough from this perspective. The courage that makes someone good with respect to the natural end is by itself insufficient for producing acts that are meritorious or make the agent good in the order of grace. However, infused moral virtue can make the acts of an acquired virtue meritorious by ordering them to a supernatural end.

A second text adds more evidence for the thesis that Thomas believed in the compatibility of infused and acquired moral virtue. In the *Commentary on the Sentences*, Thomas gives a preliminary argument for the specific distinction between acquired and infused virtue by appealing to their presence in the same adult. He writes:

> Two forms of the same species cannot be in one subject. But infused virtue exists at the same time with acquired virtue, as is clear in an adult who, having acquired virtue, enters upon baptism, who does not receive less of the infused than a boy does. Therefore the acquired and infused virtues differ in species.[82]

Since the adult has the acquired virtue before baptism and afterwards she has the infused as well, then these two virtues must be specifically distinct habits. In this case the very argument for their formal distinction assumes that they can be possessed by the same person and presumably that they can work together.

---

[81] Decosimo, "More to Love," 51–54. See Thomas, *S.T.*, II-II, q. 32, art. 1, resp.; q. 81, art. 1, ad 1.

[82] "duae formae ejusdem speciei non possunt esse in uno subjecto. Sed virtus infusa est simul cum virtute acquisita, ut patet in adulto qui habens virtutem acquisitam ad Baptismum accedit, qui non minus recipit de infusis quam puer. Ergo virtus acquisita et infusa differunt specie." Thomas, *In Sent.*, lib. 3, d. 33, q. 1, art. 2, qc. 5, sc2 (Mandonnet-Moos, 3, 1027).

Even though Thomas states that acquired and moral virtue coexist and cooperate, he gives no account of the exact way in which they do so. It seems to me that Thomas's account of the relationship between the acquired and infused virtues can be developed in a variety of ways without obviously violating his basic tenets. But in order to be in harmony with Thomas's thought, these developments must at the same time maintain the basic compatibility of the acquired and infused virtues with each other without sacrificing the fact that these distinct virtues have distinct formal objects and acts.

After introducing the distinction between acquired and infused virtues, Thomas has provided an exhaustive account of the kinds of virtue. This account incorporates material from his predecessors and contemporaries so as to account for the variety of ways in which the human good is achieved. Moreover, it shows that the definition of virtue as a "good operative habit" applies in different ways to different kinds of virtue. In previous chapters we have seen how his understanding of virtue applies to intellectual and moral virtues. Intellectual virtues are good habits that perfect the intellect. They make humans good in a limited way. These virtues include speculative virtues such as understanding and science as well as practical virtues such as prudence and the various arts or skills. Prudence is the one intellectual virtue that is concerned with the good life as a whole. Consequently, it is closely aligned with or even sometimes included in the next general group of virtues, called the moral virtues. These are operative habits that produce good acts that make the agent good. They are consequently more truly virtues than the intellectual virtues are. Thomas mentions different classifications of the moral virtues. For instance, he defends Aristotle's account of the division of moral virtue into justice, which is concerned with operations, and ten moral virtues that are about passions. But he also adopts from his patristic and philosophical predecessors the thesis that there are four cardinal virtues, namely prudence, justice, fortitude, and temperance.

In this chapter, we have seen how Thomas adds to the framework of Aristotle and other philosophers. Thomas's theological predecessors had often contrasted the moral or "political" virtues with the theological or "Catholic" virtues. Like Bonaventure, but more clearly, Thomas replaces this distinction with a threefold distinction between theological virtue, infused moral virtue, and acquired moral virtue. The three theological virtues, namely faith, hope, and charity, are directly about the ultimate end, which is God in himself. The moral virtues are about the different means towards an end. Thomas argues that these means have a twofold object or rule, insofar as they are proportionate to a good that corresponds to human nature or the supernatural good to which humans are raised by God. Consequently, although the infused moral virtues are not directly about God, they must be efficiently caused by God and are about their objects insofar as they are proportionate to eventually obtaining the vision of God in the next life. In contrast, the acquired moral virtues are achieved through human actions and proportionate to that good which belongs to humans by nature. Although Thomas does not provide a sustained or detailed account of the relationship between these two kinds of moral virtue, he does think that they are ultimately compatible and that the acquired are subordinated to the infused. He clarifies some issues in the remaining discussion of virtue in the *Prima Secundae*, which is concerned with the different properties of virtue.

CHAPTER 5

The Properties of Virtue

Thomas's discussion of the virtues in the *Prima Secundae* concludes with a series of four questions on their properties, namely their mean (q. 64), their connection with each other (q. 65), their equality (q. 66), and their duration after this life (q. 67). The order of these questions is not obvious. The question on the mean appears first perhaps because it sheds light on the nature of what a virtue is.[1] It is an intrinsic property of virtue. In the following three questions Thomas addresses the extrinsic properties of the virtues. The questions about their connection and equality are about the relationship between virtues. Can one virtue be possessed without another? Which virtues are most important and why? The final question of this section and the entire treatise is about the persistence of the virtues after death.

In these last four questions on virtue, Thomas addresses problems that arise in both philosophical and theological contexts. The philosophical issues are in some way subordinated to the theological, and the theological issues depend on and are sometimes determined by the philosophical. For example, the discussion on the survival of the virtues after death, which might seem entirely theological, draws on Cicero's philosophical claim that there is no need for virtue in the next life. In each question we see how Thomas wrestles with the complex nature of the subject matter and disagreements among his predecessors. Moreover, by looking at these questions we can better understand many of his earlier remarks on such issues as the unity of prudence, the number of the cardinal virtues, and formal differences between the acquired and infused virtues.

Mean of Virtue

Casual readers of Thomas and Aristotle might raise the question of whether there is a mean even in seeking virtue. Can an agent err in being

---

[1] Conradus Koellin, *In I–II*, q. 65, *Scolastica Commentaria in Primam Secundae* (Venice, 1602), 435.

too morally earnest in seeking the mean? Both Aquinas and Aristotle note that virtue itself is a kind of excess in being good or acting well.[2] It is not virtuous to avoid excess in virtue. The mean of virtue is a mean about the matter than belongs to the virtue, and lies between excess and deficiency in conforming to a rule. It is determined by reason and relative to the agent. Thomas writes, "the mean belongs to virtue not insofar as it is a mean, but insofar as it is a mean of reason, since virtue is the good of the human, which is to be according to reason."[3]

The mean of virtue is a measure or rule. Consequently, the mean itself must be determined by reason in a way similar to how the measure or role of a technical skill is so determined. For instance, a boat builder needs to use a certain kind of wood for the boat. The planks should not be too thin or too thick. The mean is determined by the materials and the nature of the boat. Similarly, the mean between eating too much and taking too little pleasure in food comes from the amount of food and need of the person who is eating. There is no excess or deficiency in virtue itself. It is impossible to be too temperate or too just. Even the extreme exercise of virtues such as temperance and justice involves some sort of mean in the relevant matter of the virtues.

The mean belongs to the very definition of moral virtue as "a habit of choice existing in the mean."[4] This doctrine might seem straightforward when applied to virtues such as courage and justice in exchange. Courage is a mean between cowardice and rashness. The just price is between too much and too little money. Aristotle's doctrine of the mean is developed and expounded in the context of such moral virtues. But Thomas also applies it to the intellectual and theological virtues. At first glance this application perhaps seems forced. But a closer examination shows that there is a meaningful way in which the intellectual virtues, since they involve the measure of reason, must conform to some sort of mean. The theological virtues are so unlike the moral and intellectual virtues that they do not admit of a mean in their object, which is God himself. Nevertheless, there is a significant way in which each theological virtue has a mean that is *per accidens*.

This mean of moral virtue is about the agent's own passions or some external thing.[5] Virtues such as courage and temperance regulate the

---

[2] Aristotle, *EN* 2.6.1107a7; Thomas, *S.T.*, I-II, q. 64, art. 1, ad 1.
[3] "medium competit virtuti non in quantum medium, sed in quantum medium rationis: quia virtus est bonum hominis, quod est secundum rationem esse." Thomas, *DVC*, art. 13, ad 8 (Marietti, 750).
[4] "habitus electivus in mediate existens." Aristotle, *EN* 1107a1, in Thomas, *S.T.*, I-II, q. 64, art. 1, sc.
[5] Thomas, *DVC*, art. 13, resp. (Marietti, 748–749).

passions according to a rule that takes into account the relevant circumstances.[6] For instance, Aristotle distinguishes between a wrestler such as Milo, who would eat an entire beef cow, and lesser individuals.[7] The mean of temperance for Milo differs from the mean of temperance for Aristotle. If Aristotle were to eat a whole cow at a sitting, he would be a glutton. Moreover, the mean in such virtues is not the exact midpoint between extremes. For example, temperance is a mean between gluttony and the nameless lack of care for food, but the temperate person will tend more towards the vice of caring too little for food or pleasure than towards gluttony. Temperance and other virtues that have their mean in the passions are between differently named vices of excess and deficiency. Courage considered in one way is a mean between cowardice and rashness, and liberality is a mean between avarice and wastefulness. At times, the mean is so rare as to lack a name.

Thomas does not address the distinction between acquired and infused moral virtues in this explicit discussion of moral virtue's mean. But we should remember that acquired and infused virtues are specifically distinct and that they involve a different mean.[8] For instance, a person with the infused virtue of temperance will fast more strictly than she would through merely acquired temperance. She follows a stricter rule. Consequently, although both acquired and infused temperance are about bodily pleasure, the mean of infused temperance will differ from that of acquired temperance.

Acquired temperance produces acts about food and drink that can be ordered to a higher end. The same good acts of acquired temperance might or might not be ordered to God as the ultimate end, depending on whether the agent has charity. They are ordered to this end by charity in a way similar to how they might be ordered to the common good through the virtue of justice. In contrast to acts of acquired temperance, infused temperance produces acts about food and drink that must be ordered to the higher end to which they are directed by charity. The necessary order of infused temperance to the end that exceeds nature requires that the mean of infused temperance be distinct from that of acquired temperance.

This account of the mean applies to Aristotle's account of virtues such as magnificence and magnanimity, which involve respectively great

---

[6] Thomas, *S.T., I-II*, q. 64, art. 1 and ad 2; *In Sent.*, lib. 3, d. 33, q. 1, art. 3, qstcla. 1. sol., ad 2 (Mandonnet-Moos, 3, 1035–1036).

[7] Aristotle, *EN* 1.6.1106a36–1106b8; Thomas, *SLE*, lib. 2, lect. 6 (Leonine, 47.1, 95–96).

[8] Thomas, *S.T.*, I-II, q. 63, art. 4, resp.

money and honor.[9] It might seem that the amounts of money and honor would err only through some sort of excess. But Thomas uses Aristotle's text to argue that the mean of these virtues involves not only the matter but also the way in which the matter is ruled by reason. They are concerned with the quantity of their matter with respect to "where it is needful, when it is needful, and for the reason why it is needful."[10]

This Aristotelian account of the mean might appear to conflict with the Christian notion that there are virtues such as poverty and chastity that require complete abstinence from goods such as money and sexual activity. These virtues could seem to require deficiency in the matter. But Thomas holds that these virtues require abstinence from such goods "for the reason why it is needful and according to what is needful; that is, according to the command of God and for the sake of eternal life."[11] Some exceed the mean of reason in these matters through their superstition or vainglory. Others fail to achieve the mean because they violate vows of virginity and of poverty.

As we have seen, virtues such as justice are not about the agent's own passions but instead about some external thing, such as money.[12] In this case, virtues that err through excess and deficiency share the same name, such as injustice. The mean of justice is a mean of reason that is the same as the mean of a thing. This identity can be clearly seen in transactions that are governed by commutative justice. The monetary value of a boat or a pair of shoes depends neither on the character of the one who is in possession of the money or of the one who has the boat or the shoes. Injustice in such cases can involve taking too many goods in an exchange or giving too little money. As in temperance, sometimes this mean will take into account the characteristics of an individual. Such a mean belongs to distributive justice. For instance, if the civil authorities give honors according to distributive justice, they will give more honor to the citizen who deserves more. In such cases the mean is still in the thing and not in the agent, even though it involves not only the worth of a good that is distributed but also the individual's meriting of such a good.

---

[9] Thomas, *S.T.*, I-II, q. 64, art. 1, obj. 2 and ad 2. Aristotle, *EN* 4.2–3.

[10] "ubi oportet, et quando oportet, et propter quod oportet." Thomas, *S.T.*, I-II, q. 64, art. 1, ad 2.

[11] "propter quod oportet et secundum quod oportet, idest secundum mandatum Dei, et propter vitam aeternam." Thomas, *S.T.*, I-II, q. 64, art. 1, ad 3.

[12] Thomas, *S.T.*, I-II, q. 64, art. 2; II-II, q. 58, art. 10; *In Sent.*, lib. 3, d. 33, q. 1, art. 3, qstcla. 2, sol. (Mandonnet-Moos, 3, 1036–1037). Rafael Tomás Caldera, *Le jugement par inclination chez Saint Thomas d'Aquin* (Paris: Vrin, 1980), 105–108.

Although Aristotle does not discuss the issue in any detail, Thomas maintains that there is a mean in intellectual virtues.[13] The doctrine of the mean in these contexts faces two difficulties. First, it is unclear what it would mean for there to be a mean in intellectual virtue. It seems as if statements are either true or false, and not too much or too little. Second, intellectual virtues are divided into practical and speculative virtues. It might seem that practical intellectual virtue would have its own mean since it involves action. In particular, prudence might seem to borrow the mean from whatever virtue is relevant. But Thomas argues that not only does prudence have a mean in the same way that other intellectual virtues do but it also has its own properly practical mean.

The mean of any intellectual virtue is about the thing known, since truth in the intellect is measured by the thing.[14] The intellect can lack conformity to the thing through excess and deficiency. These departures from the mean are through affirmative and negative statements. Thomas writes:

> Therefore among affirmation and opposed negations is accepted the mean of the speculative intellectual virtues, which is the true: as for example, it is true when "what is" is said to be, and "what is not" not to be; but the false will be according to excess, as "what is not" is said to be; but according to defect, when "what is" is said not to be.[15]

Cajetan uses the example of the evidently true statement "The whole is greater than the part" to indicate the different ways in which the intellect can depart from the mean.[16] Everyone who understands the terms of this statement assents to it, but its very obviousness helps us to see in what way there can be error through excess and deficiency. Someone who asserts "The whole is less than its part" would err through excess, since she affirms the whole to be something that it is not. Someone who asserts "The whole is not greater than its part" would err through deficiency, since she denies what is.

The speculative intellectual virtues, such as wisdom and science, are only concerned with truth. The mean of practical intellectual virtue differs

---

[13] Thomas, *S.T.*, I-II, q. 64, art. 3, sc, cites Aristotle's statements that there is a mean in technical skill and that technical skill is an intellectual virtue. See *EN* 2.6.1106b11–15; 6.3.1139b16.

[14] Thomas, *S.T.*, I-II, q. 64, art. 3; *In Sent.*, lib. 3, d. 33, q. 1, art. 3, sol. 3 and ad 3 (Mandonnet-Moos, 1037–1038).

[15] "Inter affirmationes ergo et negationes oppositas accipitur medium virtutum intellectualium speculativarum, quod est verum: ut puta, quia verum est cum dicitur esse quod est, et non esse quod non est; falsum autem secundum excessum erit, ut dicitur esse quod non est; secundum defectum vero, cum dicitur non esse quod est." Thomas, *DVC*, art. 3, resp. (Marietti, 749). See also *DVSpe*, art. 1, ad 7.

[16] Cajetan, *In I-II*, q. 64, art. 3, n. 3 (Leonine, 6, 415).

from that of speculative virtue because it requires not only conformity to the thing but also conformity to right appetite. Insofar as prudence is concerned with truth, it requires conformity to the thing, and consequently there can be error according to excess and deficiency in the same way that there is error in the speculative intellect. In this way the rectitude of the intellect concerns a judgment about whether the act should be done. Insofar as it requires or issues a judgment, such as "Drinking fewer than four beers is good," it is capable of being true or false. If someone under the relevant circumstances states that "Drinking fewer than four beers is not good," then she errs through deficiency. She might err thorough excess by stating that "Drinking more than four beers is good." In another way, prudence is about practice and must also be about the mean that belongs to virtue. The rectitude of the practical intellect in this context is about the execution of the act. This mean would be about the drinking itself. The mean is the drinking of three of four beers, as opposed to the deficiency of drinking one or even none at all under these circumstances and the excess of drinking nine or ten.

Since the theological virtues have God as their object, they do not have a mean in the way that the moral and intellectual virtues do.[17] God is the measure and rule of faith, hope, and charity. These virtues are regulated by God's truth, his omnipotence and care, and his goodness. It is impossible to err by excessively believing, hoping in, or loving God. But on our part, there can be an excess and deficiency *per accidens*.[18] For instance, Catholics believe through faith that the Second Person of the Trinity assumed a human nature, and consequently one divine person has two natures. According to Catholics, the Nestorian heresy correctly holds that there are two natures but errs in thinking that there are also two persons. In contrast, the Monophysite (Eutychist) heresy correctly holds that there is only one person but errs in thinking that there is also only one nature. Catholic belief is consequently in some way a mean between these two heresies. But this mean is not a *per se* mean, since it is not directly about excess and deficiency with respect to the virtue's object, namely God as First Truth. Similarly, hope is a kind of mean between presumption and despair. Through hope Catholics have confidence that heaven can be reached through God's help. Catholics can sin through presumption, by thinking that they can attain heaven too easily, or through despair, by lacking confidence in the power

[17] Thomas, *S.T.*, I-II, q. 64, art. 4; *DVC*, art. 13, resp.
[18] Thomas, *S.T.*, II-II, q. 17, art. 5, ad 2; *In Sent.*, lib. 3, d. 33, q. 1, at. 3, qstcla. 4, ad 2–3 (Mandonnet-Moos, 3, 1039); *DVSpe*, art. 1, ad 7 (Marietti, 805–806).

of God's help. But its mean is not directly about excess or deficiency with respect to its object, which is God's omnipotence.

Thomas's discussion of the mean of virtue is an illustrative example of some of the ways in which he uses Aristotle's philosophy as part of his own broader moral teaching. Aristotle himself had a somewhat meagre account of the mean that was applied to moral virtue. Thomas not only clarified and developed this account but he applied it to the intellectual virtues that were first clearly delineated by Aristotle. Unlike Aristotle, he clearly indicates how there is one sort of mean in the speculative intellectual virtues and an additional mean in prudence. Additionally, Thomas explains how this doctrine of the mean might be applied to the theological virtues. Even though they do not have the *per se* mean that the other virtues do, they have a *per accidens* mean.

Connection between Virtues

After discussing the mean, which is an intrinsic property of virtue, Thomas addresses the ways in which virtues are related to each other. His understanding of the connection of the virtues follows from his earlier accounts of what virtue is, how moral virtue depends on prudence, and how other virtues depend on charity. Like his teaching on these previous topics, his doctrine of the connection of the virtues is influenced heavily by earlier traditions, including patristic sources and scholastic debates that stretch back to the later twelfth century. The account of the connection between the acquired moral virtues naturally leads to a discussion of the infused moral virtues and the way in which the theological virtues of faith and hope are connected with charity.

In previous generations, scholastic theologians had access only to translations of Books I–III of Aristotle's *Nicomachean Ethics*. Consequently, earlier theologians were aware of Aristotle's understanding of a virtue as a distinct habit that is acquired through the repetition of certain kinds of acts but not his account of their connection through prudence. It seemed to many of them that on Aristotle's account an agent might acquire one virtue, such as temperance, without another, such as justice, simply by performing temperate acts and not just acts. Philip the Chancellor defended an early version of the thesis that the cardinal virtues are not connected with each other if they are considered as separate habits but that they are so connected if they are considered as general conditions or formalities of every virtuous act.[19]

---

[19] Philip, *Summa de Bono*, 2 vols., ed. Nikolaus Wicki (Berne: Francke, 1985), vol. 2, 1069–1076. See Lottin, *PM*, 3.1, 220–222.

Like Philip, Thomas thinks that as general conditions of every virtuous act, the cardinal virtuous must be connected.[20] Since every act is in some extended way reasonable, just, courageous, and temperate, the cardinal virtues would be connected through their presence in one act. According to Thomas, Church Fathers such as Augustine and Gregory the Great, and even later thinkers such as Peter Lombard, discuss the connection of the cardinal virtues in this context, namely insofar as these virtues are general conditions of a virtuous act. Thomas agrees with this account but holds that this way of speaking about the cardinal virtues as general conditions is less proper than the other way of speaking about them as specifically distinct habits.

More properly, the moral cardinal virtues, and in some way all the relevant moral virtues, are specifically distinct habits that are connected through one cardinal virtue of prudence. Albert the Great and Thomas were the first to discuss this kind of connection between the virtues, largely because of the newly available translation of the *Nicomachean Ethics*, Book VI.[21] In this way the virtues are not operative in every act but instead are concerned with determinate matter. For instance, temperance is about pleasure and courage about death. The connection between such virtues would be about the way in which the agent must be concerned with the moral life as a whole and not only with a part of living well.

Thomas also draws on different traditions in his description of different ways in which virtues can be perfect or complete. The various distinctions between perfect and imperfect virtues are relevant to a particular context.[22] For instance, we have already seen that the term "disposition" can mean an undeveloped or imperfect habit as opposed to a fully developed or perfect habit.[23] The imperfect habit differs from the perfect habit in the way that the child differs from the grown human being. Perfect and imperfect are used to describe imperfect and perfect members of the same species.

In the *Prima Secundae*, q. 65, which is the question on the connection of the virtues, Thomas emphasizes two other kinds of imperfection. In art. 1, he refers to what Aristotle calls "natural virtue," which is imperfect in the sense that it is not a habit at all but a natural disposition that inclines to a

---

[20] Thomas, *S.T.*, I-II, q. 65, art. 1; *In Sent.*, lib. 3, d. 36, art. 1, sol. (Mandonnet-Moos, 3, 1216); *Quodl.*, 12, q. 15, art 1, resp. For a translation of and introduction to this article of the *S.T.*, see J. Budziszewski, *A Commentary on Thomas Aquinas's Virtue Ethics* (Cambridge: Cambridge University Press, 2017), 112–132.

[21] Albert the Great, *Super Ethica*, lib. 6, lect. 18 (vol. 14.2, 510–511). Lottin, *PM*, 3.2, 271–276. For the context, see Jörn Müller, *Natürliche Moral und philosophische Ethik bei Albertus Magnus* (Münster: Ashendorff, 2001), 69–71.

[22] Thomas M. Osborne Jr., "Perfect and Imperfect Virtues in Aquinas," *The Thomist* 71 (2007), 39–64.

[23] Thomas, *S.T.*, I-II, q. 49, art. 2, ad 3.

virtue. They are imperfect in contrast to perfect moral virtues, which are habits. They are not habits and therefore do not belong to the same species as the corresponding perfect moral virtue. In the following arts. 2 and 4, a virtue is perfect because of its connection to the ultimate end, and not with respect to the ultimate end in some genus, such as the merely human good. Such perfect moral virtue is infused as opposed to acquired. In this context, the acquired virtue is a habit that is specifically distinct from the corresponding infused virtue that concerns the same matter. It is perfect as a habit but imperfect as a virtue because it does not make the agent fully good with respect to the supernatural ultimate end.

In the *De Virtutibus Cardinalibus*, art. 2, Thomas discusses this same twofold imperfection in the same context of the connection of the virtues. The first kind of imperfect virtue, namely mere natural inclinations to act, are "entirely imperfect." They are immediately contrasted with the acquired moral virtues, which are perfect in relation to natural virtues but imperfect when compared to the infused. Thomas writes, "in some way they are perfect in comparison to the human good, but they are not simply speaking perfect, since they do not attain to the first rule, which is the ultimate end."[24] Only the infused virtues are fully perfect in this sense, because of the way they make someone good simply speaking. The acquired moral virtues are real virtues, but they only make someone good with respect to an end that is proportionate to human nature.[25]

In the *Secunda Secundae*, q. 23, art. 7, Thomas discusses perfection and imperfection in another sense. In this text he distinguishes between false virtue, true but imperfect virtue, and perfect virtue. This threefold distinction corresponds to the distinction between apparent particular goods that are not true, true particular goods, and the last end, which is the principal human good. False similitudes of virtues are ordered to merely apparent goods. Acquired virtues can be true virtues in the sense that they are ordered to what is truly good. Such virtue can be perfect or imperfect, depending on whether it is ordered to the ultimate end. Thomas writes, "But if that particular good is a true good, for instance the conservation

---

[24] "aliqualiter sunt perfectae per comparationem ad bonum humanum, non tamen sunt simpliciter perfectae, quia non attingunt ad primam regulam, quae est ultimus finis." Thomas, *DVCard.*, art. 2, resp. (Marietti, 818).

[25] Brandon Dahm, "The Acquired Virtues Are Real Virtues: A Response to Stump," *Faith and Philosophy* 32 (2015): 453–470. He is responding to Eleonore Stump, "The Non-Aristotelian Character of Aquinas's Ethics: Aquinas on the Passions," *Faith and Philosophy* 28 (2011): 29–34, who emphasizes the importance of the infused virtues and the gifts of the Holy Ghost, and, as Dahm notes, may not be defending the strong version of the claim that he is attributing to her. See Dahm, "Acquired Virtues Are Real Virtues": 453, note 2.

of the city or something of this sort, it will be true virtue indeed, but imperfect, unless it is referred to the final and perfect good."[26] In this sense of the term "imperfect," an acquired virtue is imperfect if its acts are not referred to the last end, which is supernatural, through the infused virtue of charity. The stated distinction between imperfect and perfect virtue here is in the way in which its acts are referred to the last end. A true virtue is imperfect if the agent lacks charity because it produces acts that are not in fact directed to the ultimate end.

Thomas's discussion of the connection of the specifically diverse acquired moral virtues is almost entirely about their connection through prudence, and his discussion of the infused virtues is partly about such a connection, as well as their connection through charity. When reading these texts, it is of utmost importance to keep in mind the various kinds of perfection that can be attributed to a virtue. The acquired moral virtues are perfect to the extent that they are not natural inclinations that arise from the soul or the particular body. In comparison to such natural inclinations, acquired virtues are perfect virtues.

Moreover, both acquired and infused moral virtues are the kinds of habits that completely come under the nature of virtue in that they perfect both the act and the agent. Even acquired virtues are the kinds of habits that make the agent good, although they are concerned with that good which is proportionate to the agent. The connection of the specifically distinct moral virtues through the one virtue of prudence depends on two positions that we have touched on in previous chapters, namely that moral virtue and prudence are interdependent and that prudence, unlike art and moral virtue, has the whole of the moral life as its matter.

As we have seen, prudence and moral virtue are interdependent. Prudence depends on moral virtue for its end, and moral virtue depends on prudence for commanding the means to this end. One cannot correctly

---

[26] "Si vero illud bonum particulare sit verum bonum, puta conservatio civitatis vel aliquid huiusmodi, erit quidem vera virtus, sed imperfecta, nisi referatur ad finale et perfectum bonum." Thomas, *S.T.*, II-II, q. 23 art. 7. For a discussion and version of the classical Thomistic view, see Jacques Maritain, *Science et sagesse: Suivi d'eclaircissements sur la philosophie morale* (Paris: Labergerie, 1935), 241–255; Timothy J. Lopez, "United Acquired Virtue in Traditional Thomism: Distinguishing Necessities, Efficient Causes, and Finalities," in *The Virtuous Life: Thomas Aquinas on the Theological Nature of Moral Virtues*, ed. Harm Goris and Henk Schoot (Leuven, Paris, and Bristol, CT: Peeters, 2017), 183–199. Many interpreters conflate the thesis that the sinner cannot have fully developed acquired moral virtues that are connected through prudence with the thesis that the sinner cannot have true acquired moral virtue. But Thomas argues for the former and denies the latter. For a recent example, see Nicholas Austin, *Aquinas on Virtue: A Causal Reading* (Washington, DC: Georgetown University Press, 2017), 178–180. I summarize some of the arguments for the first thesis in Thomas M. Osborne Jr., "The Augustinianism of Thomas Aquinas' Moral Theory," *The Thomist* 67 (2003): 279–305.

deliberate, judge, and especially command the means to virtues such as justice or temperance without first being ordered to justice through these virtues. Similarly, one who fails to command just or temperate acts when needed lacks prudence, even if this agent has correct speculative knowledge about the matter. Prudence is fully practical.

Remember that prudence does not require the existence of every virtue but only those that are needed in common life. For instance, one who lacks money is unable to possess magnificence, which is the virtue of giving large amounts. Thomas thinks that an otherwise virtuous person will be in close potency to such virtue or that there is a preparedness for it.[27] A person who is virtuous with respect to money will quickly acquire the relevant virtues if great amounts become available.

Thomas emphasizes that specifically one prudence covers that matter of all the different moral virtues. It cannot be divided into species on the basis of their distinctive moral matter. The different subjective parts of prudence, namely individual, family, political, and military prudence, are mostly based on the distinct natural groups and not on different moral virtues.[28] For instance, there is no species of prudence that is about the matter of justice and distinct from that kind of prudence which is about the matter of temperance.

There is a significant similarity between prudence and technical skill, in that they both are concerned with the way in which different kinds of matter can be directed towards an end. Since prudence is about the good life, this similarity shows why prudence about temperance cannot be separated from prudence about justice. For instance, a carpenter knows how to use different kinds of wood, such as oak or the wood of a nut tree, in order to make a chest.[29] Similarly, the prudent person knows how the good life as a whole requires the exercise of different virtues, such as temperance and courage. The one virtue of prudence is concerned with the matter of the different virtues in the way that the one technical skill of carpentry is concerned with different kinds of wood.

Despite such similarity to technical skills, prudence about one subject matter cannot be separated from prudence about another subject matter.

---

[27] Thomas, *S.T.*, I-II, q. 65, art. 1, ad 1; II-II, q. 152, art. 3, ad 2; *DVCard.*, art. 2, ad 5 et 9, 820 (Marietti, 820).
[28] Thomas, *S.T.*, II-II, qq. 48, 50. For later controversies over Thomas's account, see Thomas M. Osborne Jr., "Thomas and Scotus on Prudence without All the Major Virtues, Imperfect or Merely Partial?," *The Thomist* 74 (2010), 1–24. For an alternative interpretation of Thomas, see Angela McKay Knobel, "Prudence and Acquired Moral Virtue," *The Thomist* 69 (2005): 535–565.
[29] Thomas, *In Sent.*, lib. 3, d. 36, art. 1, ad 2 (Mandonnet-Moos, 3, 1217).

For example, the prudence that concerns matters of justice is not a distinct habit from that which concerns matter of temperance.[30] It is impossible to be prudent about justice but imprudent about temperance. However, one might easily be a good carpenter but a bad blacksmith. Technical skills are separable from each other in a way that is somewhat similar to how one speculative science can be separated from another. For instance, one might possess the habit of geometry and yet lack the habit of physics.

In the *De Virtutibus Cardinalibus*, Thomas gives three reasons for why the intellectual virtues are not connected in the way that the moral virtues are. He writes:

> First indeed, because they are about diverse kinds of things, and are not connected to each other, as has been said about the technical skills. Second, because in the sciences principles and conclusions are not convertible; such that namely whoever has the principles has the conclusions, just as has been said about morals. Third, because intellectual virtue is not related to charity, through which a human being is ordered to the ultimate end.[31]

Although Thomas discusses each of these points in his other writings, he does not delineate them in the same way. In the *Commentary on the Sentences*, Thomas emphasizes the first point, which is that different technical skills and sciences have different principles, whereas the principles of moral knowledge are the same for all areas of the moral life.[32] For example, since the principles of the science of living things differ from the principles of geometry, it is possible for a person to have the habit of geometry and to lack the habit of the science of living things. But the same principles belong to the moral knowledge concerning the matter of each distinct virtue. Consequently, it is impossible for someone to have moral knowledge in one area and to lack it in another.

In the *Prima Secundae* and in the *De Virtutibus Cardinalibus*, Thomas draws attention to a point that is related to the second reason, which is that the premises and conclusions of moral knowledge are convertible. In these texts he argues separately for the thesis that in morals knowledge of all the relevant principles is necessary. An error in any moral principle is like an error in the particular principles of a science.[33] Someone who

---

[30] Thomas, *DVCard.*, art. 2, ad 4 (Marietti, 819–820).

[31] "Primo quidem, quia quae sunt circa rerum diversa genera, non sunt coordinata ad invicem, sicut et de artibus dictum est. Secundo, quia in scientiis non convertibiliter se habent principia et conclusiones; ita scilicet quod quicumque habet principia, habeat conclusiones, sicut in moralibus dictum est. Tertio, quia virtus intellectualis non habet respectum ad caritatem, per quam ordinatur homo ad ultimum finem." Thomas, *DVCard.*, art. 2, ad 8 (Marietti, 820).

[32] Thomas, *In Sent.*, lib. 3, d. 36, art. 1, ad 3 (vol. 3, 1217).

[33] Thomas, *S.T.*, I-II, q. 61, art. 1, resp.; q. 65, art. 1, ad 4; *DVCard.*, art. 2, resp. (Marietti, 819)

errs in any geometrical principles will fail to draw the correct conclusions. Similarly, someone who errs about any principle of morals, whether in justice, courage, or temperance, will also err in particular judgments about what should be done. Correct reasoning about morals excludes error or lack of rectitude concerning the ends of all of the virtues in the way that correct reasoning about geometry excludes error about geometrical principles. For example, someone who lacks the principles of temperance and attempts to reason about the moral life is like someone who tries to acquire Euclidean geometry without knowing what a circle is.

Thomas's description of the convertibility of premises and conclusions in morals is most clearly developed in the *Prima Secundae* and in the *De Virtutibus Cardinalibus*.[34] In sciences, the premises are often known without the conclusions. For instance, the premises of geometry are easy to grasp, whereas the conclusions are known only through demonstration. But in morals, someone who knows the premises must also know the conclusions. This convertibility is based on the way in which prudence depends on moral virtue for its end, and that in morals the end is the first principle. Someone who is fully prudent about chocolate or whisky will use principles to which she is directed by temperance. But the rectitude towards these principles itself depends on the correctness of right reason as expressed in judgments and commands about particular acts, such as those about the proper consumption of chocolate or whisky. These judgments and commands about particular acts are like conclusions in the speculative sciences. In contrast, someone might know all of the principles of a science such as geometry and yet be unaware of the conclusions. In the sciences, it is easy to know the principles without knowing the conclusions.

Thomas does not so clearly develop in other writings the third of the abovementioned reasons for the distinctive unity of prudence, which is that prudence must be ordered to the ultimate end through charity whereas the other intellectual virtues can exist without charity. In the earlier *Commentary on the Sentences*, he briefly mentions the importance of such an order for there to be virtue. But in the *De Virtutibus Cardinalibus*, the central discussion invokes this order to the end when discussing fully perfect moral virtue, which is infused. He does not introduce a similar connection between charity and acquired prudence. We will return to this perplexing question of the dependence of the moral virtues on the ultimate end after first discussing the connection between the infused

---

[34] Thomas, *DVCard.*, art. 2, ad 11 (Marietti, 820).

virtues, which sheds special light on the way in which infused prudence depends on charity.

Both infused prudence and infused moral virtues depend for their existence on the theological virtue of charity.[35] Infused prudence depends on a correct order to God as a supernatural end in the way that acquired prudence depends on a correct order to the good that is proportionate to human nature. This correct order to God as the ultimate end that exceeds human nature is achieved only through the theological virtue of charity. Consequently, the infused virtue of prudence depends on the infused and theological virtue of charity. The infused moral virtues depend on infused prudence in the same way that the acquired moral virtues depend on acquired prudence. Since they cannot exist without prudence, they too cannot exist without charity. These infused moral virtues are about the means to the supernatural end. Charity is directly about the supernatural end.

Not all infused virtues depend on charity in the same way that the infused moral virtues do.[36] Faith and hope can exist at least as habits without charity, even though charity cannot exist without them. However, without charity faith and hope are not fully virtues because their acts do not make their agents good. Such virtues are imperfect in the sense that they produce good acts that are not done well. Thomas compares faith and hope without charity to justice without prudence:

> If someone acts justly, she does something good; but it will not be an act of perfect virtue, unless she does this well, that is according to right choice, which is through prudence; and therefore justice without prudence cannot be a perfect virtue.[37]

For instance, someone without prudence might be just to the extent that she might return the correct amount of change, but she will not do so in a settled choice according to prudence. Similarly, someone without charity might believe the articles of faith and hope in God's assistance in reaching heaven. But these acts of belief and hope will not be done in the right way, which is out of a supernatural love for God over oneself. Thomas notes that without charity faith and hope are virtues in some way, but they do not have the "nature of perfect virtue." In this sense of "perfect virtue," a virtue is perfect when it makes the agent good. Faith and hope

---

[35] Thomas, *S.T.*, I-II, q. 65, art. 2.

[36] Thomas, *S.T.*, I-II q, 65, art. 4; *In Sent.*, lib. 3, d. 23, q. 3, art. 1, sol. 2 (Mandonnet-Moos, 3, 744–745).

[37] "si aliquis operetur iusta, bonum quidem facit: sed non erit opus perfectae virtutis, nisi hoc bene faciat, idest secundum electionem rectam, quod est per prudentiam: et ideo justitia sine prudentia non potest esse virtus perfecta." Thomas, *S.T.*, I-II, q. 65, art. 4, resp.

without charity are like the acquired virtues of someone who lacks charity in that they produce good acts but do not make the agent good.

Thomas makes an interesting remark about the imperfection of such virtues and their acts in the *De Veritate*, when he responds to an objection's use of Augustine as an authority for the position that virtue can exist without charity:

> Augustine accepts "virtues" in a wide sense, as every perfecting habit for performing praiseworthy acts. Or it can be said that Augustine does not mean that habits existing without grace are called virtues, but that some habits that are virtues when they are with grace, remain without grace; however they are not then virtues.[38]

Faith and hope perform praiseworthy acts and with charity these acts are meritorious. Without charity, faith and hope are the same kinds of habits and produce the same kinds of acts, but their acts lack merit. Since such habits produce good acts, they can be called virtues. Since their acts fail to make the agent good, they are not fully virtues.

The discussion of the connection between the virtues in q. 65 of the *Prima Secundae* does not discuss at any length the way in which the acquired virtues might be affected by the presence or absence of charity. In art. 2, Thomas notes that the acquired virtues were "in many gentiles" (*in multis gentilibus*). Presumably such gentiles lacked the theological and infused moral virtues even though they possessed in some way the acquired virtues. In many other texts, Thomas frequently states that unbelievers and those believers who lack charity can perform good acts, even if these acts have no supernatural merit.[39] Such agents presumably might have some sort of acquired virtue and yet lack charity. Moreover, in other texts he argues that although charity and the infused moral virtues are lost through one mortal sin, the acquired virtue remains.[40] For instance, someone who sins mortally against justice thereby loses the infused virtues of temperance and fortitude. But she does not immediately lose acquired justice. The acquired virtues are lost through repeated contrary acts. Even though the virtues are connected, someone loses

---

[38] "Augustinus accipit large virtutes, omnes habitus perficientes ad actus laudabiles. Vel potest dici quod non intelligit Augustinus quod habitus sine gratia existentes virtutes dicantur, sed quia aliqui habitus qui sunt virtutes quando sunt cum gratia, remanent sine gratia, non tamen tunc sunt virtutes." Thomas, *DV*, q. 14, art. 6, ad 6 (Leonine, 22.2, 456).

[39] Thomas, *S.T.*, II-II, q. 10 art. 4; I-II, q. 109 art. 2; *In Sent.*, lib. 2, d. 40, q. 1, art. 5, sol. and ad 2; d. 41, q.1, art. 2 (ed. Mandonnet-Moos, vol. 2, 1026, 1037–1039); *In Sent.*, lib. 4, d. 39, art. 2, ad 5 (ed. Parma, 1025); *Sup. Rom.*, cap. 14 lect. 3 n. 1141 (Marietti, vol. 1, 213); *Sup. Tit.* cap. 1 lect. 4 n. 43 (Marietti, vol. 2, 310); *DM*, q. 2, art. 5, ad 7 (Leonine, 23, 44–45).

[40] Thomas, *S.T.*, I-II, q. 63, art. 2, ad 2; q. 71, art. 4; q. 73, art. 1, ad 2; *DVC*, art. 1, ad 5 (Marietti, 709).

temperance through intemperate acts and not through acts of injustice or cowardice.

In many other texts Thomas discusses acquired virtue that is imperfect in ways that are not discussed in this question. This point is significant because the other senses of the term "imperfect" are the ones that are relevant to the ways in which a true acquired virtue might be undeveloped, unstable, and present in bad agents. Although someone can have acquired moral virtue without charity, it seems that such virtue will be imperfect in that it will fail to make the agent good, and it will also be more easily lost. Thomas's position on the imperfection of acquired moral virtue without grace can be found in several texts.

First, in several places Thomas mentions such imperfections in discussions of whether sinners can have virtue. Even in the *Prima Secundae*, q. 65, art. 2, he briefly touches on this point by mentioning as an objection Prosper of Aquitaine's claim that every virtue other than charity can exist both in the good and in the bad. Thomas responds by noting that these virtues must be imperfect because otherwise they would make not only the act but also the agent good. Moral virtue without charity consequently only halfway satisfies Aristotle's description of virtue as "what makes the one having it good, and renders his work good."[41]

As we have seen, moral virtue is dependent on the agent's overall goodness or badness in a way that the technical skills and sciences are not. Someone can be a bad human being and a good craftsman or thinker.[42] The goodness of the craftsman's technical skill rests in the product that is produced. Similarly, intellectual virtue makes someone good only in a particular way. In contrast, moral virtue makes someone good strictly speaking. Without charity acquired moral virtue produces good acts but these are not ordered to the agent's ultimate end, which is supernatural. A virtue without charity produces morally good acts but does not make the agent good. Consequently, it does not completely satisfy the full description of virtue.

In the *Secunda Secundae*, q. 23, art. 7, Thomas states that the sinner's virtue remains true virtue even if it is imperfect in the sense that it fails to make the agent good. He stresses that such imperfect virtue is true virtue because it produces good acts. Such virtue is imperfect virtue because it causes acts that are about particular goods. In this context, only perfect virtue produces

---

[41] "quae bonum facit habentem, et opus eius bonum reddit." Aristotle, *EN* 2.5.1106a22–23, cited in Thomas, *S.T.*, I-II, q. 55, art. 3sc; q. 65, art. 2, ad 1.

[42] Thomas, *S.T.*, I-II, q. 56, art. 3. For intellectual virtue, see especially Thomas, *DVC*, art. 7 (Marietti, 723–725).

acts that are directed to the good life as a whole, which involves rectitude to the supernatural ultimate end. Although the good done by these virtues is orderable to the ultimate end by charity, this good is in fact not ordered to the ultimate end, which is supernatural. This true virtue is the kind of habit that perfects both the act and the agent. It remains moral virtue. Such true virtue is imperfect because moral virtue, in order to perfectly be a virtue, must produce acts that are ordered and not merely orderable to the ultimate end. Thomas writes, "A science and a technical skill by its nature entails an order to some particular good thing, but not to the ultimate end of human life, unlike the moral virtues, which make human beings simply speaking good."[43] Thomas is not stating that the moral virtues themselves are directly about the ultimate end and that technical skills and sciences are not. But their acts are orderable to such an end in such a way that by them an agent becomes good. In this text Thomas seems to be speaking about acquired and not infused moral virtue. Only acquired virtue produces acts that might or might not be ordered to the ultimate end by charity. Infused virtue is always accompanied by charity.

This same contrast between an imperfect and perfect virtue is made in the *Secunda Secundae*, q. 47, art. 13, which addresses the question of whether sinners can have prudence. This text bases the distinction between the virtues on the same division between particular goods and the good of life as a whole. Thomas uses this division between goods to distinguish between false prudence, two kinds of imperfect prudence, and perfect prudence:

> Prudence is said in a threefold way. There is a certain false prudence, or prudence that is said by a likeness ... But second, there is indeed true prudence, since it discovers ways accommodated to a truly good end; but it is imperfect for two reasons. In one way, that good that it takes for an end is not the common end of the whole human life, but of some special business, for instance when someone finds ways accommodated to business or to sailing, he is called a prudent businessman or sailor. In another way, when he fails in the principal act of prudence, for instance when he deliberates well and rightly judges even about those things which pertain to the whole of life, but he does not efficiently command. However, the third prudence is true and perfect, which rightly deliberates about the good end of a whole life, judges, and commands. And this alone is called prudence simply speaking. Which cannot be in sinners.[44]

---

[43] Thomas, *S.T.*, II-II, q. 23, art. 7, ad 3.

[44] "prudentia dicitur tripliciter. Est enim quaedam prudentia falsa, vel per similitudinem dicta ... Secunda autem prudentia est quidem vera, quia adinvenit vias accommodatas ad finem vere bonum; sed est imperfecta, duplici ratione. Uno modo, quia illud bonum quod accipit pro fine

This threefold structure mostly corresponds to the earlier discussion of virtue without charity, in that there is a similitude of virtue that is about a false good, a true but imperfect virtue that is about only a particular good, and that virtue which is directed to the good life as a whole. The difference in this threefold division of prudence is that there are two ways in which true prudence can be true but imperfect, namely by covering only one aspect of the moral life and by being insufficiently practical. The first kind of imperfection, which is that it is not about the good of the whole of life, makes it possible to map the threefold division of prudence onto the threefold division of moral virtue into false, true but imperfect, and perfect. The second kind of imperfection, which is in prudence's failure to command, seems peculiar to prudence.

It seems to me that contemporary disputes over Thomas's understanding of the connection of the virtues partially result from the fact that the true but imperfect virtue that produces good acts in a disordered agent does not obviously correspond to any of the kinds of imperfect virtue discussed at length in Thomas's discussions of how the acquired virtues are connected. In these texts Thomas is concerned with the distinction between natural dispositions that are distinct in kind from acquired virtue and the distinction between acquired virtue and infused virtue. It is a disposition in a different sense from the way that the natural virtue that is merely an inclination is a disposition. The term "disposition" has different meanings when applied to the different virtues. True but imperfect virtue is a disposition because it is related to perfect virtue as a boy is related to a man. In contrast, the altogether imperfect virtue that Thomas mentions when discussing the connection of the virtues is a disposition because it is not an operative habit at all. It is related to the virtue in the way that a lion's courage is related to the human virtue of courage. True but imperfect virtue is not necessary for his argument that the acquired moral virtues are connected with each other through prudence and that the infused virtues are connected with each other primarily through charity. The discussion of true but imperfect virtue is necessary for us in this context primarily because of those who would later claim that connected virtue is possible without rectitude towards the supernatural last end.

non est communis finis totius humanae vitae, sed alicuius specialis negotii, puta cum aliquis adinvenit vias accommodatas ad negotiandum vel ad navigandum, dicitur prudens negotiator vel nauta. Alio modo, quia deficit in principali actu prudentiae, puta cum aliquis bene consiliatur et recte iudicat etiam de his quae pertinent ad totam vitam, sed non efficaciter praecipit. Tertia autem prudentia est et vera et perfecta, quae ad bonum finem totius vitae recte consiliatur, iudicat et praecipit. Et haec sola dicitur prudentia simpliciter. Quae in peccatoribus esse non potest." Thomas, *S.T.*, II-II, q. 47, art. 13, resp.

Unlike the virtue that is imperfect because it is merely natural, this true but imperfect moral virtue is a rational habit that produces human acts. Unlike the virtue that is imperfect merely because it is about the good proportionate to human nature and not about the supernatural ultimate end, this true but imperfect moral virtue is imperfect because the agents on the whole leads a disordered life. It seems to be the same kind of virtue as that perfect acquired moral virtue which is connected with the other moral virtues through acquired virtues. True but imperfect moral virtue does not seem to be specifically distinct from perfect acquired moral virtue in the way that merely natural virtue is distinct from acquired virtue or that acquired moral virtue is distinct from infused virtue. But this true but imperfect moral virtue differs from the perfect acquired moral virtue in three ways. First, since the subject of such true but imperfect moral virtue lacks perfect acquired prudence, this true but imperfect moral virtue lacks the connection with the other moral virtues through prudence. Moreover, such true but imperfect virtue lacks two of the essential features of such virtue, namely 1) that it makes the agent good and 2) that it is difficult to change (*difficile mobilis*). The failure of such true but imperfect virtue to make the agent good is shown through the moral disorder of its possessors. Sinners can have such true but imperfect virtue. It seems to me that such true but imperfect virtue is widely possessed.[45]

We have seen how in the *Prima Secundae*, q. 49, art. 2, ad 3, Thomas had distinguished between two kinds of changeable dispositions. One kind of easily changeable disposition, such as health or beauty, is distinct from habits that are difficult to change, such as virtue and science. But the other kind of easily changeable dispositions are imperfect forms of habits that are difficult to change. These dispositions are the same kinds of habits that the fully possessed virtues and sciences are. Such an easily changed habit is merely an inchoate virtue or science. This inchoate virtue or science does not seem to be the simply natural virtue or science that comes from one's individual nature. It differs from a perfect habit in the way that a boy differs from a grown man. This imperfection is not that of an acquired habit to an infused habit, since the acquired and infused habits differ in species. The boy and the man do not differ in species. It is the same kind of quality as the habit but merely imperfect in that it is undeveloped. It seems likely that the acquired moral virtue of someone

---

[45] Thomas, *S.T.*, I-II, q. 96, art. 2, resp.

who lacks charity is imperfect in this way as well.[46] Someone who turns away from the good life as a whole seems unlikely to consistently choose virtuous acts.

It should be clear now why such imperfect acquired virtue is discussed at length neither in the *Prima Secundae*, I-II, q. 65, art. 1 nor in the *De Virtutibus Cardinalibus*, art. 2. These two texts are about the connection of a kind of virtues, and not about imperfect members of such kinds. A sinner's true but imperfect acquired virtue is imperfect only in the sense that it fails to make the agent good. It is related to the perfect acquired virtue in the way that a boy is related to a man. It is distinct from a merely natural inclination. The acquired virtue that is imperfect in this way is the same habit as that which is connected to the others through prudence in a fully virtuous agent. In the case of an acquired virtue in a bad person, the habit is the kind of habit that is connected, although it exists in a deficient way in its subject.

Another reason for this virtue's absence from the texts about the connection of the virtues may be that such virtue and the reasons for it are only clearly delineated later in the *Summa Theologiae*. We have seen that the explicit discussions of it are in the *Secunda Secundae*. Moreover, in the *Prima Secundae*, Thomas discusses the necessity of grace for the natural moral life in the much later q. 109, when he states that without the grace that heals fallen nature it is impossible to fulfill the most important precept of the natural law, which is to love God more than oneself.[47] Without such grace the agent is not only turned away from God as a supernatural end, but she is morally deficient even on a natural level. Without such healing grace, it would seem impossible to possess even any acquired virtue that would make the agent good. Thomas never denies what he says about the connection of the virtues in the *Prima Secundae*, q. 65. The earlier text on their connection is compatible with his later account of the sinner's virtue, although it does not mention the later account.

---

[46] For the interpretation of Thomas by classical Thomists, see Réginald Garrigou-Lagrange, "L'instabilité dans l'état de péché mortel des vertus morales acquises," *Revue Thomiste* 42 (1937): 255–262. For less convincing alternative accounts, see Angela McKay Knobel, "Aquinas and the Pagan Virtues," *International Philosophical Quarterly* 51 (2011): 339–354; David Decosimo, *Ethics as a Work of Charity, Thomas Aquinas and Pagan Virtue* (Stanford, CA: Stanford University Press, 2014), 87–94.

[47] Thomas, *S.T.*, q. 109, art. 3, art. 4, ad 3; II-II, q. 26, art. 3. For additional relevant texts and problems, see Osborne, "The Augustinianism of Thomas Aquinas' Moral Theory," 285–303. For the development of Thomas's mature understanding of healing grace, see especially Bernard Lonergan, *Grace and Freedom: Operative Grace in the Thought of St. Thomas Aquinas*, ed. J. Patout Burns (London: Darton, Longman and Todd; New York: Herder and Herder, 1971), 46–55.

Although we should distinguish between the natural and supernatural goodness of acts and virtues, we should deny that there can be naturally bad agents who are supernaturally good or naturally good agents who are turned away from God through mortal sin. Given the effects of original sin, it is impossible to be naturally good without healing grace. Although individuals without such healing grace can perform some good acts, they cannot avoid serious violations of the natural law.[48] Moreover, as we have mentioned, without healing grace humans cannot perform the most important precept of the natural law, which is to love God more than self insofar as God is the source of natural goods. God has connected this healing grace with grace that elevates human nature. Humans cannot have God as their natural end by loving him more than themselves and yet be turned away from God as a supernatural end through mortal sin. Sins are both against human reason and against God as a last end.[49]

In summary, acquired moral virtue seems to depend on healing grace in order for it to make the agent good even on a natural level.[50] Without such grace, it cannot perform good acts that also make the agent good. Moreover, it is hard to see how such acquired virtue could be fully stable in the bad agent. Nevertheless, it should be kept in mind that acquired virtue does not depend on charity in the way that infused virtue does. The habit does not disappear when the agent loses charity, and it is not acquired when the agent is given charity. Acquired virtue without charity can produce the kinds of acts that would make the agent good if the agent had charity. A bad agent can have only an imperfect version of such virtue, in the way that a boy is an imperfect man. It is an imperfect instance of the same kind of virtue to which the perfect acquired virtue of the good agent belongs, but it fails to make the agent good and is unstable.

Order among Virtues

The discussion of the order of the virtues is about their inequality. It is important to distinguish between Thomas's understanding of the connection of the virtues and the Stoic understanding of their unity. We

[48] Thomas, *S.T.*, I-II, q. 109, art. 4; *Sup. Rom.*, cap. 2 lect. 3, n. 216 (Marietti, vol. 1, 39).
[49] Thomas, *S.T.*, I-II, q. 71, art. 6, resp. et ad 4–5; q. 73, art. 7, ad 3.
[50] I am passing over the details of disputes in recent literature that fail to consider these points. For a summary of the difficulties, see Thomas M. Osborne Jr., "What Is at Stake in the Question of whether Someone Can Possess the Natural Moral Virtues without Charity?," in *The Virtuous Life*, 117–130.

might say with appropriate qualifications that he defends the connection of the virtues but denies the unity of the virtues. According to Thomas, the Stoics hold not only that the moral virtues are connected so that when one virtue is possessed the others are possessed but also that they are all possessed in the highest degree. On this view, the cardinal virtues seem to be equal to each other and possessed equally by their subjects. But Thomas argues that even though the principal moral virtues are connected, they remain distinct and unequal habits. First, they are of unequal importance even in the good agent. Second, the same good agent might possess the same virtue unequally at different times or due to different inclinations. Furthermore, different individuals might possess different virtues to different extents. In the *Prima Secundae*, Thomas addresses these key differences between the virtues immediately after defending their connection.

The principal or cardinal virtues themselves are unequal because of what makes them specifically distinct from each other.[51] Considered in themselves apart from their possession by someone, there is a clear ordering. Prudence is the preeminent cardinal virtue, followed by justice, and then by fortitude and temperance. Since prudence perfects reason, and reason is the root of the other virtues, prudence is better than the moral virtues that perfect the appetite. It is more perfect than the other virtues in the way that the cause is more potent than the effects. Among the virtues that perfect the appetite, justice is superior, since it is about reason in operations.[52] Moreover, it is greater than the other moral virtues because its subject is the rational appetite, whereas the subjects of fortitude and temperance are sense appetites. Temperance is less important than fortitude because the concupiscible appetite, which it perfects, is less important than the irascible appetite, which is perfected by fortitude.

Even though these four cardinal virtues are unequal among themselves, the virtuous agent possesses them according to a proportional equality.[53] Thomas rejects the Stoic position that there can be no degrees in the possession of virtue, since an agent either reaches the mean of virtue or fails to reach it. He writes:

> It is not required for the nature of virtue, that it attains the mean of right reason in something indivisible, as the Stoics thought; but it suffices to be

[51] Thomas, *S.T.*, I-II, q. 66, art. 1; *DVCard.*, art. 3 (Marietti, 821–825).
[52] Thomas, *S.T.*, I-II, q. 66, art. 4.
[53] Thomas, *S.T.*, I-II, q. 66, art. 2., resp.; *In Sent.*, lib. 2, q. 2, art. 5, ad 6 (Mandonnet-Moos, 2, 1086–1087); *In Sent.*, lib. 3, d. 36, art. 4, sol. (Mandonnet-Moos, 3, 1223); *DM*, q. 2, art. 9, ad 8 (Leonine, 23, 56); *DVCard.*, art. 3, ad 1 (Marietti, 823).

near the mean, as is said in the Book II of the *Ethics*. For one person attains
the same indivisible target more closely and promptly than another, just as
is also clear in archers shooting at a fixed target.[54]

Different individuals might have different degrees of virtue, but an individual cannot increase in one virtue without increasing in the others.
The different virtues each grow in proportion to each other, in the way
that when a hand grows its fingers grow. The little finger and the thumb
remain shorter than the other fingers. When the hand becomes bigger,
these fingers become bigger. Similarly, prudence and justice are always
greater than the other virtues. All the virtues can grow together, but the
inferior virtues never grow so as to outshine the superior ones. Thomas
emphasizes that this proportional growth applies to the cardinal virtues
both when considered either as general conditions of virtues or as specifically distinct habits. This proportional equality between the moral virtues is based on their connection through prudence and is consequently
formal. Moreover, the infused moral virtues are proportionately equal
insofar as they are connected through charity. Despite such proportional
equality between the moral virtues in an individual, they can be present
in different individuals in different degrees.

As Although Thomas rejects the Stoic thesis that every virtue must be possessed to the maximum degree, he agrees with the Stoics that there is no
inequality in the way that a virtue extends over its matter. For example, one
temperance is not less than another because it is a temperance only about
vegetables whereas the other is about both meat and vegetables. Similarly,
it is impossible to be virtuous with respect to temperance and not with
respect to fortitude. Moral virtues are unlike intellectual habits in this way.
Different individuals can possess science to various extents depending on
the number of conclusions that they have demonstrated. But each moral
virtue must be about all of the relevant matter, and the virtuous person
must have virtues that cover the matter of the entire moral life.

As we have seen, there is inequality between virtues on account of the
way in which the same individual might possess virtues in degrees at different times and different individuals might possess the virtues in different degrees. In general, this inequality between the virtues can result from
four different causes, namely custom, natural inclination, the clarity of

---

[54] "Non enim exigitur ad rationem virtutis, quod attingat rectae rationis medium in indivisibili,
sicut Stoici putabant, sed sufficit prope medium esse, ut in II Ethic. dicitur. Idem etiam indivisi-
bile signum unus propinquius et promptius attingit quam alius, sicut etiam patet in sagittatoribus
trahentibus ad certum signum." Thomas, *S.T.*, I-II, q. 66, art. 1, resp.

reason's judgment, and grace. Thomas accepts the Aristotelian thesis that the virtues are connected through prudence and denies the Stoic thesis that the virtues are united in such a way that they are all possessed at the highest degree of perfection.

Thomas emphasizes that different individuals have different inclinations to virtuous acts. For instance, the soldier might be more inclined to courage in battle and the merchant might be more inclined to acts of justice. Thomas explains: "one human can be more prompt for the act of one virtue than for the act of another, whether from nature, or from custom, or even from the gift of grace."[55] Three of these causes are the same as the causes that he gave more generally for an inequality among virtues in the same subject. The first cause is presumably the individual nature, which comes from the agent's own bodily composition.[56] The second cause, custom, takes into account the agent's previous exercise of the virtues. The third cause is due to God. Insofar as the virtues are considered materially, they can be possessed in different degrees. Thomas remarks that such a difference exists even among the saints.[57] One virtuous individual will be more prompt for the act of one virtue than another virtuous individual might be. For example, Moses is known for his gentleness and Job for his patience.

Notice that in his discussion of the differences between individuals, Thomas does not mention the difference between the clarity of judgment that he mentioned previously when discussing the degrees of virtue. The reason could be that the clarity of judgment seems to belong to prudence and consequently is formal. Insofar as the virtues are considered formally, they must be all present in their proportionate equality. One individual might be more prudent than another and consequently have proportionately greater moral virtue than the others do. But prudence works in all of the principal moral virtues. The agent through her prudence alone cannot favor one virtue over the other. Perhaps clarity of judgment on its own would not explain why she is more inclined to acts of one virtue than to acts of another.

The proportional equality between the cardinal virtues depends on the intellectual virtue of prudence. Simply speaking, the intellectual virtues are superior to these moral virtues, and the intellectual virtue of wisdom is superior to prudence.[58] Since the universal is greater than the particular,

---

[55] "potest esse unus homo magis promptus ad actum unius virtutis quam ad actum alterius, vel ex natura, vel ex consuetudine, vel etiam ex gratiae dono." Thomas, *S.T.*, I-II, q. 66, art. 2, resp.

[56] Thomas, *S.T.*, I-II, q. 63, art. 1.

[57] Thomas, *S.T.*, I-II, q. 66, art. 2, obj. 2 and ad 2.

[58] Thomas, *S.T.*, I-II, q. 66, art. 3, 5.

the object of the intellect, which is universal, is superior to the object of
the appetite, which is a particular good. Wisdom is superior to prudence
because it is about God, whereas prudence is about merely human affairs,
although such human affairs should be considered in relation to the ultimate end, which is God. Aristotle himself stated that prudence is not
the greatest intellectual virtue because it is about merely human affairs,
whereas some beings are greater than humans.[59] Thomas, like Aristotle,
thinks that intellectual contemplation is higher than the exercise of moral
virtue. Nevertheless, in a way the moral virtues are superior to the intellectual, since they make the agent good in an unqualified way. Exercising
the intellectual virtue of wisdom is only one way of, or perhaps even something different from, being a good human being. Being good at wisdom
is being good in a particular way. On the other hand, the person who
exercises moral virtue is, precisely by doing so, good as a human being.
The acts of the moral virtues make their agents good.

The theological virtues are all about God himself and consequently in
some way are equal.[60] Nevertheless, someone comes closer to God through
charity than through faith and hope. The reason for this closeness is that
faith and hope are about the possession of God in the future. Faith is
about what is not yet seen, namely God's essence, and hope is about the
attainment of beatitude. But charity is a kind of love, and love brings a
union. The loved object is present to the lover through love. Consequently,
charity makes God present at once because through it the agent loves God
for his own sake.

Due to the way in which it makes God present, charity is superior to
faith in the way that in this life the will is superior to the intellect with
respect to objects that are above us.[61] Truth is in the intellect, whereas
goodness is in the external thing. We cannot adequately grasp through
our intellect what is above us. But we can love its goodness as it is in itself.
Thomas emphasizes that the relationship between faith and charity is not
the same as that between prudence and moral virtues. Prudence is fully
practical. Faith merely shows its object to charity insofar as it is able to.
By charity the agent is moved to God himself and not merely to God as
he is known by faith.

Thomas clearly distances himself from any account of the virtues
according to which they are unified to such a degree that they are all
equal to each other or possessed in an equal way. He directly criticizes

[59] Aristotle, *EN* 6.7; Thomas, *SLE*, lib. 6, 6 (Leonine, 47.2, 352–354).
[60] Thomas, *S.T.*, I-II, q. 66, art. 6; II-II, q. 23, art. 6.
[61] Thomas, *S.T.*, I-II, q. 66, art. 6, ad 1.

the Stoic account of their unity. He defends the Aristotelian thesis that
the moral virtues are connected through the one virtue of prudence, but
he shows that this thesis is compatible with the recognition that different
virtuous individuals possess the major moral virtues unequally. Moreover,
he argues that this inequality among the moral virtues applies to the intellectual virtues as well, and in a way even to the theological virtues.

This Life and the Next

In the *Prima Secundae*, Thomas concludes his entire discussion of the
virtues in general with a question on their duration (q. 69). Medieval
theologians, perhaps influenced by Augustine and Cicero, were concerned
with whether the moral virtues continue to exist after the agent's death.
The first problem is whether the virtues can function after death. Since
the virtues inhere in the soul's powers, one might expect them to exist
after death along with the soul. On the other hand, most of the soul's
powers have bodily organs, which no longer exist after the body corrupts.
Acts most properly belong to organs and to the whole organism. Without
the organ, the power remains only in its roots. If powers cannot function, then there would be no need for the virtue to perfect the power. The
second problem is whether there is any need for the virtues after death.
Someone who enjoys the beatific vision would seem to have little use for
ordinary acts of the cardinal virtues. The intellectual and theological virtues bring with them their own difficulties. For instance, someone who
sees God is unlikely to need faith in God or hope for heaven. Thomas
considers separately such different kinds of virtue.

In the *Commentary on the Sentences* and similar texts, Thomas stresses
the connection of the acquired moral virtues to the political life. In this
Commentary, he briefly notes that the matter of the acquired virtues is the
civil life and their end is the civic good.[62] In contrast, the infused virtues
are about the heavenly city and the Church. After death, there is no matter or end for the acquired virtues. Consequently, they cannot remain. In
contrast, the spiritual life of the heavenly city and the Church is perfected.
Therefore, the infused moral virtues remain after death. This argument
depends upon the sharp division between the civil life, which passes, and
the spiritual life, which is completed in heaven.

Thomas develops this argument in much greater length in his *De
Virtutibus Cardinalibus*, art. 4. He places the discussion in the context of

---

[62] Thomas, *In Sent.*, lib. 3, d. 33, q. 1, art. 4, sol. (Mandonnet-Moos, 3, 1040).

Augustine's rejection of Cicero's position that there will be no virtues in the next life.[63] Augustine writes:

> What justice does now in relieving the miserable, what prudence does in averting snares, what fortitude [does] in bearing troubles; what temperance [does] in restraining depraved pleasures, will not be there, where there will be nothing evil at all; but to justice, being put under the ruling God; to prudence, preferring no good to God, nor making any good equal to him; to fortitude, clinging most firmly to him; to temperance, taking pleasure in no hurtful affect.[64]

Augustine agrees with Cicero that the present acts of virtue will no longer be present. But he thinks that the same virtues can have different acts that are suitable for the next life.

Thomas defends Augustine's claim by explaining how one kind of virtue can have multiple kinds of acts by arguing that different kinds of acts can belong to the same habit if their terms are in an ordered series.[65] He rests his argument on Aristotle's description of virtue as the "peak of a power" (*ultimum potentiae*). The Latin translation of Aristotle's Greek as "*ultimum potentiae*" here is awkward. We might also translate the Latin as the "limit of a power," the "ultimate of a power," or even as the "utmost of a power." It might be best here to retain the Latin "*ultimum*." There are two ways in which something may be the *ultimum*. First, there is the *ultimum* in an ordered series, as when someone builds a house. In such a case the *ultimum* in the laying of a foundation is different from that of the erection of a column. There are two different acts. But since the two distinct acts are ordered to the same construction of a house, they belong

---

[63] Marcus Tullius Cicero, *Hortensius*, fr. 110, ed. Albertus Grilli (Milano and Varese: Instituto Editoriale Cisalpino, 1962), 51. For the context, see Paul MacKendrick, *The Philosophical Books of Cicero* (New York: St. Martin's Press, 1989), 106–113.

[64] "quod nunc agit iustitia in subveniendo miseris, quod prudentia in praecavendis insidiis, quod fortitudo in perferendis molestiis, quod temperantia in coercendis delectationibus pravis, non ibi erit, ubi nihil omnino mali erit; sed iustitiae erit regenti Deo subitum esse; prudentiae, nullum bonum Deum praeponere vel aequare; fortitudinis, ei firmissime cohaerere; temperantiae, nullo affectu noxio delectari." Augustine, *De Trin.*, lib. 14, cap. 9, in Thomas, *DVCard.*, art. 4, resp. (Marietti, 826). The critical text (CCSL 50a, 439–440) is longer and in a slightly different order: "cui regenti esse subditum si iustitiae est, immortalis est omnino iustitia nec in illa esse beatitudine desinet sed talis ac tanta erit ut perfectior et maior esse non possit. fortassis et aliae tres uirtutes, prudentia sine ullo iam periculo erroris, fortitudo sine molestia tolerandorum malorum, temperantia sine repugnatione libidinum erunt in illa felicitate ut prudentiae sit nullum deo praeponere uel aequare, fortitudinis ei firmissime cohaerere, temperantiae nullo defectu noxio delectari. nunc autem quod agit iustitia in subueniendo miseris, quod prudentia in praecauendis insidiis, quod fortitudo in perferendis molestiis, quod temperantia in coercendis delectationibus prauis non ibi erit ubi nihil omnino mali erit."

[65] Thomas, *DVCard.*, art. 4, resp. (Marietti, 826).

to the same technical skill of housebuilding. There is one technical skill of housebuilding but different kinds of acts. Similarly, the same virtue of courage or fortitude produces such specifically different acts as preparing for battle, fighting during a battle, and rejoicing in glory after a battle. The *ultima* of these different acts can belong to the same virtue because they are part of an ordered series.

The same technical skill or habit produces different acts only when such acts are part of such an ordered series. Motions that have *ultima* that lack such order must also have different technical skills or habits. For instance, laying a keel or stepping a mast are not only different acts from those connected with housebuilding, but they also belong to a different technical skill, namely that of the shipwright and not that of the house builder.

According to Thomas, acts of the acquired virtues as part of an ordered series are directed only to the civil life. They can be directed to a higher end, but need not be. Consequently, the acquired virtues do not act in the next life. On the other hand, acts of the infused virtues even in this life have an *ultimum* that is part of an ordered series. They are for the sake of heavenly glory. But the same virtues have different kinds of acts in this life and in the next.

In this text, Thomas's distinction between infused and acquired virtue allows him to argue that both Augustine and Cicero are correct in their claims about whether the virtues exist in the next life. Augustine rightly states that the virtues continue to act in the next life but only if we restrict the scope of his claim to the infused virtues. Cicero is correct to say that the virtues are unused in this next life but only if we consider the thesis as applying to the acquired virtues. This argument improves that of the *Commentary on the Sentences* in two ways. First, it explains precisely why in some cases the same virtue can have different kinds of acts and in other cases it cannot. Different acts of the same virtue must have *ultima* that are part of an essential order. Second, it explains that Cicero and Augustine can both be correct since they are speaking about different kinds of moral virtue.

This emphasis on the permanence of infused virtue and the passing nature of acquired virtue is strangely absent from the *Summa Theologiae, Prima Secundae*, q. 67, in which Thomas seems to hold that acts of both acquired and infused virtues exist in the next life. The nature of the question is the same. Moreover, to some extent Thomas approaches the issue in the same way as a dispute between Cicero and Augustine.[66] But, unlike in his other

---

[66] Thomas, *S.T.*, I-II, 67, art. 1, resp.

texts, he does not appeal to the distinction between acquired and infused virtues or between civil affairs and the heavenly city. He focuses instead on the distinction between what is material and what is formal in the virtues.

The moral virtues exist in the next life only with respect to their formal characteristics and not with respect to the matter of their acts. The moral virtues will have different but formally similar acts. With respect to what is material, the virtues cannot remain, since there will be no place for disordered desires to be ruled by temperance, or fear and daring to be ordered by courage, or infractions to be redressed by justice. On the other hand, formal characteristics will remain. For instance, reason will be correct, and the appetitive powers will be ordered by reason. When the soul is separated from the body after death but before the general resurrection, there are no sense powers or sense appetites. Consequently, fortitude and temperance will remain in the soul only insofar as the roots of the sense appetites in some way remain in the soul.[67] But after the resurrection the renewal of the sense appetites will be accompanied by the full development of these respective virtues. Every act will be subordinate to God.

In the *Secunda Secundae*, he similarly avoids discussing the persistence of virtue after death in the context of the distinction between civil life and heavenly beatitude.[68] He also fails to distinguish between acquired and infused virtues. He states here that in the next life the same habits will produce different acts. These acts will be different because the matter of these acts will no longer remain. However, the virtues will produce different acts in relation to their ends. For instance, justice will not be about buying or selling but about the correct order to God. Similarly, patience will not be about sustaining evils but instead about the joy in the goods that were attained in this way.[69] This treatment is similar to that of the *Prima Secundae* in that Thomas emphasizes that the matter of the present virtuous acts disappears. But here he focuses on the end rather than the formal aspect. It seems to me that there is no real difference between the two approaches in the *Prima Secundae* and in the *Secunda Secundae*. He can emphasize the end in the later text because of the way in which the end of an act is formal. He does not deny what he said in the *Prima Secundae*. On the other hand, it is perhaps significant that Thomas never seems to settle on the terminology used in the *Prima Secundae*, even in the following part of the *Summa Theologiae*.

---

[67] Thomas, *S.T.*, I-II, 67, art. 1, ad 3. For the powers of the separated soul, see Thomas, *S.T.*, I, q. 77, art. 8.

[68] Thomas, *S.T.*, II-II, q. 136, art. 1, ad 1.

[69] For patience, see also Thomas, *DVCard.*, art. 4, ad 12 (Marietti, 827).

It is much harder to square the texts from the *Summa Theologiae* with those of his other works. How is the use of the formal aspects or ends of moral virtue in the *Summa Theologiae* compatible with the use of the distinction between the civil and heavenly in the relevant early passage of the *Commentary on the Sentences* and the later or contemporaneous passage from the *De Virtutibus Cardinalibus*? It might be tempting to think that in all of these texts Thomas thinks that the acquired virtues disappear and the infused remain because there is only matter for the infused virtues in the next life. Such a solution would make both positions thoroughly compatible, but it seems to stretch the texts. The more plausible interpretation is that in the *Summa Theologiae* Thomas argues that both the acquired and infused moral virtues endure after death. Thomas does not state that he is discussing both kinds of virtue, but his arguments seem to apply to both kinds.

In his commentary on the *Prima Secundae*, q, 67, art. 1, Conradus Koellin gives three arguments for the position that Thomas holds in the *Summa Theologiae*, that acts of both the acquired and infused virtues are in the next life.[70] First, Conrad notes that, in the response, Thomas's discussion of Cicero and Augustine seems to be about the acquired moral virtues. Second, ad 3 of the article states that only the seeds of fortitude and temperance (*seminalia*) exist in the soul between death and the resurrection of the body. These seeds resemble the seeds (*seminalia*) of intellectual and moral virtues that are discussed in the earlier q. 63, art. 1. Moreover, in art. 2, ad 3, of that earlier question, Thomas states that only the principles of acquired virtues are naturally present in the soul. This second argument seems to me the weakest of Conrad's three, since it is not clear whether the seeds of the question concerning the duration of the virtue are the same as that of the earlier discussion or whether these seeds are the same as the innate principles of acquired virtue. Conrad's third argument is that the account of the acquired intellectual virtues in the following art. 2 corresponds to the discussion of moral virtue in this art. 1. As we will see, in art. 2 acquired intellectual virtue exists with respect to what is formal but not with respect to what is material. For similar reasons, we might take Thomas to say in the earlier article that acquired virtue has such existence.

In this art. 2, which is about the intellectual formal virtues, Thomas uses a distinction between the formal and material aspects that departs at least verbally from the earlier discussions of the same issue in the *Commentary*

---

[70] Conradus, *In I-II*, q. 67, art. 1 (ed. 1602, 461).

on the Sentences. The development in his understanding of the persistence of the intellectual virtues parallels the change in his account of the persistence of the moral virtues. In the earlier work, Thomas states that the same intellectual habits remain after death but that there will be a difference in the mode of knowing and the acts.[71] The mode of knowing will be different because there will be no phantasms. The acts will be different since there will be no discursive reasoning. In this *Commentary on the Sentences*, Thomas's discussion of the intellectual virtues is similar to that of his alternative discussions of the persistence of infused moral virtue according to which the same habit remains, although it produces specifically distinct acts.

In the *Summa Theologiae*, Thomas argues that the intellectual virtues will remain with respect to what is formal but not with respect to what is material. He uses the distinction between the formal and the material in this context in the same way that he uses it when arguing for the persistence of the moral virtues. But he does not seem to be basing his discussion of intellectual virtue on that of moral virtue. He develops the persistence of the formal aspect of intellectual virtue much earlier, in the *Prima Pars* of the *Summa Theologiae*.[72] Consequently, the shift in his treatment of the persistence of intellectual virtue seems temporally prior to the shift in his understanding of moral virtue.

In the later q. 67 of the *Prima Secundae*, he develops this distinction in the context of the absence of phantasms and the kinds of intellectual acts. The intelligible species is formal and the phantasms are material. Since the intellect remains but the internal senses do not, the separated soul will have the same intelligible species but not the sense images that are normally used. Consequently, these intellectual habits use the intelligible species in a different way to produce different acts from those that are produced when the soul is united to the body. This thesis closely resembles the thesis that the moral virtues exist after death only with respect to what is formal. Conrad's use of the discussion of intellectual virtue in art. 2 rests on the similarity of treatment of the duration of intellectual virtues with that of the duration of moral virtues.

Whether he changes his mind or not, Thomas does not argue in the *Summa Theologiae* that the acquired moral virtues disappear at death. He seems to think that they persist in the way that the intellectual virtues

---

[71] Thomas, *In Sent.*, lib. 3, d. 31, q. 2, art. 4, sol. (Mandonnet-Moos, 3, 996–997). See also Thomas, *In Sent.*, lib. 4, d. 50, q. 1, art. 2 (Parma, vol. 2, 1248–1249).

[72] Thomas, *S.T.*, I, q. 89, art. 6.

persist. However, unlike the moral and intellectual virtues, both faith and hope cease to exist after death.[73] Even their formal characters include imperfections that are due to the present life. The imperfections belong to what these virtues are. For example, faith by definition is "the substance of things to be hoped for, the evidence of what does not appear."[74] It is an imperfect knowledge because its object is obscure. In the next life, this imperfect knowledge will be replaced by the vision of God. Similarly, hope by its very nature is about a happiness that has not yet been attained. Since in the next life such happiness will be possessed, there is no need for hope.

In the *Prima Secundae*, Thomas concludes his discussion of both his question on the virtues and his whole treatment of virtue with an account of the way in which charity remains in heaven. Unlike faith and hope, charity involves no imperfection. Unlike moral and intellectual virtues, it lacks a material aspect that belongs only to the present life. Not only does the habit of charity endure but its act remains the same. Loving God has the same object both in this life and the next. The only difference is that the beatific vision will increase charity because the greater knowledge will cause a greater love. Charity is not only the preeminent theological virtue but it is also the most enduring.

These four questions on the properties of the virtues can seem to be more or less sloppily added on to the otherwise orderly section on virtue in the *Prima Secundae*. But they clarify central points that must be considered. The question on the mean clears up some possible confusion about what virtue is. The question on the connection of the virtues is of central importance both historically and doctrinally. The question on the inequality of the virtues depends on and develops what is said about their connection. The last question, on the duration of the virtues, is a staple of the medieval debates, and Thomas fittingly uses it to close the set of questions on virtue.

These questions provide a fitting end to the treatise in part because of the way in which they depend upon the earlier questions. Understanding the role of the mean in the different virtues depends on a precise account of the differences between the moral, the intellectual, and the theological virtues. An exact account of their connection depends not only on the previous discussion of their nature but also on discussions of what habits

---

[73] Thomas, *S.T.*, I-II, q. 67, art. 3–4. For hope, see also Thomas, *In Sent.*, 3, d. 26, q. 2, art. 5, qstcla. 2, sol. (ed, Mandonnet-Moos, 3, 845–846); *DVSpe*, art. 4 (Marietti, 809–812). For both faith and hope, see Thomas, *In Sent.*, lib. 3, d. 31, q. 2, art. 1, qsctla. 3, sol. (Mandonnet-Moos, 3, 989–990).
[74] "*Substantia sperandarum rerum, argumentum non apparentium.*" Heb. 11:1, in Thomas, *S.T.*, I-II, q. 67, art. 3, resp.

are and how they are acquired. The equality of the virtues, or perhaps more clearly their inequality, depends on all of these previous accounts. For instance, the proportional growth of the virtues can only be understood in light of their connection. Finally, the discussion of their duration in the next life depends on all of what has passed previously concerning their formal and material aspects, their connection, and their importance. In particular, it emphasizes continuing relevance of moral virtue even after death and the supremacy of the theological virtue of charity. The preeminence of charity readies the reader for the questions that immediately follow, which are on the gifts of the Holy Ghost, the fruits of the Holy Ghost, and the beatitudes. The reader is reminded that the *Summa Theologiae* is after all a work of theology, even if it includes and depends on philosophy.

CHAPTER 6

Thomistic Virtue and Contemporary Thought

The previous chapters are an attempt at a precise and accurate account of Thomas's understanding of virtue in light of its philosophical, theological, and historical context. We should now be in a better position to determine whether his account has intrinsic importance and, a different issue, contemporary relevance. Many of my claims in this last chapter are tentative, and they may be more suggestive than convincing. First, we will distinguish between Thomas's discussion of virtue and some trends in the contemporary virtue ethics movement. Such a consideration leads to revisiting the overall purpose of Thomas's own description of virtue, which is to provide an account of the human good and a way of organizing the study of moral matters. After looking at Thomas's understanding of virtue and the human good, we can consider some problems concerning whether it might be compatible with contemporary science and, though it is not the same, with contemporary philosophical "naturalism."

Virtue Ethics

Current scholarship on Thomas's account of virtue usually refers to the virtue ethics movement, which began in the middle of the last century as rejection of modern moral theories such as Kantianism and utilitarianism. It is a broad movement and impossible to define precisely. Elizabeth Anscombe and Philippa Foot, who were in some ways founders of this movement, argued against the attempts of their philosophical contemporaries to practice moral philosophy without a well-developed moral psychology.[1] They looked for an alternative to the philosophical practice

---

[1] For representative texts, see G. E. M. Anscombe, "Modern Moral Philosophy," *Philosophy* 33 (1958): 1–19; repr. in *Virtue Ethics*, ed. Roger Crisp and Michael Slote (Oxford: Oxford University Press, 1997), 26–44; Philippa Foot, "Virtues and Vices," in *Virtues and Vices and Other Essays in Moral Philosophy* (Oxford: Clarendon Press, 2002), 1–18; repr. in *Virtue Ethics*, ed. Crisp and Slote, 163–177.

of their time. Alasdair MacIntyre similarly argued for the bankruptcy of modern moral theories and a return to a broadly Aristotelian moral philosophy.[2] These philosophers were suspicious of the way that philosophy was done by their contemporaries. Their work was to some extent outside of the established parameters. More recently many followers of virtue ethics have become a small part of the philosophical establishment. The "virtue ethicists" develop and defend their views much in the same way that other moral philosophers now do. As Jonathan Sanford has shown, most or at least many philosophers in the virtue ethics movement eventually began to practice virtue ethics as an option within modern moral philosophy, as a rival to other contemporary theories.[3] What Anscombe arguably introduced as an alternative to modern moral philosophy has in some way itself become part of modern moral philosophy.

It is difficult to describe what characteristics are now shared by the various philosophers who see themselves as practicing virtue ethics.[4] For some, virtue ethics seems to include the view that the virtues are more fundamental than any rules or ends, and for others it seems instead, or also, to be a revival of a "naturalistic" Aristotelianism, which is compatible with contemporary science. In general, they seem to hold that the virtues overshadow other topics of moral philosophy. In contrast to such versions of virtue ethics, Thomas's account of virtue does not on its own provide a basis for an ethical system.

We will see that there are consequently two distinct ways in which Thomas seems to differ from many practitioners of contemporary virtue ethics, in particular from such philosophers as Rosalind Hursthouse and Daniel C. Russell.[5] First, Thomas does not replace rules, ends, or goods with virtues. Second, he does not think that the nature of moral goodness

[2] Alasdair MacIntyre, *After Virtue: A Study in Moral Theory*, 2nd ed. (Notre Dame, IN: University of Notre Dame Press, 1984).

[3] Jonathan J. Sanford, *Before Virtue: Assessing Contemporary Virtue Ethics* (Washington, DC: The Catholic University of America Press, 2019), 114–142. For the relationship between this movement and Thomas, see Andrew Pinsent, *The Second-Person Perspective in Aquinas's Ethics: Virtues and Gifts* (New York: Routledge, 2012), 1–14; Candace Vogler, "Aristotle, Aquinas, Anscombe, and the New Virtue Ethics," in *Aquinas and the Nicomachean Ethics*, ed. Tobias Hoffmann, Jörn Müller, and Matthias Perkams (Cambridge: Cambridge University Press, 2013), 239–257.

[4] For an overview, see Christopher Miles Coope, "Modern Virtue Ethics," in *Values and Virtues: Aristotelianism in Contemporary Ethics*, ed. Timothy Chappell (Oxford: Oxford University Press, 2007), 20–52; Timothy Chappell, "Virtue Ethics in the Twentieth Century," in *The Cambridge Companion to Virtue Ethics*, ed. Daniel C. Russell (Cambridge: Cambridge University Press, 2013), 149–171.

[5] Sanford, *Before Virtue*, 117–120, 131–132. For representative texts, see especially Rosalind Hursthouse, *On Virtue Ethics* (Oxford: Oxford University Press, 1999), 25–42; Daniel C. Russell, *Practical Intelligence and the Virtues* (Oxford: Clarendon, 2009), 37–71, 103–142.

or rightness ultimately depends on moral virtue. For him, the order is reverse. Nevertheless, we should keep in mind that there are many varieties of contemporary virtue ethics, and not all of them would necessarily disagree with Thomas on these two areas.

On Thomas's account, virtues, rules, and goods all play central but distinct roles.[6] As we have seen, moral virtue in its very definition includes a mean that is determined by reason, and reason's rules are needed to determine this mean. This determination of the mean by rules of reason is perhaps most obvious in the virtue of justice that considers external operations, and perhaps most particularly in commutative justice, which is about a relatively straightforward equality. But reason also applies rules to matter that involves the passions. For instance, overeating involves a mean between too much and too little food. Sometimes overeating straightforwardly violates a rule of ecclesiastical, natural, or perhaps even civil law. The mean of virtue itself varies between persons. For example, the greater need of larger persons for more food can be expressed in a rule of reason. Virtues require and do not replace moral rules.

Moral rules are primarily used in evaluating acts. As David Gallagher argues, the moral goodness of the virtues is not primary. It derives from the moral goodness of acts.[7] He mentions various texts in which Thomas distinguishes between the goodness of nonrational powers and habits, widely speaking, and the goodness of moral virtues, which are habits of choice.[8] These texts are significant insofar as they show the importance of choice for moral goodness, but they are not all directly about the difference between the goodness of an operative habit and its own acts. The important text for this last issue, and consequently for comparing Thomas's view with that of those contemporary virtue ethicists who think that the moral goodness of virtue is primary, is that which is about whether a vicious act is worse than a vice. In addressing this question, Thomas states that the relationship between a vice and its act is like that between a virtue and its act. He writes:

> But is clear that an act exceeds a potency in good or in bad, as is said in Book IX of the *Metaphysics*; for it is better to act well than to be able to act

---

[6] For the place of moral rules in relation to virtue and goods, see Thomas M. Osborne Jr., *Aquinas's Ethics* (Cambridge: Cambridge University Press, 2020), 41–53.
[7] David M. Gallagher, "Aquinas on Goodness and Moral Goodness," in *Thomas Aquinas and His Legacy*, ed. David M. Gallagher (Washington, DC: The Catholic University of America Press, 1994), 37–60.
[8] Gallagher, "Aquinas on Goodness," 56, note 57, mentions Thomas, *S. T.*, I-II, q. 55, art. 3, ad 2; q. 56, art. 4, resp.; q. 71, art. 3, resp.; q. 58, art. 4, resp.

well; and similarly it is more blameworthy to act badly than to be able to act badly ... Which even is clear from this, that a habit is not said to be good or bad except from this that it inclines to a good or bad act. So, a habit is said to be good or bad on account of the goodness or badness of the act. And thus the act is better or worse than the habit is.[9]

Thomas does qualify this claim. A habit might be better or worse than an individual act because of the many acts that it causes. Nevertheless, the operative habit's ability to cause many acts makes it better or worse in only a limited way.[10] Acts remain primary. The habits are better or worse only on account of the acts that they produce.

As we have seen in Chapter 3, operative habits are defined by the kinds of acts that they produce. One virtue such as justice or courage might have different acts that share in the object of the virtue, and perhaps a more specific object by which the act is specified. The objects that specify virtues and acts are determined by reason. The object is good insofar as the act perfects the agent. Eating unhealthy amounts is generally bad because it is incompatible with achieving the human good. Acts such as adultery and murder by definition undermine the human good and consequently should never be done. Both acts are against justice, and the first is also against temperance. Most importantly, even when they are about passions, the moral virtues perfect the agent as part of the political community and thereby make the agent well-ordered with respect to the political common good. The individual's good, which is a part of the common good, gives rise to the rules according to which virtuous acts are measured. The various goods achieved through virtue either constitute or lead to the individual's ultimate end, which can only be understood in light of the different wholes to which the individual belongs, such as the family, the political community, the universe, and the Church.

If, as Thomas and Aristotle think, virtue makes acts and the agent's good, then there is a necessary order of virtue to action. Virtue not only causes good action, but it makes the agent good precisely by making the acts good. It is hard to see what worth justice or courage would have just in themselves as adornments to an agent. Those who would prioritize

9 "Manifestum est autem quod actus in bono et in malo praeeminet potentiae, ut dicitur in IX Metaphys., melius est enim bene agere quam posse bene agere; et similiter vituperabilius est male agere quam posse male agere ... Quod etiam ex hoc apparet, quod habitus non dicitur bonus vel malus nisi ex hoc quod inclinat ad actum bonum vel malum. Unde propter bonitatem vel malitiam actus, dicitur habitus bonus vel malus. Et sic potior est actus in bonitate vel malitia quam habitus est." Thomas, S.T., I-II, q. 71, art. 3, resp. Aristotle, Met. 9.8.1051a4. See also Thomas, In Met., lib 9, lect. 10 (Marietti, 453); SLE, lib. 3, lect. 6 (Leonine, 47.1, 136).
10 Thomas, S.T., I-II, q. 71, art. 3, ad 1, 2.

virtues over acts would seem to be modelling virtue on a disposition such as physical health, which has some desirability even apart from its effects. But physical health is not an operative habit. It is a distinct nonoperative disposition of the body. It is desirable in itself even apart from any human operation. Unless it is joined to something bad and consequently bad on account of such a connection, health is desirable. Like physical health, moral virtue is a good that is desirable for its own sake and for the sake of happiness. Unlike physical health, moral virtue is morally good, and moral goodness primarily consists in proper operations, which belong to the intellect and will. Moral virtue is morally good only because it produces such morally good acts. Those who would make virtue desirable primarily for its own sake and apart from morally good acts seem to misunderstand what a virtue is, in particular how it is distinct from dispositions such as health or beauty.

For Thomas, virtues are not a tool for evaluating different possible moral scenarios in the way that a rule of reason or an account of the human good might be. He does not appeal to virtue on its own to explain why an act might or might not be bad, in the way that a contemporary consequentialist might appeal to preference satisfaction or a deontologist might appeal to moral principle. Virtue on its own does not exhaust or even provide a primary instance of what it means for the act or agent to be morally good.

The Role of Virtue in Thomas's Ethics

As we have seen in Chapter 1, following Aristotle, Thomas includes virtue in the definition of the human good. Virtue is part of the definition of the ultimate end or the human good, and as such it has an organizing role in ethics. This description of the human good itself presupposes a particular understanding of human nature. Human happiness and consequently the operation of virtue are varied according to the different ways in which human nature is capable of being perfected.

Thomas's account of the human good arguably includes but is certainly not limited to Aristotle's account. First, there is a good that is proportionate to human nature. But for Thomas, and not for Aristotle, there is a supernatural human good that exceeds the capacities of human nature. It is made possible for us by God's elevation of human nature through grace. This elevation presupposes and adds a further determination to the natural human good and depends on the capacity of human nature to be elevated in this way. Consequently, even though the ultimate end of humans surpasses that which can be achieved by human nature and known through human reason, it is consonant with and depends on an account of a human good that is proportioned to human nature.

This twofold human goodness explains the distinction between moral goodness and the goodness that belongs to the supernatural order. Moral goodness primarily consists in operations that perfect human nature. Since reason is proper to humans, the human good consists in operations that belong to or somehow come under the influence of reason. Consequently, as we have seen in Chapter 1, Thomas accepts Aristotle's account of happiness as "the human good will be an operation according to virtue, but if there are many virtues, according to the most perfect and best."[11] So defined, virtue is necessary for the human good because this good consists in virtuous operation. Thomas agrees with this overall account, although he distinguishes sharply between the different ways in which the ultimate end can be considered as a thing and as the possession of the thing.[12] The ultimate end of human beings considered as a thing is God. But the ultimate end of human beings considered as the possession of good is an activity of the soul.

For Thomas, the ultimate end of humans insofar as it is an activity is the contemplation of God in the beatific vision. He denies that human happiness consists merely in the contemplation of God through the intellectual virtue of wisdom, or first philosophy. In his *Commentary on the Gospel of St. Matthew*, Thomas is particularly critical of attempts to identify happiness with the exercise of moral virtue or the contemplation of God in this life.[13] Consequently, the happiness that Aristotle describes is the ultimate end only when considered as a description of unaided human nature in this life. Given the reality of grace and the possibility of the beatific vision, Aristotle's account of happiness is imperfect to a great extent.

Thomas applies the term "happiness" primarily to the contemplation of God that belongs to the saints in heaven.[14] This ultimate end consists in the activity of some infused virtues and is reached to some extent through the practice of the infused virtues in this life and even through the exercise

---

[11] See Chapter 1, note 75.
[12] Thomas, *S.T.*, I-II, q. 2, art. 7; q. 3, art. 2. The term "thing" (*res*) in Latin does not have the connotation or meaning of not being a person, which it seems to have in English.
[13] Thomas, *Super Mat.*, cap. 5, lect. 5 (Marietti, 65–66, 69–70). See Servais Pinckaers, "La voie spirituelle du bonheur selon Saint Thomas," in *Ordo Sapientiae et Amoris: Image et message de Saint Thomas d'Aquin*, ed. Carlos-Josaphat Pinto de Oliveira (Fribourg: Éditions Universitaires, 1993), 276–281; trans. Mary Thomas Noble as "Aquinas's Pursuit of Beatitude: From the Commentary on the Sentences to the Summa Theologiae," in *The Pinckaers Reader*, ed. John Berkman and Craig Steven Titus (Washington, DC: The Catholic University of America Press, 2005), 104–108.
[14] Thomas, *SCG* 3, cap. 48 (ed. Leonina Manualis, 277–279); *S.T.*, I-II, q. 3, art. 8.

of naturally virtuous acts that are ordered to God through the infused virtue of charity.[15] Such acts are not only morally good but also meritorious of eternal life.[16] Merit presupposes ordinary moral goodness. Moreover, Thomas's account of infused moral virtue is patterned after philosophical accounts of acquired virtue, which by itself is only morally good. All the acts of the acquired moral virtues are good and in a limited way make the agent good. The infused moral virtues produce acts that are also meritorious and cause acts that have merit for attaining the ultimate end of contemplating God directly.

For Thomas, the various virtues indicate different areas in which human nature is perfected. In contrast to Thomas, many contemporary virtue ethicists are imprecise or unclear about the relationship between virtue and happiness, and some might be read as holding that the virtues are merely instruments for achieving happiness.[17] But Thomas holds that the virtues are good because virtuous operations are good, and these virtuous operations are not good in a merely instrumental way. They are worthwhile in themselves and also achieve either a natural or even a supernatural good. In explaining Aristotle's account of happiness, Thomas writes:

> Truly we choose pleasure and understanding and virtue certainly for their own sake. For we would choose them or desire them even if nothing else originated for us from them. And for all that we choose them for the sake of happiness, in as much as through them we believe that we will be happy.[18]

The ultimate end is the only end that can be desired for its own sake alone. But the virtues are desired for their own sake and for making the agent happy. Aristotle was unaware of the beatific vision. Thomas thinks that it is our ultimate end. Since it is the perfect happiness of knowing God in heaven, it entails loving God through the infused virtue of charity.[19] Various operations that are under the direction of charity, even if they are not part of this perfect happiness, are valuable because they perfect the agent and by doing so in a way merit this perfect happiness.

---

[15] Thomas, *S.T.*, I-II, q. 5, art. 7.

[16] Thomas, *S.T.*, I-II, q. 114, art. 3–4.

[17] David Copp and David Sobel, "Morality and Virtue: An Assessment of Some Recent Work in Virtue Ethics," *Ethics* 144 (2004): 525–532.

[18] "Honorem vero et voluptates et intelligentiam et virtutem eligimus quidem propter se ipsa, eligeremus enim vel appeteremus ea etiam si nihil aliud ex eis nobis proveniret, et tamen eligimus ea propter felicitatem in quantum per ea credimus nos futuros felices." Thomas, *SLE*, lib. 1, lect. 9 (Leonine, 47.1, 32).

[19] Thomas, *S.T.*, I-II, q. 3, art. 4; q. 67, art. 6. For the question of whether virtues remain in heaven, see Chapter 5, pp. 183–189.

Like Aristotle, Thomas holds that happiness, or, as many contemporary authors prefer, "flourishing," includes virtuous activity. Its necessary connection to virtue might appear to indicate that he has a "moralised concept of flourishing," as if such a "moralised" concept belonged to a separate moral realm.[20] Such a description of human virtue as "moralised" presupposes that there is some separate concept of morality that needs to be connected with human happiness or flourishing and consequently virtue. But Thomas thinks that moral goodness consists in those virtuous operations that make humans good in a way that is proportionate to human nature. He does not seem to have the disconnected concept of "morality" that is used by many philosophers during the past several centuries. The separation of the moral good from the human good is an artifact of later philosophical and theological debates, although it may have roots in ancient philosophy. Thomas Aquinas and most of his contemporaries deny the possibility of such a separation. Elizabeth Anscombe suggested that philosophers should refuse to use the term "moral" and the "moral ought" unless they show how it make sense in light of their account of human nature.[21] If, as many philosophers suspect, the modern concept of such a separate "morality" is confused beyond repair, its absence from Thomas's ethics would be a strength.[22]

As somehow constitutive of either imperfect or perfect human flourishing, the virtues provide Thomas with a way of organizing his account of the good life.[23] In particular, his description of ethical material is not ordered around the Ten Commandments or some alternate set of rules but instead largely around the cardinal and theological virtues. His use of the virtues in this context reflects the way in which ethical matters are about objects that are determined by reason. In particular, his moral discussions follow the rule of reason that is used in determining the mean of moral virtue.

As we have seen in Chapter 2, the multiplicity of the moral virtues is partially based on the complexity of human nature. Although the human good is ultimately and completely found in the perfect happiness of the beatific vision, there are many partial goods that only lead to such happiness

---

[20] Copp and Sobel, "Morality and Virtue," 531.
[21] See also Coope, "Modern Virtue Ethics," 22–23.
[22] Bernard Williams, *Ethics and the Limits of Philosophy* (Cambridge, MA: Harvard University Press, 1985), 174–196; Alasdair MacIntyre, *Ethics in the Conflicts of Modernity: An Essay on Desire, Practical Reasoning, and Narrative* (Cambridge: Cambridge University Press, 2016), 114–165.
[23] Thomas, *S.T.*, II-II, prol.

or make it present in an inchoate way.[24] It is important to recognize that there is only one ultimate end, but this ultimate end allows for a variety of other ends, of which some are supernatural and others are proportionate to human nature. Most obviously there is a disparity of goods even on the natural level. The distinction between intellectual and moral virtue follows the distinction between the intellect and the appetites, in particular the sense appetites. As animals, humans are concerned about death, reproduction, and the education of the young. The concerns are properly moral for humans on account of which these activities, like all human activities, are subject to the rule of reason. Moral virtues that regulate the passions are necessary on account of our animality.

In contrast, the intellectual virtues and some moral virtues, such as justice, are not directly concerned with the passions. They perfect rational powers. But since the intellectual virtues perfect only the human reason in its operations, they do not perfect the human precisely as human. They do not directly rectify the will. They are higher than the moral virtues in that they perfect a more important power, namely the intellect, but they do not simply speaking make the agent good, even in a way that is proportionate to human nature. In contrast, the moral virtues make the agent good. Justice, which in some way is the most important moral virtue, perfects the highest human appetite, which is the rational appetite, or the will. The distinction between moral and intellectual virtue and some distinctions within moral virtue reflect the way in which humans are both intellectual and animal.

The moral virtues assist in the production of operations by which individuals achieve their individual goods, which are part of and inseparable from the common goods of the wholes to which they belong. As rational animals, humans are parts of different wholes, such as families and political communities, and as raised by grace, they have a role in the supernatural order. Such common goods consist in the coordinated activity of parts that have a common end. The virtues assist in the individual's part in that coordinated activity. In particular, justice is concerned with perfecting these operations. Legal justice is concerned with the activity of the part towards the whole, distributive justice perfects activities of those who represent the whole towards its parts, and commutative justice is about the activities between parts. In this political context Thomas plausibly develops the work of earlier philosophers, and most importantly Aristotle. But for Thomas there is a more important

---

[24] For the way in which these various goods are united in one ultimate end, see especially Steven Jensen, *Sin: A Thomistic Psychology* (Washington, DC: The Catholic University of America Press, 2018), 15–65.

community, namely the Church, and a higher common good, namely God insofar as he is himself a shared supernatural good. The infused virtues are concerned with this supernatural common good.

The strength of Thomas's theory is that it takes into account these various human roles. Moreover, as we have seen, in doing so it draws upon a variety of philosophical traditions that are rooted in different cultural contexts. Thomas's division between moral and intellectual virtues, and between virtues concerning operations and those concerning the passions, is rooted in Aristotle and his commentators. Thomas adds many virtues to Aristotle's schema, but he takes all of Aristotle's virtues into account. His use of the four cardinal virtues to organize the moral life draws on such disparate Greek and Roman authors as the Pseudo-Andronicus, Cicero, and Macrobius. Moreover, he draws on a variety of Church Fathers, and particularly on Augustine. Much of his discussion of the infused and theological virtues relies not only on these Fathers but also on medieval theologians. Despite these disparate sources, or perhaps because of their wide range, Thomas is able to use the moral virtues to give an overall account of the good human life. This account is based on the structure of the human being and the multifarious objects of human action.

There may be room for more virtues to be added to Thomas account, or for changes in his descriptions of the virtues, but I do not know of successful attempts to do so. Contemporary virtue ethicists have added new virtues to the traditional lists and changed descriptions of earlier virtues. For instance, contemporary writers in virtue ethics often hold that there is a virtue of charity or benevolence, which is obviously not drawn from Aristotelian or Stoic lists of the virtues. To many contemporary philosophers, this virtue seems to be something like the neighbor-regarding aspect of Christian charity but devoid of the theological context that gives it meaning and makes it reasonable.[25] Contemporary accounts of charity and other such virtues seem to reflect contemporary prejudices and customs rather than sustained reflection on the good life or the practices of healthy societies. It might be more helpful to consider whether Thomas's account might be enriched by lists of virtues from other premodern traditions.

Contemporary Science and Naturalism

Although contemporary philosophers may be inclined to lists of the virtues that differ from those upon which Thomas draws, a greater obstacle to Thomas's

---

[25] Sanford, *Before Virtue*, 66–69; Coope, "Modern Virtue Ethics," 33–36.

contemporary reception might be the current penchant for naturalism. Many contemporary philosophers are "naturalists." Before addressing such difficulties, we should recognize that the term "naturalism" itself is vague and even ambiguous.[26] It can be a belief that the only subjects of human inquiry are those that can be studied by contemporary science, and perhaps more particularly contemporary natural science. Sometimes this methodological approach is based on or assimilated to the stronger metaphysical position that the only objects that exist are those that can be studied by such science. Thomas's emphasis on the superiority of the supernatural common good itself seems incompatible with the "naturalism" of these contemporary philosophers, and there are additional difficulties with his account of the infused moral virtues, as well as with his understanding of the moral virtue of religion and the natural requirement to love God more than oneself. Moreover, naturalism seems incompatible with the Aristotelian claim that the highest intellectual virtue is wisdom, which considers the first immaterial cause or causes.

Some contemporary virtue ethicists are naturalistic in that they attempt to base their ethical theories on contemporary natural science. They think that the moral philosophy and more narrowly the study of virtue is rooted in such science in the same way that the moral theories of Aristotle and Thomas are rooted in the natural sciences of their time. For instance, Julia Annas writes:

> Contemporary virtue ethics with the ambitions of the classical theories ... looks at human nature as we find out about that from the best contemporary science. Here the relevant sciences are biology, ethology, and psychology, studies of humans and other animals as parts of the life of our planet.[27]

Her examples of the relevant sciences points to a vagueness or ambiguity even about what a science is. It is hard to know or perhaps articulate precisely what, aside from sociological considerations, might group together biology, ethology, and psychology as sciences and yet exclude the basic principles of Aristotle's understanding of the physical world or his more precise account of human nature. Many philosophers deny that there is one scientific account of the world or one scientific method according to which the world should be investigated.[28]

---

[26] David Papineau, "Naturalism," *The Stanford Encyclopedia of Philosophy* (Summer 2021 Edition), ed. Edward N. Zalta, forthcoming URL = <https://plato.stanford.edu/archives/sum2021/entries/naturalism/>.

[27] Julia Annas, "Virtue Ethics," in *The Oxford Handbook of Ethical Theory*, ed. David Copp (Oxford: Oxford University Press, 2006), 526–527.

[28] John Dupré, *The Disorder of Things. Metaphysical Foundations of the Disunity of Science* (Cambridge, MA: Harvard University Press, 1993); Nancy Cartwright, *The Dappled World: A Study of the Boundaries of Science* (Cambridge: Cambridge University Press, 1999).

It may be that Annas is appealing to those who think that only exist-ing objects relevant to the study of human action and virtue are in fact studied by such sciences. Some philosophers assume that the immaterial cannot be subject to rational inquiry, which poses a problem for medieval philosophers and those ancient philosophers who hold that human under-standing requires the existence of some or many immaterial beings. Even those philosophers who admit the existence of such immaterial objects as propositions and sets might balk at the existence of an immaterial intellect or will. Whatever their views on other matters, naturalists and many other philosophers describe immaterial human and superhuman intellects as "supernatural," even if they do not think that immaterially existing math-ematical objects or propositions are.

There are at least two ways in which there is clearly a conflict between most varieties of contemporary naturalism and Thomas's account of the virtues. First, as we have seen, Thomas holds that the definition of virtue entails that it is not merely a bodily modification but instead involves an immaterial human reason and will. Nonrational and consequently merely physical animals might have certain dispositions, such as beauty and strength, but they cannot have virtues in the fullest sense. Second, accord-ing to Thomas, some intellectual and even moral virtues must take into account an immaterial God, either as an object of contemplation or as an end of worship. This twofold importance of the immaterial to ethics and the virtues more particularly is not unique to Thomas or Christian writers but can be found among Jewish and Muslim philosophers as well. It is not supernatural in the sense that the supernatural depends on a particular revealed religion. More significantly, these kinds of immateriality are also central to the moral theories of Plato, Aristotle, and Plotinus, as well as of their major followers. By setting aside the immateriality of the intellect and immaterial beings, contemporary naturalistic philosophers are primar-ily rejecting not Christianity but more broadly the whole philosophical tradition that has its roots in the teachings of Aristotle and Plato. Such naturalistic philosophy rarely gives reasons for excluding the immaterial. This naturalism usually seems to result from arbitrary definitions or cultur-ally formed but questionable intuitions.

Although Thomas's moral theory is not entirely dependent on natural philosophy or "naturalistic" in the contemporary sense, it does in some way depend on or entail certain theses in natural philosophy. However, knowl-edge of moral philosophy depends only on a very general understanding of natural philosophy. For instance, in the *Nicomachean Ethics*, Book III, chapter 13, Aristotle connects the division between the intellectual and moral virtues to the division between the different parts of the soul. He states that the study of the soul is relevant to this enquiry and a precise description of this division belongs to the study of the soul and not to ethics.[29]

Thomas's account of the virtues not only depends on beings whose very existence seems to be incompatible with naturalistic intuitions, but it also relies on an understanding of the natural world that seem inconsistent with the claims of some naturalists that the contemporary sciences exhaust what can be known about the physical world. It relies on an understanding of human nature that does not seem reducible to what is studied by contemporary biology or even by contemporary psychology. Virtues are about different kinds of human goods and the various ways in which the human good is attained. According to Thomas, the goodness of the human being or any other being depends on its nature. It is relative to the species. For instance, being a good oak is different from being a good palm tree, which in turn is different from being a good dolphin or wolf.

In many respects Philippa Foot follows Thomas and Aristotle on this point.[30] Rosalind Hursthouse accepts and develops Foot's understanding of how "ethical evaluations are analogous to evaluations of tigers (or wolves or bees) as good, healthy, specimens of their kind."[31] However, Hursthouse's own descriptions of evaluating animals seems at least questionable.[32] For example, she seems to think that a peculiarly animal good is pleasure and the absence of pain. As we have seen, for Aristotle and Thomas pleasures and pains are subordinate to the goods that they accompany, for instance, the pleasure of eating with reference to the goodness of food and the proper functioning of an animal's nutritive powers. By focusing on pleasure and pain rather than on the goods that are objects of animal appetites, she departs from the way in which Aristotelians such as Thomas understand the connection between the good and natural inclination. But this connection is necessary to the way that Aristotelians account for human goodness.

Since Thomas thinks that goodness is relative to the specific nature, we might be tempted to say that his ethics should primarily draw on the biological study of humans. But biological species are not obviously the same as the species that Aristotle describes. For example, contemporary

[29] Thomas, *SLE*, lib. 1, lect. 19 (Leonine, 47.1, 69).
[30] Foot's argument is perhaps best developed in her *Natural Goodness* (Oxford: Clarendon, 2001), 25–51.
[31] Hursthouse, *Virtue Ethics*, 197.
[32] Hursthouse, *Virtue Ethics*, 199–200.

scientists might consider *homo erectus* and *homo neanderthalensis* to be specifically distinct from *homo sapiens.*[33] These scientists might rely on various criteria that are useful but not "scientific" in an Aristotelian sense. But Thomas's account of the virtues depends on the way of considering the properly human good, which involves reason. If members of the former two groups possessed reason, then they would be capable of acquiring human virtues, even if the majority of contemporary scientists were to place them in a distinct biological species. For this and other reasons, contemporary philosophers such as Michael Thompson and Philippa Foot appeal not to the biological species but to what they describe as the "life form."[34] Such an appeal would be compatible with Thomas's approach if the life form is understood as that which belongs to a natural species of the kind described by Thomas and his predecessors.

If by "life form" we mean activities that achieve certain true goods, then it seems plausible that such life forms are shared by members of the same species and that the virtues are relative to both the species and the life form or forms. But this congruity between life form and Aristotelian natural species presupposes that humans by nature are inclined to the relevant goods. There may perhaps be different life forms within the same human species, if we keep in mind the indeterminacy of the human good, which is due to the indeterminacy of reason. Different virtues will be needed depending on the particular nature and circumstance of the agent. Soldiers will develop courage in a way that teachers of small children might not. Farmers in a small city-state will presumably develop prudence and justice in ways different from how they will be developed by physicians who work in an industrialized city. However, even though individuals achieve the human good in different ways, they still achieve a properly human good. They will need all of the cardinal and other major moral virtues in at least some way, and they will avoid such actions as theft, adultery, murder, and blasphemy. It is not clear that the goods that are achieved through these virtues can be fully reduced to characteristics that are studied by any contemporary natural or social science.

We might be tempted to think that notions of natural function and goodness might be explained in terms of evolutionary adaptations.

---

[33] Kenneth W. Kemp, "Science, Theology, and Monogenesis," *American Catholic Philosophical Quarterly* 85 (2011): 217–236; Nicanor Pier Giorgio Austriaco, "Defending Adam after Darwin: On the Origin of *Sapiens* as a Natural Kind," *American Catholic Philosophical Quarterly* 92 (2018): 337–352; Marie I. George, "Aquinas's Teachings on Concepts and Words in His Commentary on John contra Nicanor Austriaco, OP," *American Catholic Philosophical Quarterly* 94 (2020): 357–378.

[34] Michael Thompson, *Life and Action: Elementary Structures of Practice and Practical Thought* (Cambridge, MA: Harvard University Press, 2008), 49–82; Foot, *Natural Goodness*, 31–32, 38–51.

Although these adaptations are valuable for biological research, they do not seem to capture fully what is meant as good for any biological species, never mind the human good.[35] For example, the evolutionary history of an oak or a dolphin helps us to understand what is good for an oak and a dolphin and why they are good in different ways. But we seem to know and use evaluative language about them without any reference to this evolutionary history, and it seems unlikely that our notions of what is good for them can simply be reduced to statements about adaptations for survival. The goodness of animals and plants is ultimately rooted in the way in which their nature seems directed to certain ends, such as growth and reproduction. Thomas and other Aristotelians recognize some form of goodness and direction to goals in all of nature, including humans, animals, plants, and even inanimate substances. Evolutionary adaptations help us to think about some such natures, but they do not obviously explain everything about them.

Thomas's account of the human good depends on a natural teleology, which is common to our ordinary discussion of living beings, and all of our ordinary language about human action. Some philosophers have thought that goodness is a nonnatural property that humans see or that it is somehow rooted originally in human desire. On this account, goodness is rooted in the first human appetite. Whether this account of goodness is true is central for any ethical theory.[36] Neither Thomas nor his predecessors think that we add goodness to the world or that it is some special property that is applicable only to humans. Our desires correspond in some way to goods that are objects of our natural inclinations. Goods are suitable objects of our appetite even if we do not desire them. We desire objects because they are good; objects are not good simply because we desire them.

The existence of such goods might seem unlikely, especially if one attends only to mechanistic accounts of nature. On the other hand, it should seem at least as unlikely that humans are able on their own to add to the world the very notion of goodness. The ability to endow the natural world with goodness and purpose would on this account be a sort of inexplicable, mystical property of our minds and perhaps the minds of other animals. In contrast, Thomas contends that goods are known and discovered. They are not created by us. If our contemporary scientific practices are unable to account for such goods, we should not immediately conclude that they do not exist.

---

[35] Foot, *Natural Goodness*, 30, note 10.
[36] This point is missed by Copp and Sobel, "Virtue Ethics," 542.

It may be even more difficult to see how contemporary sciences could touch on the goods that are achieved through the exercise of the intellectual and infused virtues. In particular, Thomas and Aristotle recognize that the highest philosophical activity is the contemplation of the separate substances, in particular of the First Mover, whom Thomas and much of the philosophical tradition identified with the God of revelation. The intellectual virtues are acquired through ordinary human abilities and do not require grace. Nevertheless, it is difficult to see how his account of them is compatible with contemporary philosophical naturalism. More importantly, the infused virtues depend on the way in which humans, as intellectuals, can be raised to live with God. God could not give such infused virtues to fish or dolphins. Thomas thinks that this supernatural life is compatible with human nature but exceeds its abilities. Contemporary naturalists are likely to hold that such an elevation of human nature is impossible.

The various goods that are proportionate to human nature are difficult for contemporary sciences to address. Supernatural goods are inaccessible to such sciences. This consideration of the supernatural good adds another level to Thomas's account of the way in which the human goods can be regarded as heterogeneous. The acquired virtues achieve a good that is merely proportionate to human nature. Since human nature is complex, these acquired virtues are complex. In contrast, the infused virtues help in the attainment of a good that far exceeds human nature. Infused virtue holds the highest importance in Thomas's ethical thought. But we should keep in mind how even infused virtue ultimately depends on a particular account of human nature as the kind of nature that can be raised and assisted. Thomas's theory of virtue is not "naturalistic" in most or all of the contemporary senses of the term, but it depends on an account of human nature.

Although Thomas allows for human goods that are heterogeneous in some way, he thinks that the ultimate end includes and exceeds all the goods that can be attained by human nature. The perfect happiness of heaven essentially contains all that humans could need or want, although it can be increased in certain accidental ways. Ultimately, even the particular goods of this life in some way are good insofar as they lead to or participate in the goodness of this ultimate end, either considered as the source of all goodness or as the object of the beatific vision. This end is not supernatural merely because it includes God but because it includes the elevation of human nature so that God is attained in a higher manner, namely as himself the object of immediate knowledge. Although the various goods proportionate to human nature might in some way be studied by contemporary science, they are more easily addressed from the standpoint of an Aristotelian science. The contemporary counterparts to Thomas's Aristotelian philosophical science might be some sort of enriched notion of science or a philosophy of nature. If Thomas's account of the human good is correct, even such contemporary counterparts cannot consider the complete human good. The ultimate end of a human nature that is elevated by grace does not conflict with that of a human nature considered apart from such elevation. Nevertheless, it exceeds it in such a way that it no longer belongs to the study of the philosophical disciplines.

Thomas's account of the virtues consequently depends on an account of human nature that for several reasons cannot be reduced to that of the contemporary physical sciences. First, such sciences do not seem to consider the relevant features that are necessary for moral philosophy, more particularly the various goods that are proportionate to human nature. Reason, which is proper to human nature and essential to any human good, does not seem to be studied as such by them, and certainly not by contemporary biologists. Thomas and the weight of the preceding philosophical tradition argue that human reason is immaterial, which might make it opaque to science as currently practiced, and outside the purview of contemporary naturalism. The acquired virtues, as habits, are intrinsically connected to such reason. They cannot be reduced to merely biological factors. If such reduction were possible, it might be conceivable that they could be caused by medicines. Instead, they are acquired through repeated actions of the intellect and will.

It might seem at first that the requisite scientific account of the human good can be found in the contemporary social sciences. But it is even less clear that social sciences explain human behavior in a way similar to how sciences such as contemporary physics explain material phenomena and sciences such as biological explain living substances. Insofar as such sciences use the same approaches as contemporary natural sciences, it is unclear how they would help us to consider the human good. Inasmuch as such sciences differ from the currently accepted natural sciences, we might question what it means to say that they are scientific and why they should be preferred to other ways of thinking about the human good.

According to Thomas, the objects of the virtues are not only about matters such as eating and reproducing but more importantly involve lives that are ordered by justice to the political common good and by natural love to God as the source of natural goods and to God Himself as the Trinity insofar as he is the source of supernatural goods. Human individuals are parts of non-artificial wholes such as families and political communities, and some are part of the supernatural community that is the Church. The contemporary social sciences are unable to take into account the last community, and they seem to enrich but not exhaust our understanding of the first two communities. Contemporary social sciences should be valuable for completing Thomas's ethical account and correcting some mistakes. But they should not be expected to play the same role in any recuperation of Thomas's ethical theory that the Aristotelian account of nature plays. The contemporary sciences are too limited by their own natures and sociological factors to provide the necessary framework in which to develop such an ethical theory.

We should consider Thomas's account of the virtues in light of contemporary science without setting aside the way that it depends on a broadly Aristotelian account of nature and metaphysics and is rooted in ordinary pre-Christian and Christian practice. However, we should not claim that it is easy to reconcile contemporary views with Thomas's notions of goodness, more particularly moral goodness, and the immaterial aspects of human beings and God. Indeed, contemporary followers of Thomas and Aristotle sharply disagree over the nature of contemporary science and its compatibility with Aristotelian thought. For instance, some Thomists have thought that contemporary science is a different kind of inquiry from that pursued by Aristotle and Thomas.[37] Others have argued that the modern science is a precision and development of medieval Aristotelian science and that the general Aristotelian science of nature remains true and important for our contemporary inquiries.[38] Several recent philosophers have argued for the compatibility of a modified Aristotelianism with very recent science.[39] It is impossible here to argue for any such view or for possible alternatives. It seems sufficient to recognize that the viability of Thomas's account of the virtues depends only broadly on an account of human nature that has not been shown to be incompatible with what we know through contemporary sciences but also has not been shown to be obviously true by them.

The difficulty of addressing these issues should not lead us to think that the contemporary sciences have nothing to contribute to our knowledge of the virtues. The sheer amount of specialized information available now

---

[37] Yves Simon, "Maritain's Philosophy of Science," *The Thomist* 4 (1943): 85–102.

[38] William A. Wallace, *The Modeling of Nature: Philosophy of Science and Philosophy of Nature in Synthesis* (Washington, DC: The Catholic University of America Press, 1996); James A. Weisheipl, *Nature and Motion in the Middle Ages*, ed. William E. Carroll (Washington, DC: The Catholic University of America Press, 1985).

[39] William M.R. Simpson, Robert C. Koons, and Nicholas J. Teh, eds., *Neo-Aristotelian Perspectives on Contemporary Science* (London: Routledge, 2018).

far exceeds what few empirical findings were available to Thomas. The contemporary sciences, when used judiciously, should be able to fill in many details that were opaque to Thomas and correct some of his more obvious mistakes. For instance, Thomas had little of worth to say about the material characteristics of the emotions or the way in which the brain was involved in practical reasoning. Nevertheless, insofar as Thomas's account of the virtues is general and rooted in inquiries that are based on widespread human experience, it should not be particularly affected by discoveries in the contemporary sciences. Moreover, insofar as Thomas's account of the virtues rests on supernatural revelation, it should be inaccessible to contemporary science. Whether or not we accept his account of these religious matters depends both on whether we accept his religious authorities and interpret them in a similar manner.

The challenge of reconciling Thomas's account of the virtues with contemporary sciences seems to me significant, but not fatal, to Thomas's account. It is arduous (if not impossible) to define contemporary science or to delineate what falls under its province. It would be a strange accident of history if all that can be known through human reason were the same as that which has been studied by the more recently developed sciences. At least on the surface, the contemporary sciences seem to be a collection of loosely related methods and achievements rather than natural kinds of inquiry that give comprehensive accounts of the world. Consequently, they do not seem to replace previously achieved philosophical knowledge.

The widespread contemporary assumption of naturalism by the philosophical establishment not only presents questions concerning the relevance of contemporary science to Thomas's account of the virtues but it also raises the concern that his account is vitiated by its appeal to supernatural religious revelation. This appeal is problematic for two groups of scholars who might be otherwise open to at least some of his insights. First, many professional philosophers are suspicious of religion as dangerous, obfuscating, and an outdated attempt at explain the world. At times moral philosophers seem to set up arbitrary barriers to religious assertions.[40] Second, academics who study religion often carry similar biases. Many professional religious scholars dismiss discussions of the reasonableness of religion and reject that the Christian faith is a kind of knowledge about God. Those religious scholars who are also theologians often are preoccupied

[40] John M. Rist, *On Inoculating Moral Philosophy against God* (Milwaukee, WI: Marquette University Press, 2000).

with making their religion palatable and up-to-date. Whatever the merits of these various outlooks, they make it difficult to consider the whole of Thomas's ethical theory. His philosophy is at the service of and perhaps even absorbed by the theological concerns, and he understands theology to be a science in the Aristotelian sense, and resting upon principles that are known through faith.

Thomas thinks that the infused virtues, more particularly the theological virtues, are preeminent. But those who lack his faith may still find his philosophical account convincing, even though his philosophical insights are intertwined with his theology. For instance, we saw in Chapter 4 that Thomas's attempt to differentiate the acquired from the infused virtues causes him to consider more carefully the relationship between the virtues and the passions and to explain why the virtues are needed. Moreover, the category of infused virtue helps him to distinguish how and by what subjects the various virtues are acquired. Similarly, his discussion of how the infused virtues are connected through infused virtue is conducted alongside discussions of the connection of the acquired virtues through prudence. Although Thomas is indebted to Aristotle's account of the connection of the virtues, Thomas develops the connection through prudence in far greater detail than Aristotle did. On all of these issues concerning acquired virtue, as well as on others, the reader of Aristotle can profitably consult Thomas to consider where Aristotle's basic thoughts might ultimately lead.

Thomas develops and draws on previously established traditions of enquiry. He uses the later writers to consolidate and deepen the insights of their predecessors. His development of the tradition applies not only to the Bible and Christian tradition but also to the thought of Aristotle, Cicero, minor philosophers such as Macrobius, Arabic and Jewish philosophers, and the philosophical tradition as retained by Christians. He is not principally concerned with merely reporting the thought of any one previous thinker but instead with studying the thinkers to understand better what is being studied. His theological goals cause him to attempt philosophical progress. This attempt to understand ethics and in particular human virtue led him to considerations that should be profitable to anyone interested in classical virtue theory and perhaps more broadly in thinking about ordinary human moral behavior. Contemporary physical and social sciences might add content and precision to his account, but, like that of the ancient philosophers, his work would retain basic relevance.

Conclusion

This book has shown how Thomas's account of virtue should be considered in its historical and intellectual context. Thomas's thought is perhaps best understood by looking at how he responds to and develops issues raised by his predecessors and contemporaries. Although his work is primarily theological, his theology develops and depends on philosophy. Thomas's teaching on the virtues draws on disparate philosophical and theological sources to cover a wide range of distinct and yet related difficulties. By focusing on this account in its historical and intellectual context, we should have come to a better understanding of his dialectical approach and the way in which he incorporates moral philosophy into his theology. He does not develop any of his philosophical positions in an intellectual vacuum. His account of the various virtues draws not only upon Aristotle but also upon Stoic and Neoplatonic sources. His use of philosophical authorities in his theology indicates how his dialectical method works.

Thomas's use of the definition of virtue in the *Summa Theologiae* shows the dialectical structure of his thought and the way in which his later discussions depend upon his earlier ones.

For example, in Chapter 1 we saw how Thomas does not begin his discussion of virtue by immediately defining it as a "good operative habit" and assuming that such a definition will be immediately grasped by his readers. Although he has regular recourse to principles and definitions, he does not always start from such foundations. He bases his teaching on what has been established by his predecessors and attempts to find whatever is true in the various accounts that are available to him. Following Albert, he uses Aristotle's placement of habits in the genus of quality as an explanation of why Lombard's Augustinian definition refers to virtue as a "habit of the mind." He uses the Aristotelian definition of virtue as that which makes both the act and the agent good in order to explain that aspect of the Augustinian definition which states that virtue is "that by which one lives rightly and which no one uses badly."

In Chapter 2, it was shown how the related Aristotelian definition of the virtue as making the act and agent good allows Thomas to distinguish between the different ways in which the term "virtue" can be applied to the intellectual and moral virtues. Thomas uses this definition in one context to distinguish between the way in which the intellectual and moral virtues are virtues. Intellectual virtues only partly share in the nature of virtue, since they cause good acts but do not make the agent good. Indeed, they produce acts that are in a way better than the acts of the moral virtues. But they do not on their own make the agent better. In contrast, moral virtues produce good acts that make their agents better. This definition shows why although the intellectual virtues are better in themselves, the moral virtues are better simply as virtues, since they make the agent good.

In Chapter 3, we saw that Thomas develops his description of how virtue involves the passions by recounting Augustine's influential description of the disagreement between Stoics and Peripatetics over whether the virtuous agent even has passions. Thomas seems to agree with Augustine's evaluation of the difference as primarily verbal, but he gives a clearer account of the related substantive issues and how the disagreement might be resolved. Thomas notes that the passions are acts of the sense appetites, which in themselves are not rational, although in humans they are rational through participation in reason. They are ruled indirectly, in a political or royal way. Consequently, the sense appetites need to be perfected by virtues such as courage and temperance in order for them to be regulated by reason. The Stoics were correct to recognize the possibility of opposition to reason, which results in part from the fact that they are not essentially rational. Nevertheless, they misunderstood the way in which sense powers can be ruled. Thomas does not criticize Aristotle on this point, but he explains Aristotle's account in light of his own, more developed, understanding of the distinction between the sensitive appetitive powers and the rational appetite. Aristotle himself never clearly articulated such a distinction.

This distinction between the various appetites allows Thomas to accommodate the Stoic and Platonic theory of the cardinal virtues. He states that these virtues differ from each other in part on account of their subjects. Prudence is the only cardinal virtue that inheres in the intellect. The other three inhere in the various distinct appetites that were not clearly delineated by ancient and patristic writers. Justice perfects the will, temperance perfects the concupiscible appetite, and fortitude perfects the irascible appetite. Thomas gives reasons why these powers need the virtues. Sense appetites need habits precisely because they are rational only by participation. In contrast, the will is intrinsically rational. It needs a habit in order to will something more than its own good, such as the good of another individual or of the political community.

Even though Thomas relies heavily on Aristotle's thought, he does not simply repeat what Aristotle says or follow lines clearly indicated by Aristotle. For example, Thomas quickly passes over Aristotle's description of eleven virtues and instead gives central place to the theory of the four cardinal virtues, which at first glance might seem foreign to Aristotle. Thomas explains that of the eleven moral virtues that Aristotle addresses, ten are about passions and one is about operations. Unlike Aristotle, Thomas explains how these latter virtues are distinguished according to a diversity of passions, matter, and objects. In his later descriptions of these virtues, he often relies on Aristotle's text. Nevertheless, he also relies on Cicero, Macrobius, and the author of the *De virtutibus et vitiis*. He finds in these other authors many moral virtues that Aristotle does not mention and a way of organizing the entire moral life around the four cardinal virtues.

In the *Summa Theologiae*, Thomas follows his discussion of the cardinal virtues with an account of the Neoplatonic distinction between political, purgative, purged, and exemplar virtue. He describes the last as belonging to God and the first three as stages of virtue that eventually led to the contemplation of God. Moral virtues are categorized according to whether they are merely political, or purifying the soul for later contemplation, or as possessed by those purified agents who contemplate God in heaven or more perfectly in this life. Thomas's discussion of these stages allows him to make a transition from the cardinal virtues that were recognized by the philosophers to the three theological virtues of faith, hope, and charity, which are discussed in Chapter 4.

We have also seen how his distinction between infused and acquired virtue allowed him to provide a more precise description of the relationship between the cardinal virtues and grace than was given by his theological predecessors. Thomas applies the definition of virtue as making the act and agent good to the distinction between infused and acquired moral virtue. Acquired moral virtue produces acts that make the agent good, but by itself it does not perfect the agent with reference to the ultimate end. It makes the agent good only with respect to that good which is proportionate to human nature. In contrast, infused moral virtue makes the agent good with respect to the ultimate end, which exceeds nature. Infused moral virtue is always accompanied by charity, which accomplishes such rectitude towards this end. Consequently, infused moral virtue is more of a virtue than the acquired virtue precisely because it more completely exemplifies the characteristic of virtue that it makes the agent good.

In Chapter 5, we saw how Thomas's reworking of the various traditions on the virtues allows him to more adequately address contemporary
debates over the properties of the virtues. Thomas's discussion of the connection of the virtues illustrates how theology and moral philosophy can
assist each other. We see that he makes use of the description of virtue
as making act and agent good in order to argue that strictly speaking
faith and hope without charity are not virtues. If the agent lacks charity,
then the agent is disordered with respect to the ultimate end and bad.
Consequently, such an agent cannot perform acts that make the agent
good. An agent who lacks charity can possess faith and hope and perform
the good acts that belong to these virtues. But these good acts of faith and
hope do not make the agent good when the agent lacks charity.

Thomas's discussion of how the virtues are connected, which is explicitly addressed in Chapter 5, shows how we should keep in mind all of
his more significant texts on an issue when reading any text on an issue.
In his discussion of the connection of the virtues, Thomas also uses the
description of virtue as making both the act and agent good to distinguish between the different ways in which virtue can be perfect, both
between and within kinds of virtue. What Aristotle would describe as
a natural virtue, which was discussed in Chapter 1, is unconnected and
imperfect because it is not regulated by reason. For example, natural fortitude, which is entirely nonrational, is imperfect, whereas the acquired
habit of fortitude is perfect in this context. Strictly speaking, such natural
virtue is imperfect in that it is not really a virtue at all. Such purely natural
fortitude not only fails to make the agent good but it might even produce
bad acts, such as acts of cruelty. Natural and acquired virtues belong to
different species. In contrast, as we also saw in Chapter 1, a virtue such as
fortitude can be imperfect in another way, namely as a kind of disposition
that is imperfect because it is not fully developed. Such imperfect acquired
courage is related to perfect acquired courage in the way that a boy is
related to a man. It is the kind of disposition that lack's a habit's stability
even though it belongs to the same category as the habit. It produces good
acts that make the agent good, but it is more easily lost than a perfect
acquired virtue is. This imperfect fortitude belongs to the same species
as perfect acquired fortitude does. But acquired virtue that is perfect in
comparison with the purely natural virtue is in another way imperfect in
comparison with the infused.

In Chapters 4 and 5, we have seen how true virtue is imperfect when its
agent is bad. It produces good acts but does not make the agent good. In
this way, the same acquired moral virtue can exist in some way not only

in the good but also in the wicked. For instance, someone with acquired courage retains such courage even after committing a mortal sin. She can still perform morally good courageous acts but she is fundamentally disordered even on a natural level. Acquired virtues, unlike infused virtues, are not lost alongside charity or through merely one opposed act. The person who loses charity through mortal sin does not thereby immediately become a coward, even if she sins mortally through cowardice. But the agent's acts of courage and other virtuous acts will not make that agent good. Such acquired virtues of a bad agent in some way resemble the faith and hope of someone who lacks charity. Such an agent produces good acts, but these good acts are not referred to the ultimate end in the way that they should be. Similarly, the sinner can have prudence about some moral matters but does not possess prudence with respect to the good life as a whole. If a sinner has true prudence, then the prudence must be in some way imperfect. In general, an agent who is disordered with respect to the ultimate end can have true virtue, but such virtue must be imperfect because the agent is not good.

A natural inclination is imperfect in kind in comparison to an acquired moral virtue. An acquired moral virtue in a sinner is imperfect in comparison with the same kind of moral virtue in a good agent who has developed the virtue. In a different way, infused moral virtue is more perfect than acquired moral virtue because it makes the agent good in a way that acquired virtue does not. An acquired virtue can be perfect in its species but must always be imperfect in comparison to infused moral virtue. On its own, this acquired virtue produces acts that are the kind that can but might not be referred to the ultimate end by charity. It produces the kind of act that can be ordered to the ultimate end by charity. In contrast, the acts of an infused moral virtue are always directed to the ultimate end. The mean and end of such infused virtue require that it can be possessed only by someone with charity. Every act of such an agent is ordered to the ultimate end is by charity. The infused virtue is consequently perfect because it makes the agent good in order to the supernatural ultimate end. Acquired virtue is imperfect in comparison. Its mean and end on their own have no essential connection with charity.

This summary of the different kinds of perfection and imperfection in virtue provides one of many instances in which Thomas's reader must always keep in mind the place of any one text in his overall account. Similarly, Thomas's discussion of the connection of the cardinal virtues also depends on his assimilation of the historical tradition. When addressing the connection between the virtues in the *Prima Secundae*, q. 65, arts. 1–2, Thomas adopts Philip the Chancellor's distinction between two different ways of thinking about the cardinal virtues, namely as general conditions and as specifically distinct habits. However, he rejects Philip's solution, according to which the separate habits are unconnected. The reason is that he has read Book VI of Aristotle's *Nicomachean Ethics*, according to which specifically distinct moral virtues are connected through one prudence. In q. 65, these issues are mentioned but unexplained. Thomas discussed the two ways of considering the cardinal virtues much earlier in q. 61, without mentioning their connection. He considers the connection of prudence with moral virtue in detail even earlier, in q. 58. It is important to analyze Thomas's arguments, but we should do so only in the context of his work as a whole. Although each article of each question might seem to be an independent discussion, Thomas assumes that the reader will be familiar with previous questions and articles. Moreover, a reader who is unfamiliar with the views of Philip the Chancellor on the formalities of virtue might be confused about why Thomas mentions the general conditions of virtue. Similarly, a reader who has not considered Thomas's use of Book VI of the *Nicomachean Ethics* might misunderstand his description of the connection of the virtues through prudence.

These examples indicate that, in order to fully understand one of Thomas's texts on a variety of issues, such as the connection of the virtues, we must attend to a text's historical context and place in his wider account of virtue. A partial approach obscures his dialectical method and can cause confusion about the main lines of his teaching. A relatively short discussion in an article or two of the *Summa Theologiae* about the connection of the virtues can turn on distinctions and discoveries that Thomas makes in other places and more broadly on the way in which he thinks through what his Christian and non-Christian predecessors have said about the virtues. From such considerations, we see that moral philosophy is necessary although far from sufficient for Thomas's theology.

This book also attempts to show that we should guard against assuming that Thomas is concerned with the same issues that are discussed by later scholastics or by our own contemporaries. For instance, later Thomists sometimes discuss at length why there need to be infused moral virtues and how they are related to the acquired ones. Thomas himself did not address these issues at length because he was one of the first to describe such virtue. Later generations develop criticisms and difficulties that Thomas would foresee inchoately if at all. It is pointless to try to find developed answers to later questions in Thomas's own texts. Later Thomists have developed Thomas's thought in much the same way that Thomas develops the thought of his own predecessors.

Although it might seem complex, Thomas's account of virtue is important both historically and for its own philosophical and even theological interest. The main philosophical and theological positions have never been definitively shown to be inadequate or inconsistent. Historically speaking, it has been one of the more influential approaches to moral theory both in the late scholastic period and in some contemporary circles. It is also one of the more defensible versions of Aristotelian ethics and incorporates the insights of many other thinkers and traditions. Thomas provides a way of thinking about moral virtue that is coherent and part of a plausible overall approach. Aspects of his thought need development. We should remember that neither Thomas nor his contemporaries thought that they could establish a complete, personal philosophy. They were assimilating, developing, and passing on what was taught to them by previous philosophers and theologians.

Bibliography

Primary Literature

Albert the Great (Albertus Magnus). *Opera Omnia*. Edited by Auguste Borgnet. 38 vols. Paris: Vivès, 1890–1899.

Opera Omnia. Edited by Bernhard Geyer and Wilhelm Gubel. Monasterium Westfalorum: Aschendorff, 1951–.

Alvarez, Diego. *Disputationes Theologicae in Iam-IIae S. Thomae*. Trani: Per Costantinum Vitalem, 1617.

Ambrose of Milan (Ambrosius Mediolanensis). *De Spiritu Sancto*. Edited by Otto Faller. CSEL 79. Vienna: Österreichischen Akademie der Wissenschaften, 1964.

Augustine of Hippo (Augustinus Hipponensis). *Confessionum Libri XIII*. Edited by L. Verheijen. CCSL 27. Turnhout: Brepols, 1981.

De Civitate Dei Libri XXII. Edited by B. Dombart and A. Kalb. 2 vols. CCSL 47–48. Turnhout: Brepols, 1955.

De Diversis Quaestionibus Octoginta Tribus. Edited by Almut Mutzenbecher. CCSL 44A. Turnhout: Brepols, 1975.

De Libero Arbitrio Libri Tres. Edited by W. M. Green. CCSL 29. Turnhout: Brepols, 1970.

De Moribus Ecclesiae Catholicae et De Moribus Manichaeorum Libri Duo. Edited by J. B. Bauer. CSEL 90. Vienna: Hoelder-Pichler-Tempsky, 1992.

De Sermone Domini in Monte. Edited by Almut Mutzenbecher. CCSL 35. Turnhout: Brepols, 1967.

De Trinitate Libri XV. Edited by W. J. Mountain. 2 vols. CCSL 50–50a. Turnhout: Brepols, 1968.

Retractationum Libri Duo. Edited by Almut Mutzenbecher. CCSL 57. Turnhout: Brepols, 1984.

Boethius. *In Categoria Aristotelis Libri IV*. Edited by J.-P.Migne. PL 64. Paris: Migne, 1847.

Bonaventure (Bonaventura). *Opera Omnia*. 10 vols. Quaracchi and Grottaferrata: Editiones Collegii S. Bonaventurae ad Claras Aquas, 1882–1902.

Cicero (Marcus Tullius Cicero). *Cicero on the Emotions: Tusculan Disputations 3 and 4*. Translated by Margaret Graver. Chicago: University of Chicago Press, 2014.

Hortensius. Edited by Albertus Grilli. Testi e Documenti per lo Studio dell'Antichita. Milan and Varese: Instituto Editoriale Cisalpino, 1962.

Collegium Salmanticense Fr. Discalceatorum B. Mariae de Monte Carmeli. *Cursus Theologicus.* 20 vols. Paris: Palme, 1870–1883.

Conradus Koellin. *Scholastica Commentaria in Primam Secundae.* Venice: Apud R. Meiettum, 1602.

Durandus of Saint-Pourçain (a Sancto Porciano). *In Petri Lombardi Sententias Theologicas Commentariorum Libri IIII.* 2 vols. Venice: Typographica Guerrae, 1571; repr. Ridgewood, NJ: Gregg Press, 1964.

John (Johannes) Capreolus. *Defensiones Theologiae Divi Thomae Aquinatis.* Edited by Ceslaus Paban and Thomas Pègues. 7 vols. Tours: Alfred Cattier, 1900–1907; repr. Minerva: Frankfurt, 1967.

On the Virtues. Translated by Kevin White and Romanus Cessario. Washington, DC: The Catholic University of America Press, 2001.

John (Joannes) Duns Scotus. *Opera Omnia.* Edited by the Scotistic Commission. Vatican City: Typis Vaticanis, 1950–.

John of St. Thomas (Joannes a Sancto Thoma). *Cursus Theologicus In I-II: De Donis Spiritus Sancti.* Edited by Armand Mathieu and Hervé Gagné. Québec: Les Presses Universitaires Laval, 1948.

Cursus Theologicus In I-II: De Virtutibus. Edited by Armand Mathieu and Hervé Gagné. Québec: Les Presses Universitaires Laval, 1952.

Macrobius. *Ambrosii Theodosii Macrobii Commentarii in Somnium Scipionis.* Edited by James Willis. Bibliotheca scriptorum Graecorum et Romanorum Teubneriana. Leipzig: Teubner, 1963.

Medina, Bartholomew. *Expositio in Tetiam Divi Thomae Partem.* Renaut: Salamanca, 1596.

Scholastica Commentaria in D. Thomae Aquinatis Doct. Angelici Primam Secundae. Cologne: Sumptibus Petri Henningij, 1618.

Peter Aureol (Petrus Aureoli). *Commentarium in Primum Librum Sententiarum, pars prima.* Rome: Zannetti, 1605.

Peter Lombard (Petrus Lombardus). *Sententie in IV Libris Distinctae.* Spicilegium Bonaventurianum, 4–5. Rome: Collegium S. Bonaventurae, 1971, 1981.

Philip the Chancellor (Philipus Cancellarius Parisiensis). *Summa de Bono.* 2 vols. Edited by Nikolaus Wicki. Corpus Philosophorum Medii Aevi Opera Philosophica Mediae Aetatis Selecta, 2. Bern: Francke, 1985.

Suarez, Francisco. *Opera Omnia.* 26 vols. Paris: Vivès, 1856–1878.

Thomas Aquinas. *Expositio et Lectura super Epistolas Paul Apostoli.* 2 vols. Edited by Raphael Cai. Turin: Marietti, 1953.

In Duodecim Libros Metaphysicorum Expositio. Edited by M.-R. Catala and R. Spiazzi. Turin: Marietti, 1964.

In Librum Beati Dionysii de Divinis Nominibus Expositio. Edited by Ceslaus Pera. Turin: Marietti, 1950.

Opera Omnia. Rome: Commissio Leonina, 1884–.

Opuscula Theologica, vol. 1: De Re Dogmatica et Morali. Edited by Raymund A. Verardo. Turin: Marietti, 1954.

Quaestiones Disputatae. Edited by P. Bazzi et al. 2 vols. Turin: Marietti, 1953.

Sancti Thomae Aquinatis, Doctoris Angelici, Ordinis Praedicatorum Opera Omnia, ad fidem optimarum editionum accurate recognita. 25 vols. Parma: Typis Petri Fiaccadori, 1852–1873.

Scriptum super Libros Sententiarum. Edited by Pierre Mandonnet and M. F. Moos. 4 vols. Paris: Lethielleux, 1927–1947.

Summa Contra Gentiles. Editio Leonina Manualis. Rome: Commissio Leonina, 1934.

Somme Théologique: La prudence. Translated by T.-H. Deman. Paris, Tournai, and Rome: Desclée, 1949.

Somme Théologique: La vertu. 2 vols. Translated by R. Bernard. Paris, Tournai, and Rome: Desclée, 1933.

Super Evangelium S. Matthaei Lectura [Reportatio Petri de Andria]. Edited by R. Cai. 5th ed. Turin and Rome: Marietti, 1951.

Treatise on the Virtues. Translated by John A. Oesterle. Notre Dame, IN: University of Notre Dame Press, 1984.

William of Auxerre (Gulelmus Altissodorensis). *Summa Aurea.* 5 vols. Edited by Jean Ribaillier. Spicilegium Bonaventurianum, 26–20. Paris: Éditions du Centre National de la Recherche Scientifique; Rome: Collegium Bonaventurae, 1980–87.

William (Gulielmus) of Ockham. *Opera Theologica.* 10 vols. Edited by G. Gál et al. St. Bonaventure, NY: Franciscan Institute, 1967–1986.

William (Gulielmus) Peraldus. *Summa aurea de virtutibus et vitiis.* Venice: P. de Paganinis, 1497.

Scholarly Literature

Allers, Rudolf. "The *Vis Cogitativa* and Evaluation." *New Scholasticism* 15 (1941): 195–221.

Annas, Julia. "Virtue Ethics." In *The Oxford Handbook of Ethical Theory*, 515–540. Edited by David Copp. Oxford: Oxford University Press, 2006.

Anscombe, G. E. M. "Modern Moral Philosophy." *Philosophy* 33 (1958): 1–19; repr. in *Virtue Ethics*, 26–44. Edited by Roger Crisp and Michael Slote. Oxford: Oxford University Press, 1997.

  "Under a Description." *Nous* 13 (1979): 219–233; repr. in *Collected Philosophical Papers of G.E.M. Anscombe*, vol. 2: *Metaphysics and the Philosophy of Mind*, 208–219. Oxford: Blackwell; Minneapolis: University of Minneapolis Press, 1981.

Austin, Nicholas. *Aquinas on Virtue: A Causal Reading.* Washington, DC: Georgetown University Press, 2017.

Austriaco, Nicanor Pier Giorgio. "Defending Adam after Darwin: On the Origin of *Sapiens* as a Natural Kind." *American Catholic Philosophical Quarterly* 92 (2018): 337–352.

Backus, Irena and Goudriaan, Aza. "'Semipelagianism': The Origins of the Term and Its Passage into the History of Heresy." *Journal of Ecclesiastical History* 65 (2014): 25–46.

Bejcvy, Istvan. "The Problem of Natural Virtue." In *Virtue and Ethics in the Twelfth Century*, 133–154. Edited by Istvan Bejcvy and Richard Newhauser. Leiden: Brill, 2005.

"The Cardinal Virtues in the Medieval Commentaries on the Nicomachean Ethics, 1250–1350." In *Virtue Ethics in the Middle Ages: Commentaries on Aristotle's Nicomachean Ethics, 1200–1500*, 199–221. Edited by Istvan Bejcvy. Leiden: Brill, 2007.

Bielinski, Maureen. "At the Crossroads of Epistemology and Ethics: Aquinas and the Impact of Moral Perception on Prudence and the Moral Virtues." PhD diss. University of St. Thomas (Houston), 2021.

de Blic, Jacques. "Pour l'historie de la théologie des dons avant Saint Thomas." *Revue d'ascétique et de mystique* 22 (1936): 117–179.

Bouillard, Henri. *Conversion et grâce chez S. Thomas d'Aquin*. Aubier: Montaigne, 1944.

Bourke, Vernon J. "The Background of Aquinas's Synderesis Principle." In *Graceful Reason: Essays in Ancient and Medieval Philosophy Presented to Joseph Owens, CSSR*, 345–360. Edited by Lloyd Gerson. Toronto: Pontifical Institute of Mediaeval Studies, 1983.

Boyle, Leonard. "The Setting of the *Summa Theologiae* of St. Thomas – Revisited." In *The Ethics of Aquinas*, 1–16. Edited by Stephen J. Pope. Washington, DC: Georgetown University Press, 2002.

Brock, Steven L. *Action and Conduct: Thomas Aquinas and the Theory of Action*. Edinburgh: T&T Clark, 1998.

The Philosophy of Saint Thomas Aquinas: A Sketch. Eugene, OR: Cascade Books, 2015.

Budziszewski, J. *A Commentary on Thomas Aquinas's Virtue Ethics*. Cambridge: Cambridge University Press, 2017.

Bullet, Gabriel. *Vertus morales infuses et vertus morales acquises selon Saint Thomas d'Aquin*. Fribourg: Éditions Universitaires, 1958.

Butera, Giuseppe. "On Reason's Control of the Passions in Aquinas's Theory of Temperance." *Medieval Studies* 68 (2006): 133–160.

Cacouros, Michel. "Le traité pseudo-Aristotélicien *De virtutibus et vitiis*." In *Dictionnaire des philosophes antiques. Supplément*, 506–546. Edited by Richard Goulet et al. Paris: CNRS, 2003.

Caldera, Rafael Tomás. *Le jugement par inclination chez Saint Thomas d'Aquin*. Paris: Vrin, 1980.

Cartwright, Nancy. *The Dappled World: A Study of the Boundaries of Science*. Cambridge: Cambridge University Press, 1999.

Caulfield, Joseph. "Practical Ignorance in Moral Actions." *Laval théologique et philosophique* 7 (1951): 69–122.

Cessario, Romanus. "The Theological Virtue of Hope (IIa IIae, qq. 17–22)." In *The Ethics of Aquinas*, 103–115. Edited by Stephen J. Pope. Washington, DC: Georgetown University Press, 2002.

The Moral Virtues and Theological Ethics. 2nd ed. Notre Dame, IN: University of Notre Dame Press, 2009.

Chappell, Timothy. "Virtue Ethics in the Twentieth Century." In *The Cambridge Companion to Virtue Ethics*, 149–171. Edited by Daniel C. Russell. Cambridge: Cambridge University Press, 2013.

Cleveland, W. Scott and Dahm, Brandon. "The Virtual Presence of Acquired Virtues in the Christian." *American Catholic Philosophical Quarterly* 93 (2019): 75–100.

Coerver, Robert Florent. *The Quality of Facility in the Moral Virtues*. Washington, DC: The Catholic University of America Press, 1946.

Coope, Christopher Miles. "Modern Virtue Ethics." In *Values and Virtues: Aristotelianism in Contemporary Ethics*, 20–52. Edited by Timothy Chappell. Oxford: Oxford University Press, 2007.

Copp, David and Sobel, David. "Morality and Virtue: An Assessment of Some Recent Work in Virtue Ethics." *Ethics* 144 (2004): 514–554.

Cunningham, Stanley. *Reclaiming Moral Agency: The Moral Philosophy of Albert the Great*. Washington, DC: The Catholic University of America Press, 2008.

Dahm, Brandon. "The Acquired Virtues Are Real Virtues: A Response to Stump." *Faith and Philosophy* 32 (2015): 453–470.

Decosimo, David. *Ethics as a Work of Charity: Thomas Aquinas and Pagan Virtue*. Stanford, CA: Stanford University Press, 2014.

"More to Love: Ends, Ordering, and the Compatibility of Acquired and Infused Virtues." In *The Virtuous Life: Thomas Aquinas on the Theological Nature of Moral Virtues*, 47–72. Edited by Harm Goris and Henk Schoot. Leuven, Paris, and Bristol, CT: Peeters, 2017.

Deman, T.-H. Review of *Surnaturel: Études Historiques*, by Henri de Lubac. *Bulletin Thomiste* 7 (1943–46, pub. 1950): 422–446.

"Le 'précepte' de la prudence chez Saint Thomas d'Aquin." *Recherches de Théologie ancienne et médiévale* 20 (1953): 40–59.

DeSpain, Benjamin. "Quaestio Disputata: Aquinas's Virtuous Vision of the Divine Ideas," *Theological Studies* 8 (2020): 453–466.

De Hart, Paul. "Quaestio Disputata: Divine Virtues and Divine Ideas of Virtues," *Theological Studies* 8 (2020): 467–477.

Dupré, John. *The Disorder of Things. Metaphysical Foundations of the Disunity of Science*. Cambridge, MA: Harvard University Press, 1993.

Farrell, Dominic. *The Ends of the Moral Virtues and the First Principles of Practical Reason in Thomas Aquinas*. Rome: Gregorian & Biblical Press, 2012.

Ferry, Leonard. "Sorting Out Reason's Relation to the Passions in the Moral Theory of Aquinas." *Proceedings of the American Catholic Philosophical Association* 88 (2015): 227–244.

Flood, Anthony T. *The Metaphysical Foundations of Love: Aquinas on Participation, Unity, and Union*. Washington, DC: The Catholic University of America Press, 2018.

Foot, Philippa. *Natural Goodness*. Oxford: Oxford University Press, 2001.

"Virtues and Vices." In her *Virtues and Vices and Other Essays in Moral Philosophy*, 1–18. Oxford: Clarendon Press, 2002; repr. in Virtue Ethics, 163–177. Edited by Roger Crisp and Michael Slote. Oxford: Oxford University Press, 1997.

Frede, Michael. "The Stoic Doctrine of the Affections of the Soul." In *The Norms of Nature: Studies in Hellenistic Ethics*, 93–110. Edited by Malcolm Schofield and Gisela Striker. Cambridge: Cambridge University Press, 1986.

Gallagher, David M. "Aquinas on Goodness and Moral Goodness." In *Thomas Aquinas and His Legacy*, 37–60. Edited by David M. Gallagher. Washington, DC: The Catholic University of America Press, 1994.

"The Will and Its Acts." In *The Ethics of Aquinas*, 69–89. Edited by Stephen J. Pope. Washington, DC: Georgetown University Press, 2002.

Garrigou-Lagrange, Réginald. "La prudence: sa place dans l'organisme des vertus." *Revue Thomiste* 31 (1926): 411–426.

"L'instabilité dans l'état de péché mortel des vertus morales acquises." *Revue Thomiste* 42 (1937): 255–262.

Gauthier, René-Antoine. "Comptes Rendus" of *Psychologie et morale aux xiie et xiiie siècles*, vols. 2–3, by Odon Lottin. Louvain: Mont César; Gembloux: Duculot, 1948–49. *Bulletin Thomiste* 8 (1947–1953): 60–86.

"Saint Maxime le Confesseur et la psychologie de l'acte humain." *Recherches de théologie ancienne et médiévale* 21 (1954): 51–100.

George, Marie I. "Aquinas's Teachings on Concepts and Words in His Commentary on John contra Nicanor Austriaco, OP." *American Catholic Philosophical Quarterly* 94 (2020): 357–378.

Gillon, L.-B. "Aux origines de la 'Puissance Obédientielle.'" *Revue Thomiste* 48 (1947): 304–310.

Glenn, Mary Michael. "A Comparison of the Thomistic and Scotistic Concepts of Hope." *The Thomist* 20 (1957): 27–74.

Gondreau, Paul. *The Passions of Christ's Soul in the Theology of St. Thomas Aquinas*. Scranton, PA: University of Scranton Press, 2009.

Graf, Th. *De subiecto psychico gratiae et virtutum*. 2 vols. Rome: Herder, 1934.

De Haan, Daniel. "Moral Perception and the Function of the *Vis Cogitativa* in Thomas Aquinas's Doctrine of Antecedent and Consequent Passions." *Documenti e studi sulla traditione filosofica medievale* 25 (2014): 289–330.

Harvey, John. "The Nature of the Infused Moral Virtues." *Catholic Theological Society of America Proceedings* 10 (1955): 172–217.

Hause, Jeffrey. "Aquinas on the Function of Moral Virtue." *American Catholic Philosophical Quarterly* 81 (2007): 1–20.

Herdt, Jennifer. "Aquinas's Aristotelian Defense of Martyr Courage." In *Aquinas and the Nicomachean Ethics*, 110–128. Edited by Tobias Hoffmann, Jörn Müller, and Matthias Perkams. Cambridge: Cambridge University Press, 2013.

Hibbs, Thomas. "The Fearful Thoughts of Mortals: Aquinas on Conflict, Self-Knowledge, and the Virtue of Practical Reasoning." In *Intractable Disputes about the Natural Law: Alasdair MacIntyre and Critics*, 273–312. Edited by Lawrence Cunningham. Notre Dame, IN: University of Notre Dame Press, 2009.

Hochschild, Joshua. "Porphyry, Bonaventure, and Thomas Aquinas: A Neo-Platonic Hierarchy of Virtues, and Two Christian Appropriations." In *Medieval Philosophy and the Classical Tradition*, 245–259. Edited by John Inglis. Richmond, Surrey: Curzon Press, 2002.

Hoenen, Petrus. "De origine primorum principiorum scientiae." *Gregorianum* 14 (1933): 153–184.

Hoffmann, Tobias. "Prudence and Practical Principles." In *Aquinas and the Nicomachean Ethics*, 165–183. Edited by Tobias Hoffmann, Jörn Müller, and Matthis Perkams. Cambridge: Cambridge University Press, 2013.

"Aquinas on Moral Progress." In *Aquinas's Summa Theologiae: A Critical Guide*, 131–149. Edited by Jeffrey Hause. Cambridge: Cambridge University Press, 2018.

Houser, Rollen Edward, Trans and Ed. *The Cardinal Virtues: Aquinas, Albert, and Philip the Chancellor*. Toronto: Pontifical Institute for Mediaeval Studies, 2004.

Hursthouse, Rosalind. *On Virtue Ethics*. Oxford: Oxford University Press, 1999.

Hursthouse, Rosalind and Pettigrove, Glen. "Virtue Ethics." *The Stanford Encyclopedia of Philosophy* (Winter 2018 Edition). Edited by Edward N. Zalta, URL = <https://plato.stanford.edu/archives/win2018/entries/ethics-virtue/>.

Inagki, Bernard. "*Habitus* and *Natura* in Aquinas." In *Studies in Medieval Philosophy*, 159–175. Edited by John F. Wippel. Washington, DC: The Catholic University of America Press, 1987.

Inglis, John. "Aquinas's Replication of the Acquired Moral Virtues. *Journal of Religious Ethics* 27 (1999): 3–27.

Irwin, Terence. "Who Discovered the Will?" *Philosophical Perspectives* 6 (1992): 453–473.

"Practical Reason Divided: Aquinas and His Critics." In *Ethics and Practical Reason*, 189–214. Edited by Garrit Cullity and Berys Gaut. Oxford: Clarendon, 1997.

The Development of Ethics, vol. 1: *From Socrates to the Reformation*. Oxford: Oxford University Press, 2011.

Jenkins, John. "Expositions of the Text: Aquinas's Aristotelian Commentaries." *Medieval Philosophy and Theology* 5 (1996): 39–62.

Knowledge and Faith in Thomas Aquinas. Cambridge: Cambridge University Press, 1997.

Jensen, Steven. "Of Gnome and Gnomes: The Virtue of Higher Discernment and the Production of Monsters." *American Catholic Philosophical Quarterly* 82 (2008): 411–428.

"The Error of the Passions," *The Thomist* 73 (2009): 349–379.

"Virtuous Deliberation and the Passions." *The Thomist* 77 (2013): 193–227.

Sin: A Thomistic Psychology. Washington, DC: The Catholic University of America Press, 2018.

Johnson, Mark. "St. Thomas, Obediential Potency, and the Infused Virtues: *De virtutibus in communi*, a. 10, ad 13." *Recherches de Théologie ancienne et médiévale*, suppl. 1: *Thomistica* (1995): 27–34.

Kahm, Nicholas. *Aquinas on Emotion's Participation in Reason*. Washington, DC: The Catholic University of America Press, 2019.

Kemp, Kenneth W. "Science, Theology, and Monogenesis." *American Catholic Philosophical Quarterly* 85 (2011): 217–236.

Kenny, Anthony. *Aquinas on Mind*. New York and London: Routledge, 1993.

Kent, Bonnie. "Transitory Vice: Thomas Aquinas on Incontinence." *Journal of the History of Philosophy* 27 (1989): 199–223.

Virtues of the Will: The Transformation of Ethics in the Late Thirteenth Century. Washington, DC: The Catholic University of America Press, 1995.

"Habits and Virtues." In *The Ethics of Aquinas*, 116–130. Edited by Stephen J. Pope. Washington, DC: Georgetown University Press, 2002.

"Losable Virtue: Aquinas on Character and Will." In *Aquinas and the Nicomachean Ethics*, 91–109. Edited by Tobias Hoffmann, Jörn Müller, and Matthias Perkams. Cambridge: Cambridge University Press, 2013.

Keys, Mary M. *Aquinas, Aristotle, and the Promise of the Common Good*. Cambridge: Cambridge University Press, 2006.

King, Peter. "Aquinas on the Passions." In *Aquinas's Moral Theory: Essays in Honor of Norman Kretzmann*, 101–132. Edited by Scott MacDonald and Eleonore Stump. Ithaca, NY: Cornell University Press, 1999; repr. in *Thomas Aquinas: Contemporary Philosophical Perspectives*, 353–384. Edited by Brain Davies. Oxford: Oxford University Press, 2002.

Klima, Gyula. "What Ever Happened to Efficient Causes?" In *Skepticism, Causality and Skepticism about Causality*, 31–42. Edited by Gyula Klima and Alexander W. Hall. Proceedings of the Society for Medieval Logic and Metaphysics 10. Newcastle upon Tyne: Cambridge Scholars Publishing, 2013.

Knobel, Angela McKay. "Prudence and Acquired Moral Virtue." *The Thomist* 69 (2005): 535–565.

"Two Theories of Christian Virtue." *American Catholic Philosophical Quarterly* 84 (2010): 599–618.

"Can the Infused and Acquired Virtues Coexist in the Christian Life?" *Studies in Christian Ethics* 23/4 (2010): 381–396.

"Aquinas and the Pagan Virtues." *International Philosophical Quarterly* 51 (2011): 339–354.

"Relating Aquinas's Infused and Acquired Virtues: Some Problematic Texts for a Common Interpretation." *Nova et Vetera, English Edition* 9 (2011): 411–431.

"A Confusing Comparison: Interpreting *DVC* A. 10 AD 4." In *The Virtuous Life: Thomas Aquinas on the Theological Nature of Moral Virtues*, 97–115. Edited by Harm Goris and Henk Schoot. Leuven, Paris, and Bristol, CT: Peeters, 2017.

Knuuttila, Simo. *Emotions in Ancient and Medieval Philosophy*. Oxford: Clarendon, 2004.

De Letter, P. "Hope and Charity in St. Thomas." *The Thomist* 13 (1950): 204–324, 325–352.

van Lieshout, H. *La théorie Plotinienne de la vertu: Essai sur la genèse d'un article de la Somme théologique de Saint Thomas.* Freiburg: Studie Friburgensia, 1926.

Lisska, Anthony. *Aquinas's Theory of Perception: An Analytic Reconstruction.* Oxford: Oxford University Press, 2016.

Lombardo, Nicholas. *The Logic of Desire: Aquinas on Emotion.* Washington, DC: The Catholic University of America Press, 2010.

Lonergan, Bernard. *Verbum: Word and Idea in Aquinas.* Edited by David B. Burrell. Notre Dame, IN: University of Notre Dame Press, 1967.

Grace and Freedom: Operative Grace in the Thought of St. Thomas Aquinas. Edited by J. Patout Burns. London: Darton, Longman and Todd; New York: Herder and Herder, 1971.

Long, Steven. *Natura Pura: On the Recovery of Nature in the Doctrine of Grace.* New York: Fordham University Press, 2010.

"Creation *ad imaginem Dei*: The Obediential Potency of the Human Person to Grace and Glory." *Nova et Vetera* 14 (2016): 1175–1192.

Lopez, Timothy J. "United Acquired Virtue in Traditional Thomism: Distinguishing Necessities, Efficient Causes, and Finalities." In *The Virtuous Life: Thomas Aquinas on the Theological Nature of Moral Virtues,* 183–199. Edited by Harm Goris and Henk Schoot. Leuven, Paris, and Bristol, CT: Peeters, 2017.

Lottin, Odon. *Psychologie et morale aux xiie et xiiie siècles.* 6 vols. Louvain: Mont César; Gembloux: Duculot, 1942–1960.

Études de Morale: Histoire et Doctrine. Gembloux: Duculot, 1961.

De Lubac, Henri. *Surnaturel: Études Historiques.* Paris: Aubier, 1946.

MacIntyre, Alasdair. *After Virtue: A Study in Moral Theory,* 2nd ed. Notre Dame, IN: University of Notre Dame Press, 1984.

Ethics in the Conflicts of Modernity: An Essay on Desire, Practical Reasoning, and Narrative. Cambridge: Cambridge University Press, 2016.

Mansfield, Richard K. "Antecedent Passion and the Moral Quality of Human Act." *Proceedings of the American Catholic Philosophical Association* 71 (1997): 221–231.

Maritain, Jacques. *Science et sagesse: Suivi d'eclaircissements sur la philosophie morale.* Paris: Labergerie, 1935.

McGinnis, Jon. *Avicenna.* Oxford: Oxford University Press, 2010.

McGrath, Alister. *Iustitia Dei: A History of the Christian Doctrine of Justification.* 2nd ed. Cambridge: Cambridge University Press, 1998.

MacKendrick, Paul. *The Philosophical Books of Cicero.* New York: St. Martin's Press, 1989.

Mattison, William. "Thomas' Categorizations of Virtue: Historical Background and Contemporary Significance." *The Thomist* 74 (2010): 189–235.

"Can Christians Possess the Acquired Cardinal Virtues?" *Theological Studies* 72 (2011): 558–585.

McCluskey, Colleen. *Thomas Aquinas on Moral Wrongdoing.* Cambridge: Cambridge University Press, 2017.

Miller, Marianne Therese. "The Problem of Action in the Commentary of St. Thomas Aquinas on the *Physics* of Aristotle." *The Modern Schoolman* 23 (1945–46): 135–167.

Miner, Robert. "Non-Aristotelian Prudence in the *Prima Secundae*." *The Thomist* 64 (2000): 401–422.

Thomas Aquinas on the Passions: A Study of Summa Theologiae 1a2ae 22–48. Cambridge: Cambridge University Press, 2009.

"Aquinas on Habitus." In *A History of Habit: From Aristotle to Bourdieu*, 67–87. Edited by Tom Sparrow and Adam Hutchinson. Lanham, MD: Lexington Books, 2013.

Mirkes, Renée. "Aquinas's Doctrine of Moral Virtue and Its Significance for Theories of Facility." *The Thomist* 61 (1997): 189–218.

"Aquinas on the Unity of Perfect Moral Virtue." *American Catholic Philosophical Quarterly* 71 (1998): 589–605.

Morriset, Paul. "Prudence et fin selon Saint Thomas." *Sciences ecclésiastique* 15 (1963): 73–98, 439–458.

Mulcahy, Bernard. *Aquinas's Notion of Pure Nature and the Christian Integralism of Henri de Lubac.* New York: Peter Lang, 2011.

Müller, Jörn. *Natürliche Moral und philosophische Ethik bei Albertus Magnus.* Münster: Ashendorff, 2001.

Murphy, Claudia Eisen. "Aquinas on Our Responsibility for Our Emotions." *Medieval Philosophy and Theology* 8 (1999): 163–205.

Naus, John E. *The Nature of the Practical Intellect according to Saint Thomas Aquinas.* Rome: Analecta Gregoriana, 1959.

Nicolas, J.-H. *Les profondeurs de la grace.* Paris: Beauchesne, 1969.

O'Daly, Gerard. *Augustine's Philosophy of Mind.* Berkeley, CA: University of California Press, 1987.

Osborne Jr., Thomas M. "The Augustinianism of Thomas Aquinas' Moral Theory." *The Thomist* 67 (2003): 279–305.

Love of Self and Love of God in Thirteenth-Century Ethics. Notre Dame, IN: University of Notre Dame Press, 2005.

"Perfect and Imperfect Virtues in Aquinas." *The Thomist* 71 (2007): 39–64.

"The Separation of Interior and Exterior Acts in Scotus and Ockham." *Mediaeval Studies* 69 (2008): 111–139.

"The Threefold Referral of Acts to the Ultimate End in Thomas Aquinas and His Commentators." *Angelicum* 85 (2008): 715–736.

"Thomas and Scotus on Prudence without All the Major Virtues: Imperfect or Merely Partial?" *The Thomist* 74 (2010): 1–24.

"Unbelief and Sin in Thomas Aquinas and the Thomistic Tradition." *Nova et Vetera*, English Edition 8 (2010): 613–626.

"Thomas Aquinas and John Duns Scotus on Individual Acts and the Ultimate End." In *Philosophy and Theology in the Long Middle Ages: A Tribute to Stephen F. Brown*, 351–374. Edited by Kent Emery, Jr., Russell L. Friedman, and Andreas Speer. Studien und Texte zur Geistesgeschichte des Mittelalters. Leiden: Brill, 2011.

"Natura Pura: Two Recent Works." *Nova et Vetera*, English Edition 11 (2013): 265–279.

Human Action in Thomas Aquinas, John Duns Scotus, and William of Ockham. Washington, DC: The Catholic University of America Press, 2014.

"What Is at Stake in the Question of whether Someone Can Possess the Natural Moral Virtues without Charity?" In *The Virtuous Life: Thomas Aquinas on the Theological Nature of Moral Virtues*, 117–130. Edited by Harm Goris and Henk Schoot. Leuven, Paris, and Bristol, CT: Peeters, 2017.

"Natural Reason and Supernatural Faith." In *Aquinas's Summa Theologiae: A Critical Guide*, 188–203. Edited by Jeffrey Hause. Cambridge: Cambridge University Press, 2018.

"Spanish Thomists on the Need for Interior Grace in Acts of Faith." In *Beyond Dordt and De Auxiliis: The Dynamics of Protestant and Catholic Soteriology in the Sixteenth and Seventeenth Centuries*, 66–86. Edited by Jordan Ballor, Matthew Gaetano, and David Sytsma. Brill: Leiden, 2019.

Aquinas's Ethics. Cambridge: Cambridge University Press, 2020.

"Thomas, Scotus, and Ockham on the Object of Hope." *Recherches de Théologie et Philosophie Médiévales* 87 (2020): 1–26.

Papineau, David. "Naturalism." *The Stanford Encyclopedia of Philosophy* (Summer 2021 Edition). Edited by Edward N. Zalta, forthcoming URL = <https://plato.stanford.edu/archives/sum2021/entries/naturalism/>.

Pasnau, Robert. *Thomas Aquinas on Human Nature: A Philosophical Study of Summa Theologiae 1a 75–89.* Cambridge: Cambridge University Press, 2002.

Pinckaers, Servais. "Comptes Rendus – Deman et Gauthier." *Bulletin Thomiste* 9 (1955): 345–362.

"Le vertu est tout autre chose q'une habitude." *Nouvelle Revue Théologique* 82 (1960): 387–403.

"L'instinct de l'Esprit au coeur de l'éthique chrétienne." *Novitas et Veritas vitae: aux sources du renouveau de la morale chrétienne: mélanges offerts au professeur Servais Pinckaers à l'occasion de son 65e anniversaire*, 213–224. Edited by Carlos Pinto de Oliveira and Jean Marie Aubert. Fribourg: Editions Universitaires; Paris: Cerf, 1991. Translated by Craig Steven Titus as "Morality and the Movement of the Holy Spirit" in *The Pinckaers Reader*, 385–395. Edited by John Berkman and Craig Steven Titus. Washington, DC: The Catholic University of America Press, 2005.

"La voie spirituelle du bonheur selon Saint Thomas." In *Ordo Sapientiae et Amoris: Image et message de Saint Thomas d'Aquin*, 267–284. Edited by Carlos-Josaphat Pinto de Oliveira. Fribourg: Éditions Universitaires, 1993. Translated by Mary Thomas Noble as "Aquinas's Pursuit of Beatitude: From the *Commentary on the Sentences* to the *Summa Theologiae*." In *The Pinckaers Reader*, 93–114.

The Sources of Christian Ethics. 3rd ed. Translated by Mary Thomas Noble. Washington, DC: The Catholic University of America Press, 1995.

The Pinckaers Reader. Edited by John Berkman and Craig Steven Titus. Washington, DC: The Catholic University of America Press, 2005.

Pinsent, Andrew. *The Second-Person Perspective in Aquinas's Ethics: Virtues and Gifts*. New York: Routledge, 2012.

Porro, Pasquale. *Thomas Aquinas: A Historical and Philosophical Profile*. Translated by Joseph G. Trabbic and Roger W. Nutt. Washington, DC: The Catholic University of America Press, 2016.

Porter, Jean. *The Perfection of Desire: Habit, Reason, and Virtue in Aquinas's Summa Theologiae*. The Père Marquette Lecture in Theology 2018. Milwaukee, WI: Marquette University Press, 2018.

Ramirez, Santiago. *De Actibus Humanis: In I-II Summa Theologiae Expositio (QQ. VI-XXI)*. Madrid: Instituto de Filosofia "Luis Vivès." 1972.

De Habitibus in Communi: In I-II Summae Theologiae Divi Thomae Expositio (QQ. XLIX-LIV). 2 vols. Madrid: Instituto de Filosofia "Luis Vivès." 1973.

De Donis Spiritus Sancti Deque Vita Mystica: In II P. Summa Theologiae Divi Thomae Expositio. Madrid: Instituto de Filosofia "Luis Vivès." 1973.

Richardson, Kara. "Avicenna and Aquinas on Form and Generation." In *The Arabic, Hebrew and Latin Reception of Avicenna's Metaphysics*, 251–274. Edited by Dag Hasse and Amos Bertolacci. Berlin and Boston: Walter de Gruyter. 2011.

Rist, John M. *On Inoculating Moral Philosophy against God*. Milwaukee, WI: Marquette University Press, 2000.

Russell, Daniel C. *Practical Intelligence and the Virtues*. Oxford: Clarendon, 2009.

Saarinen, Risto. "The Parts of Prudence: Buridan, Odonis, Aquinas." *Dialogue* 42 (2003): 749–765.

Sanford, Jonathan J. Sanford. *Before Virtue: Assessing Contemporary Virtue Ethics*. Washington, DC: The Catholic University of America Press, 2019.

Shanley, Brian. "Aquinas on Pagan Virtue." *The Thomist* 63 (1999): 553–577.

Sherwin, Michael. "Infused Virtue and the Effects of Acquired Vice: A Test Case for the Thomistic Theory of the Infused Cardinal Virtues." *The Thomist* 69 (2005): 29–52.

Simon, Yves. "Maritain's Philosophy of Science." *The Thomist* 4 (1943): 85–102.

Simpson, William M. R., Koons, Robert C., and Teh, Nicholas J., Editors. *Neo-Aristotelian Perspectives on Contemporary Science*. London: Routledge, 2018.

Sorabji, Richard. "Infinite Power Impressed: The Transformation of Aristotle's Physics and Theology." In *Aristotle Transformed: The Ancient Commentators and Their Influence*, 1–198. Edited by Richard Sorabji. Ithaca, NY: Cornell University Press, 1990.

Emotion and Peace of Mind: From Stoic Agitation to Christian Temptation. Oxford and New York: Oxford University Press, 2000.

Stump, Eleonore. "The Non-Aristotelian Character of Aquinas's Ethics: Aquinas on the Passions." *Faith and Philosophy* 28 (2011): 29–34.

Suto, Taki. "Virtue and Knowledge: Connatural Knowledge according to Thomas Aquinas." *The Review of Metaphysics* 58 (2004): 61–79.

Thompson, Michael. *Life and Action: Elementary Structures of Practice and Practical Thought*. Cambridge, MA: Harvard University Press, 2008.

Titus, Craig Steven. "Passions in Christ: Spontaneity, Development, and Virtue," *The Thomist* 73 (2009): 53–87.

"Moral Development and Connecting the Virtues: Aquinas, Porter, and the Flawed Saint." In *Ressourcement Thomism: Sacred Doctrine, the Sacraments, and the Moral Life: Essays in Honor of Romanus Cessario, O.P.*, 330–352. Edited by Reinhard Hütter and Matthew Levering. Washington, DC: The Catholic University of America Press, 2010.

Torrell, Jean-Pierre. *St. Thomas Aquinas*, vol. 1: *The Person and His Work*, rev. ed. Translated by Robert Royal. Washington, DC: The Catholic University of America Press, 2005.

Uffenheimer-Lippens, Elisabeth. "Rationalized Passion and Passionate Rationality: Thomas Aquinas on the Relation between Reason and the Passions." *The Review of Metaphysics* 56 (2003): 525–558.

Vogler, Candace. "Aristotle, Aquinas, Anscombe, and the New Virtue Ethics." In *Aquinas and the Nicomachean Ethics*, 239–257. Edited by Tobias Hoffmann, Jörn Müller, and Matthias Perkams. Cambridge: Cambridge University Press, 2013.

Wallace, William. *The Role of Demonstration in St. Thomas Aquinas: A Study of Methodology in St. Thomas Aquinas*. River Forest, IL: The Thomist Press, 1962.

The Modeling of Nature: Philosophy of Science and Philosophy of Nature in Synthesis. Washington, DC: The Catholic University of America Press, 1996.

Weisheipl, James A. *Nature and Motion in the Middle Ages*. Edited by William E. Carroll. Washington, DC: The Catholic University of America Press, 1985.

Westberg, Daniel. *Right Practical Reason: Aristotle, Action and Prudence in Aquinas*. Oxford: Clarendon Press, 1994.

White, Kevin. "The Passions of the Soul." In *The Ethics of Aquinas*, 103–115. Edited by Stephen J. Pope. Washington, DC: Georgetown University Press, 2002.

White, Leo A. "Instinct and Custom." *The Thomist* 66 (2002): 577–605.

Williams, Bernard. *Ethics and the Limits of Philosophy*. Cambridge, MA: Harvard University Press, 1985.

William, Mary. "The Relationships of the Intellectual Virtue of Science and Moral Virtue." *New Scholasticism* 36 (1962): 475–505.

Wippel, John F. *The Metaphysical Thought of Thomas Aquinas: From Finite Being to Uncreated Being*. Washington, DC: The Catholic University of America Press, 2000.

Wolf, Raphael. *Cicero: The Philosophy of a Roman Skeptic*. London and New York: Routledge, 2015.

Index

adultery, 47, 143, 194, 204
affability, 102, 104, 106
Alan of Lille, 119
Albert the Great, 2, 10, 15, 36, 37, 41–43, 109,
 165, 211
Ambrose of Milan, 4, 108
Anaxagoras, 146
Annas, Julia, 201
Anscombe, Elizabeth, 191–192, 198
Augustine of Hippo, 10, 17–18, 37, 85–87,
 90–92, 140, 165, 172, 184
Aureol, Peter, 29
Avicenna, 145–146

blasphemy, 63–64, 204
Bonaventure, 109, 120–121, 126, 148, 156

Cajetan, Thomas de Vio, 50–51, 61, 63,
 106, 162
Capreolus, John, 50
cardinal virtues, 1, 7, 8, 125, 127, 200
 and parts, 116–118
 as general conditions and as habits, 108–119
 more properly habits rather than general
  conditions, 165
 order among, 178–179
 principal but not most important virtues,
  118–119
charity, 49, 51–52, 55, 56, 120, 125, 138–140,
 142, 197
 and acquired moral virtue, 150, 151, 153–156
 and contemporary "charity" or
  benevolence, 200
 preeminent virtue, 182
 remains in heaven, 189
choice, 14, 18, 35, 36, 47, 63, 70, 114, 140, 142,
 171, 193
 and means, 71, 73, 77
 judgment of choice, 69
Cicero, 3, 13, 67, 85, 90–92, 114, 184
cogitative power, 21–23, 25, 39, 41, 45, 61–62, 77

common good, 49, 52–53, 68, 101, 139–140,
 160, 194
 supernatural, 138, 199–200, 207
connatural
 acts, 15, 26
 ends, 127
 knowledge, 72, 80–81
continence, 50
courage or fortitude (*fortitudo*), 67, 82, 100, 102,
 103, 105, 107, 114, 134, 149, 151, 154, 172,
 179, 181, 183–187
 "courage" of lion, 175
 translations of "*fortitudo*", 8
cowardice, 103, 134, 149, 150, 159, 160, 173, 215

De Virtutibus et Vitiis, 3
Decosimo, David, 155
deliberation, 64, 66, 69, 71, 73, 81, 84, 86,
 87, 115
disposition, 150, 165, 175, 176, 195
 three distinct meanings of term, 29
 translation of "*constantia*" of Stoic sage, 90–91
docility, 67, 79
Durandus of Saint-Pourçain, 29

elevation of human nature, 52, 128, 141, 195, 206
Epictetus, 86–87
eubulia, 68–69, 71, 115
eutrapelia, 102, 104, 106, 107, 117

faith, 46, 131, 140–142, 189, 209
 and the mean, 163
 essentially supernatural, 136
 object of, 137
 without charity not fully a virtue, 172
Foot, Philippa, 191, 203, 204
formal object, 60
 of acquired and infused virtues, 153, 156
 of habits, 40
 of powers, 21
 of sciences, 42

231

For EU product safety concerns, contact us at Calle de José Abascal, 56–1°,
28003 Madrid, Spain or eugpsr@cambridge.org.

www.ingramcontent.com/pod-product-compliance
Ingram Content Group UK Ltd.
Pitfield, Milton Keynes, MK11 3LW, UK
UKHW020353140625
459647UK00020B/2448